The Moral
Foundations
of Politics

The Institution for Social and
Policy Studies at Yale University

THE YALE ISPS SERIES

The Moral

Foundations

of Politics

IAN SHAPIRO

YALE UNIVERSITY PRESS
NEW HAVEN & LONDON

Set in Scala type by Keystone Typesetting, Inc. Printed in the
United States of America.

ISBN: 0-300-07907-9

A catalogue record for this book is available from the Library of
Congress and the British Library.

The paper in this book meets the guidelines for permanence and
durability of the Committee on Production Guidelines for Book
Longevity of the Council on Library Resources.

10 9 8 7 6 5 4 3 2 1

For all the graduates of Political Science 118

. . . certainty is beautiful,
but uncertainty is more beautiful still.

Wisława Szymborska

CONTENTS

This book grew out of a lecture course called The Moral Foundations of Politics that I have been teaching at Yale since the early 1980s. The course, a version of which I inherited from Douglas Rae, has changed out of all recognition since that time. Yet it has evolved more in the manner of rebuilding a ship at sea than redesigning it from scratch. As a result, my debt to Rae is greater than he might realize from perusing the present text. The idea to turn the course into a book came in the mid-1990s from John Covell, then my editor at Yale University Press. These two people have my enduring gratitude as the project's step-parents. Bruce Ackerman, Robert Dahl, Clarissa Hayward, Nancy Hirschman, Nicoli Nattrass, Jennifer Pitts, Mark Stein, and two anonymous readers for Yale University Press all read the manuscript from stem to stern, offering helpful suggestions large and small. A fleet of research assistants, all graduates of Moral Foundations, worked on different aspects of the project under the helpful supervision of Katharine Darst. They were Carol Chang, Karl Chang, Clinton Dockery, Dan Kruger, George Maglares, Melody Redbird, David Schroedel, and Michael Seibel. Jeffrey Mueller served as a sterling research assistant as I wrote the final manuscript; his assistance was invaluable. Jennifer Carter's help in the final stages was also most welcome.

The book is conceived of as introductory in the sense that no prior knowledge of political philosophy is assumed. Its central focus is on different theories of political legitimacy in the utili-

tarian, Marxist, social contract, anti-Enlightenment, and democratic traditions. My discussion of these different theories is
meant to give readers a grasp of the major intellectual traditions
that have shaped political argument in the West over the past
several centuries. The theories are set in historical context, but the
main focus is on current formulations as applied to contemporary problems. Although introductory, the book is written from a
distinctive point of view and advances a particular argument. I
will not be disappointed if instructors find it to be a helpful teaching tool, yet feel the need to argue with it as they teach it.

Some of the material in §§1.2, 4.2.3, and 5.5 appeared previously
in my article "Resources, capacities, and ownership: The workmanship ideal and distributive justice," *Political Theory*, vol. 19,
no. 1 (February 1991), pp. 28–46. It is copyright © 1991 by Sage
Publications, Inc., and drawn on by permission here.

When do governments merit our allegiance, and when should they be denied it? This most enduring of political dilemmas motivates our inquiry. Socrates, Martin Luther, and Thomas More remind us of its vintage; Vaclav Havel, Nelson Mandela, and Aung San Suu Kyi underscore its continuing force. They are moral heroes because they faced down wrongful political authority, just as surely as Adolph Eichmann was a moral villain for his failure to do so. His motivation and behavior as a middle-level officer in Nazi Germany exemplify obedience to a technically legitimate authority. Yet his actions in sending countless thousands to Nazi concentration camps suggest that there must be limits to any government's legitimate authority.[1]

As the events surrounding Eichmann's own death underscore, it is a good deal easier to say that there should be such limits than to say what they should be or how they should be enforced. Captured by Israeli commandos in violation of Argentinean and international law, he was spirited to Israel, tried and executed for crimes against humanity and against the Jewish people. Many who shed no tears for Eichmann were nonetheless troubled by the manner of his apprehension: he was tried in a country and by courts that did not exist when he committed his crimes and a law was tailor-made to facilitate his sentencing and execution. These actions seem at odds with the hallmarks of legitimate political authority that rule out illegal searches and seizures, post hoc crafting of laws to fit particular cases, and bills of attainder. Yet if

1

we are unnerved both by Israel's acting on what its leaders saw as a moral imperative despite the legal institutions of the day and by Eichmann's slavish adherence to the legal institutions of *his* day, our question is thrown into sharp relief. Who is to judge, and by what criteria, whether the laws and actions of states that claim our allegiance measure up? In this book we explore the principal answers given to these questions in the modern West.

One set of answers grows out of the utilitarian tradition, famously associated with the name of Jeremy Bentham (1748–1832). His *Introduction to the Principles of Morals and Legislation*, first published in 1789, is its locus classicus, although utilitarianism has older roots than this, and it has since been reformulated and refined in numerous ways as we will see. Utilitarians answer our question with a variant of the claim that the legitimacy of governments is tied to their willingness and capacity to maximize happiness. What counts as happiness, whose happiness is to count, how it is measured, and who does the counting are among the contentious issues that distinguish different utilitarians from one another as will become plain in chapters 2 and 3. Despite disagreements about these and other consequential matters, utilitarians generally agree that we should judge governments by reference to Bentham's memorable, if ambiguous, dictum that they should be expected to maximize the greatest happiness of the greatest number of people.

The Marxist tradition that occupies us in chapter 4 takes the idea of exploitation as the benchmark for judging political legitimacy. Marxists differ substantially from one another on the definition of exploitation, its relations both to labor and to the economic and political systems, and on the role of political institutions in eradicating it. On all Marxist understandings, however, political institutions lack legitimacy to the degree that they underwrite exploitation and they gain it to the degree that they promote its antithesis, human freedom. Every political system in history has countenanced some kind of exploitation from the Marxist point of view, but socialism and communism are thought to hold out the possibility of a world that is free of exploitation. History has not looked kindly on these possibilities since Karl Marx (1818–1883) wrote, but, even if desirable variants of them are unavailable, we will see that aspects of Marxist theory may nonetheless be helpful in understanding the normative properties of capitalism and in distinguishing the relative legitimacy of different types of capitalist systems.

The social contract tradition examined in chapter 5 offers a third sort of answer to my initial question. Social contract arguments are as old as the hills, but in their modern form they are generally thought to originate with Thomas Hobbes's *Leviathan*, published in 1651, and John Locke's *Second Treatise on Government* which first appeared as an anonymous tract in England in the 1680s. For social contract theorists, the state's legitimacy is rooted in the idea of agreement. From the beginning they have disagreed among themselves about the nature of the agreement, who the parties to the agreement are, and how, if at all, the agreement is to be enforced, but they agree that consent of the governed, somehow understood, is the source of the state's legitimacy. We owe the state allegiance if it embodies our consent, and we are free (and in some formulations even obliged) to resist it when it does not.

Each of the utilitarian, Marxist, and contractarian traditions brings a distinctive focus and set of questions about political legitimacy to the fore, but the traditions also overlap a good deal more than is often realized. I will argue that this is mainly because they have all been decisively shaped by the Enlightenment. This is the philosophical movement aimed at rationalizing social life by basing it on scientific principles and in which there is a powerful normative impetus to take seriously the ideal of human freedom as expressed in a political doctrine of individual rights. The

Enlightenment project, as Alasdair MacIntyre has dubbed it, is generally associated with the writings of such European thinkers as René Descartes (1596–1650), Gottfried Leibnitz (1646–1716), Benedict Spinoza (1632–1677) and Immanuel Kant (1724–1804), though it was also greatly influenced by the English Empiricists, John Locke (1632–1704), George Berkeley (1685–1753), and David Hume (1711–1776). We will see how Enlightenment values have shaped the utilitarian, Marxist, and social contract traditions, and, in the course of examining those traditions, we will also evaluate their understandings of the Enlightenment values of science and individual rights.

The Enlightenment has always had its detractors; they are our focus in chapter 6. Critics of Enlightenment political thinking range from traditionalists like Edmund Burke (1729–1797) to various postmodern and communitarian theorists in the contemporary literature. Despite their many differences, they share in common considerable skepticism, not to say hostility, to the goal of rationalizing politics along scientific lines as well as to the idea that the freedoms embodied in individual rights are the most important political value. Instead they are inclined to attach normative weight to inherited norms and practices, linking the legitimacy of political institutions to how well they embody communal values that shape, and give meaning to, the lives of individuals. The sources of the self, as Charles Taylor describes them, are seen as rooted in systems of attachment and affiliation that precede and survive individuals, shaping their expectations of political legitimacy.[2]

By the end of chapter 6 it becomes plain that, despite serious difficulties with the utilitarian, Marxist, and social contract traditions, wholesale rejection of the Enlightenment project in politics is infeasible and would be undesirable even if it were feasible. Some of the difficulties with the different theories are specific to them; others flow from the particular understandings of Enlightenment values they embody. With respect to the former, each of the three traditions contains insights that survive their failures as comprehensive political doctrines and should inform our thinking about of the sources of political legitimacy. With respect to the latter, I distinguish the early Enlightenment, which is vulnerable to the arguments of anti-Enlightenment critics, from the mature Enlightenment, which is not. Attacks on the Enlightenment's preoccupation with foundational certainty are not telling against the fallibilist view of science that informs most contemporary thinking and practice and, whatever the difficulties with the idea of individual rights, they pale in comparison with trying to develop a theory of political legitimacy without them.

This raises the question: What political theory best embodies mature Enlightenment values? My answer in chapter 7 is democracy. The democratic tradition has ancient origins, but the modern formulations that shape contemporary political argument spring from, or react against, Jean-Jacques Rousseau's discussion of the general will in *The Social Contract*, published in 1762. Democrats hold that governments are legitimate when those who are affected by decisions play an appropriate role in making them and when there are meaningful opportunities to oppose the government of the day, replacing it with an alternative. Democrats differ on many particulars of how government and opposition should be organized, who should be entitled to vote, how their votes should be counted, and what limits, if any, should be placed on the decisions of democratic majorities. Yet they share a common commitment to democratic procedures as the most viable source of political legitimacy. My claim that they are correct will seem vulnerable to some, at least initially. Democracy has long and often been criticized as profoundly hostile both to the truth and to the sanctity of individual rights. However, I make the case that on the mature Enlightenment understandings of these values that make the most sense, the critique is wrongheaded. The democratic tradition offers better resources than the going alternatives for ensuring that political claims and counter-claims are tested for their veracity in the public arena, and for protecting those individual rights that best embody the aspiration for human freedom.

CHAPTER 1

Enlightenment Politics

The philosophical movement known as the Enlightenment was really several distinct, if overlapping, intellectual movements. Its roots can be traced at least to the 1600s, and its influence has been felt in every walk of life. From philosophy, science, and invention, to art, architecture, and literature, to politics, economics, and organization, every field of human activity bears the indelible stamp of one aspect or another of the Enlightenment. Despite innumerable assaults that have been leveled against different aspects of its philosophical assumptions and practical consequences from the beginning, the Enlightenment outlook has dominated intellectual consciousness in the West for the better part of four centuries.[1]

If there is a single overarching idea shared in common by adherents to different strands of Enlightenment thinking, it is faith in the power of human reason to understand the true nature of our circumstances and ourselves. The Enlightenment outlook is optimistic to its core, supplying impetus to the idea of progress in human affairs. As reason's reach expands, it seems plausible to think that understanding will yield the possibility to control and perhaps even improve our environments and our lives. Enthusiasts of the Enlightenment have always found this possibility of progress seductive, even if fraught with attendant danger—as current debates about advances in genetics underscore. When knowledge advances, so too does the possibility of genetic engineering to eradicate inherited diseases and birth defects. The

7

same advances in knowledge might, however, be pressed in the service of Orwellian manipulation of people's psyches. Partisans of the Enlightenment think the best bet is that the potential advantages of gaining knowledge outweigh the risks, or in some cases that human beings are incapable of resisting the allure of authentic knowledge. Whether the product of unvarnished enthusiasm or a more chastened desire to direct the inevitable in felicitous directions, the Enlightenment enterprise is one of deploying reason in the service of improvement in human affairs.

The aspirations to understand the social and natural world through the deployment of reason, and to press understanding into the service of human improvement, are by no means new with the Enlightenment. One need not read far into Plato's *Republic* to discover an abiding value being placed on the pursuit of knowledge through reason, and a central preoccupation of Aristotle's *Nicomachean Ethics* is with improvement that can be achieved by shaping the malleable aspects of the human psyche in accordance with objectively identifiable virtues. Yet the Enlightenment understandings of reason and human improvement are distinctive. Reason's pursuit of knowledge is seen as mediated by, and achieved through, science; and human improvement is measured by the yardstick of individual rights that embody, and protect, human freedom.

1.1 Science's Ascendancy

The preoccupation with science stemmed from a program to make all knowledge secure, measured by a standard first articulated by Descartes when he announced that he was in search of propositions that are impossible to doubt. His famous example, known as the *cogito,* was "I think, therefore I am."[2] The very act of trying to doubt it seems necessarily to affirm it. Different Enlightenment thinkers would comprehend knowledge and science in strongly differing ways over the next several centuries, but they all have been consumed with the task, as Immanuel Kant defined it in *The Critique of Pure Reason* (1781), of placing knowledge "on the secure path of a science."[3] These developments in philosophy reflected and reinforced the emergence of modern scientific consciousness. That consciousness involved not merely a commitment to the idea that science provides the only genuine knowledge but also a massive and optimistic faith in its liberating effects. Francis Bacon's (1561–1626) declaration that "knowledge is power"[4] embodied a programmatic commitment to a double faith in science as the only reliable means of authentic understanding of the universe and the best tool for transforming it in accordance with human aspirations.

It is important for our purposes to note that the status of the human sciences evolved considerably over the course of the Enlightenment. During the seventeenth and eighteenth centuries, when the hallmark of scientific knowledge was indubitable certainty, ethics, political philosophy, and the human sciences were regarded as superior to the natural sciences. This view seems strange from the vantage point of the twenty-first century, when fields like physics, chemistry, astronomy, geology, and biology have all advanced with astonishing speed to discoveries that would have been unimaginable in the eighteenth century. The human sciences, by contrast, have produced little, if any, enduring knowledge, and many doubt that ethics and political philosophy can be studied scientifically at all. Understanding why contemporary views of the relative statuses of these various fields of inquiry differ so radically from those prevalent in the early Enlightenment requires attention to two features of its distinctive epistemology that would subsequently be abandoned.

1.1.1 The Workmanship Ideal of Knowledge

The first distinctive feature of the early Enlightenment concerns the range of a priori knowledge, the kind of knowledge that either follows from definitions or is otherwise deduced from covering principles. This is the kind of knowledge Descartes had in mind when he formulated his *cogito* and that Kant located in the realm of "analytic judgments." Kant distinguished these from "synthetic" judgments. They always involve a leap from a subject to a predicate, "which has not been in any wise thought in it [the subject], and which no analysis could possibly extract from it."[5] Analytic judgments are best thought of as being logically implied by the meanings of terms, whereas synthetic judgments are not— usually because they depend for their veracity on the world beyond deductive meanings. Some twentieth-century philosophers challenged the existence of an analytic/synthetic distinction,[6] but most would still accept a version of it.

Where most, today, *would* differ sharply from the philosophers of the early Enlightenment concerns the epistemological status of ethics, political philosophy, and the human sciences. These endeavors were all classified within the realm of a priori knowledge by the earlier Enlightenment thinkers, because the relevant criterion was not a distinction between knowledge that is true by definition versus knowledge that is derived from experience. Instead, it was a distinction between knowledge that depends on the human will versus knowledge that is independent of it. As Thomas Hobbes put it in *De Homine,* the pure or "mathematical" sciences can be known a priori, but the "mixed mathematics," such as physics, depend on "the causes of natural things [which are] not in our power."[7] He put it more fully in the Epistle Dedicatory to his *Six Lessons to the Professors of Mathematics:*

> Of arts, some are demonstrable, others indemonstrable; and the demonstrable are those the construction of the subject whereof is in the power of the artist himself, who, in his demonstration does no more but deduce the consequences of his own operation. The reason whereof is this, that the science of every subject is derived from a precognition of the causes, generation, and construction of the same; and consequently where the causes are known, there is

place for demonstration, but not where the causes are to seek for. Geometry therefore is demonstrable, for the lines and figures from which we reason are drawn and described by ourselves; and civil philosophy is demonstrable, because we make the commonwealth ourselves. But because natural bodies we know not the construction, but seek it from effects, there lies no demonstration of what the causes be we seek for, but only what they may be.[8]

This "creationist" or "workmanship" theory conferred a vastly superior epistemological status on moral matters in pre-Humean Enlightenment thought to any they have enjoyed since. Consider Hobbes's statement at the end of his introduction to *Leviathan:* that when he has laid out his own argument "orderly, and perspicuously," the only task for the reader was to consider whether he also finds the same in himself, "for this kind of Doctrine, admitteth no other Demonstration."[9] Far from suggesting that readers must see how their intuitions compare with Hobbes's, he is underscoring his belief that the argument of *Leviathan* has the force of a mathematical proof.

John Locke held a similar view, though its underpinning lay in theological controversies that will initially seem arcane. However, the way he dealt with these controversies influenced many of the doctrines discussed in this book. A basic issue for Locke and many of his contemporaries was the ontological status of natural law and in particular its relation to God's will. If one took the view, common among natural law theorists of his day, that natural law is eternal and unchanging, then this view threatened another notion many of them thought compelling: that God is omnipotent. By definition, an all-powerful God could not be bound by natural law. Yet if God has the capacity to change natural law, we cannot assume it to be timeless and fixed. Locke wrestled with this tension without ever resolving it to his own satisfaction, but in his moral and political writings he came down decisively in the voluntarist, or will-centered, camp.[10] He could not relinquish the

proposition that for something to have the status of a law, it must
be the product of a will. By adopting this voluntarist view, Locke
aligned himself with other will-centered theorists of the early
Enlightenment, notably German philosopher and natural law theorist Samuel von Pufendorf.[11]

The voluntarist theory of natural law dovetailed neatly with
Locke's general epistemology, which mirrored the Hobbesian one
just described. Locke distinguished "ectype" from "archetype"
ideas: ectypes are general ideas of substances, and archetypes are
ideas constructed by man. This distinction generated a radical
disjunction between natural and conventional knowledge, under-
pinned by a further distinction between "nominal" and "real"
essences. In substances that depend on the external world for
their existence (such as trees or animals), only nominal essences
can be known to man. The real essence is available only to the
maker of the substance, God. In the case of archetypes, however,
nominal and real essences are synonymous so that real essences
can by definition be known by man. Because social practices are
always a function of archetype ideas, it follows that real social
essences can be known by man. We know what we make. For
Locke, as for Hobbes, man can thus have incontrovertible knowledge of his creations—most importantly, for our purposes, of
political arrangements and institutions.[12]

1.1.2 The Preoccupation with Certainty

Insisting that will-centeredness is the hallmark of the highest
form of knowledge involved an archaic gloss on what we today
think of as analytic truth. No less archaic was the related depreca-
tion of forms of knowledge that are not will-dependent. The post-
Humean Enlightenment tradition has been marked, in contrast,
by a fallibilist view of knowledge. All knowledge claims are fallible, on this account, and science advances not by making knowl-

edge more certain but by producing more knowledge. Recognizing the corrigibility of all knowledge claims and the possibility that one might always be wrong exemplifies the modern scientific attitude. As Karl Popper (1902–1994) noted, the most that we can say, when hypotheses survive empirical tests, is that they have not been falsified so that we can accept them provisionally.[13] As a dramatic illustration, a recent study by a distinguished group of astrophysicists suggests that what have been accepted as the basic laws of nature may not be unchanging. If true, the consequences for our understanding of modern science will be at least as profound as was Einstein's theory of relativity.[14]

Ethics, political philosophy, and substantial parts of the human sciences would thus come to face a double threat as the Enlightenment matured. The abandonment of creationist theories of knowledge would deprive them of their early Enlightenment identification with logic and mathematics as preeminent sciences, but it was far from clear that they contained propositions that could be tested empirically by the standards of a critical, fallibilist science. Neither certain nor subject to falsification, these fields of inquiry were challenged to escape the bugbear of being "merely subjective," to be cast, as A. J. Ayer argued so dramatically in *Language, Truth, and Logic* in 1936, along with metaphysics, into the trashcan of speculation. "Since the expression of a value judgment is not a proposition," Ayer insisted, "the question of truth or falsehood does not here arise."[15] Theorists of ethical science "treat propositions which refer to the causes and attributes of our ethical feelings as if they were definitions of ethical concepts." As a result, Ayer held, they fail to recognize "that ethical concepts are pseudo-concepts and consequently indefinable."[16] Ayer's doctrine of logical positivism is often attacked, but we will see that his view of the nonscientific character of normative inquiry has endured in both the academy and the public mind.

1.2 The Centrality of Individual Rights

In addition to faith in science, the Enlightenment's central focus on individual rights differentiates its political philosophy from the ancient and medieval commitments to order and hierarchy. This focus brings the freedom of the individual to the center of arguments about politics. This move was signaled in the natural law tradition by a shift in emphasis from the logic of law to the idea of natural right. Hobbes contended in *Leviathan* that it was customary to conflate *"Jus,* and *Lex, Right* and *Law;* yet they ought to be distinguished; because RIGHT, consisteth in liberty to do, or to forbeare; Whereas LAW, determineth, and bindeth to one of them; which in one and the same matter are inconsistent."[17] We find similar reasoning in Locke's *Essays on the Law of Nature,* written in 1663. Rejecting the traditional Christian correlativities between right and law, he insisted instead that natural law "ought to be distinguished from natural right: for right is grounded in the fact that we have the free use of a thing, whereas law is what enjoins or forbids the doing of a thing."[18] Just how distinctive these moves were can be gleaned from the fact that European languages other than English lack this linguistic distinction. The German word *Recht,* the Italian *diritto,* and the French *droit* are all used to signify law in the abstract as well as right; so closely bound are the etymologies of these ideas historically. Although the English social contract theorists spearheaded this change, we will see that it has left its indelible stamp on a much wider swath of the political terrain.

We have already seen that in Locke's voluntarist theology, God's omnipotence is foundational. What humans perceive as natural law is in fact God's natural right, an expression of his will.[19] Locke's theory of ownership flows naturally out of this scheme, transforming the workmanship model of knowledge into a normative theory of right. It is through acts of autonomous making that rights over what is created come into being: making entails ownership so that natural law is at bottom God's natural right over his creation.[20] Locke's frequent appeals to metaphors of workmanship and watch making in the *Two Treatises* and elsewhere make it fundamental that men are obliged to God because of his purposes in making them. Men are "the Workmanship of one Omnipotent, and infinitely wise Maker. . . . They are his Property, whose Workmanship they are, made to last during his, not one another's pleasure."[21]

For Locke, human beings are unique among God's creations because he gave them the capacity to make, to create rights of their own. We will see that this idea, in a secularized form, would long outlive the workmanship theology and epistemology that spawned it. In Locke's formulation, natural law dictates that man is subject to divine imperatives to live in certain ways, but, within the limits set by the law of nature, men can act in a godlike fashion. Man as maker has a maker's knowledge of his intentional actions, and a natural right to dominion over man's products. Provided we do not violate natural law, we stand in the same relation to the objects we create as God stands to us; we own them just as he owns us.[22] Natural law, or God's natural right, thus sets outer boundaries to a field within which humans have divine authority to act as miniature gods, creating rights and obligations of their own.

1.3 Tensions Between Science and Individual Rights

How the preoccupation with science and the commitment to individual rights have influenced arguments about the source of political legitimacy will be explored in subsequent chapters. A general point to bear in mind, already suggested by my discussion of Locke's theology, is that these two Enlightenment values live in potential tension with one another. Science is a deterministic enterprise, concerned with discovering the laws that govern the universe. In the social and political realms this point has obvious potential for conflict with an ethic that emphasizes individual freedom: if human actions are law-governed, how can there be the freedom of action that gives the commitment to individual rights its meaning and point? This is an instance of the long-standing tension between free will and determinism that reared its head in Locke's theological concerns, but it takes on a characteristic Enlightenment hue when formulated as a tension between science and individual rights.

Even Hobbes and Locke, who placed so much emphasis on the existence of definitive answers to normative questions, could not escape this tension completely. Both believed that people are free to act as they choose when natural law is silent, but, when it is not, neither was entirely comfortable with the proposition that free human will must always succumb to natural law's requirements. This was so despite the fact that both of them believed natural law had the full force of both science and theology behind it. Hobbes held that rational individuals would agree to submit to an absolute sovereign because the alternative was horrific civil war. This thinking implies that the sovereign could legitimately order his subject to lay down his life in battle, but Hobbes felt compelled to warn the sovereign not to be surprised if subjects were unwilling to do this.[23] Although Locke thought natural law as expressed in the Scriptures binding on human beings, he recognized that the Scriptures are sufficiently ambiguous to allow room for interpretive disagreement. One of his main arguments with Sir Robert Filmer in the *First Treatise* concerned Locke's insistence that God speaks directly to every individual who reads the Scriptures, and that no human authority is entitled to declare one interpretation authoritative in the face of a conflicting one.[24] This freedom to comprehend natural law by one's own lights supplied the basis of Locke's right to resist that could be invoked against the sovereign, and to which he himself appealed when opposing the English crown during the 1680s. His conviction that right answers can be discovered about the meaning of the Scriptures, and, hence, what natural law requires, was not understood to obliterate human freedom to disagree even about that very subject.

In short, although the workmanship ideal is an attempt to synthesize the deterministic injunctions of science with an ethic that gives centrality to individual freedom, that ideal contains tensions for human beings that are analogous to the natural law paradox that concerned Locke. If there are unassailable right answers about political legitimacy that any clearheaded person must affirm, in what sense do people really have the right to decide this for themselves? But if they are free to reject what science reveals on the basis of their own convictions, then what is left of science's claim to priority over other modes of engaging with the world? We will see this tension surface repeatedly in the utilitarian, Marxist, and social contract traditions, without ever being fully resolved. The tension is recast in the democratic tradition and managed through procedural devices that diminish it, but there, too, the tension is never entirely dispatched. Its tenacity reflects the reality that the allure of science and the commitment to individual rights are both basic to the political consciousness of the Enlightenment.

CHAPTER 2 | # Classical Utilitarianism

Jeremy Bentham was nothing if not bold. On the first page of his only systematic treatise about politics he reduced his doctrine to a single paragraph:

> Nature has placed mankind under the governance of two sovereign masters, *pain* and *pleasure*. It is for them alone to point out what we ought to do, as well as to determine what we shall do. On the one hand the standard of right and wrong, on the other the chain of causes and effects, are fastened to their throne. They govern us in all we do, in all we say, in all we think: every effort we can make to throw off our subjection, will serve but to demonstrate and confirm it. In words a man may pretend to abjure their empire: but in reality he will remain subject to it all the while. The *principle of utility* recognizes this subjection, and assumes it for the foundation of that system, the object of which is to rear the fabric of felicity by the hands of reason and law. Systems which attempt to question it, deal in sounds instead of senses, in caprice instead of reason, in darkness instead of light.[1]

Bentham further explains that the principle of utility "approves or disapproves of every action whatsoever, according to the tendency which it appears to have to augment or diminish the happiness of the party whose interest is in question: or, what is the same thing in other words, to promote or to oppose that happiness."

Bentham believed that his happiness principle applies equally to the actions of individuals and to those of governments, and, when applied to governments, that it requires us to maximize the greatest happiness of the greatest number in the community.[2]

This would prove to be a complex undertaking as we will see, but he had no doubt that it was possible and that governments that followed his directives would prosper and be perceived as legitimate, whereas those that failed to do so would inevitably be stuck in the dark ages of dysfunctional misery. Bentham spent much of his life trying to implement his utilitarian scheme for the design of social and political institutions—ranging from prisons to parliaments—and he traveled the world advocating it to rulers and politicians. His confidence was matched by his theoretical ambition. He never doubted that the system could be worked out in all its particulars to govern every facet of human interaction, reducing political and moral dilemmas to technical calculations of utility. A century later Marx and Engels would write of a utopian order in which politics could be replaced by administration.[3] Bentham believed that it could be done in eighteenth-century England.

2.1 The Scientific Basis of Classical Utilitarianism

An unabashed creature of the Enlightenment, Bentham was contemptuous of the influential natural law tradition of his day, famously declaring all theories of natural law and natural rights to be "simple nonsense . . . rhetorical nonsense,—nonsense upon stilts."[4] He defended an extensive system of political rights, but he saw rights as human artifacts, created by the legal system and enforced by the sovereign. He insisted that there are no rights without enforcement and no enforcement without government,[5] a blunt statement of the view that would subsequently become known as legal positivism. Whereas natural law had traditionally been seen as providing the benchmark for evaluating the positive legal systems humans create, for Bentham there is nothing but positive law, and it should be evaluated by utilitarian principles rooted in science.

Bentham had no doubt that utilitarianism has the undeniable

force of the Cartesian *cogito*. "When a man attempts to combat the principle of utility," he insisted, "it is with reasons drawn, without his being aware of it, from that very principle."[6] Thus if an ascetic moralist eschews pleasure, it is really "in the hope of honour and reputation at the hands of men," and this prospect of honor is the true source of this pleasure. By the same token someone who denies himself pleasure, or martyrs himself on religious grounds, reflects "fear of future punishment at the hands of a splenetic and vengeful Deity." This fear is nothing more than "the prospect of pain," a fully utilitarian motivation.[7] It does not take much reflection to realize that the notions of pleasure seeking and pain avoidance as Bentham deploys them here are sufficiently capacious that any conceivable motivation could be re-described in their terms. This merits suspicion today on the grounds that a theory of human psychology that is not falsifiable in principle cannot be evaluated scientifically. Bentham was operating in the mainstream of the early Enlightenment, however, so he quite naturally regarded this feature of his argument as validating the utilitarian outlook.

For Bentham, utilitarianism had a naturalistic basis that is rooted in the human organism's imperatives for survival. This is remarkable, given that he was writing seventy years before Charles Darwin.[8] Bentham recognized the existence of religious, moral, and political sources and sanctions of pain and pleasure, but he insisted that they are all based on, and secondary to, physical sources and sanctions of pain and pleasure. The physical is the "groundwork" of the political, moral, and religious; it is "included in each of these."[9] We are bound to the principle of utility by the "natural constitution of the human frame";[10] often unconsciously and when our conscious accounts of our actions are inconsistent with it. If we did not abide by the principle, he tells us in *The Psychology of Economic Man*, "the species could not continue in existence," and "a few months, not to say weeks or days would suffice for the annihilation of it."[11] Bentham takes it as an "axiom," comparable to those "laid down by Euclid" that, "successfully or unsuccessfully," man aims at happiness, and so "will continue to aim as long as he continues to be man, in every thing he does."[12]

2.2 Individual Versus Collective Utility and the Need for Government

Given this utterly deterministic view of human nature, the question arises: What place is there for government? If people pursue pleasure and avoid pain both relentlessly and regardless of all other considerations, this does not seem to leave much of a role for government to enhance the pursuit of utility. Add to this the fact that Bentham says that the legislature has little to do with the causes of pleasure, that its primary activities have to do with the prevention of mischievous acts,[13] and it seems clear that he sees the private actions of individuals, particularly in the production of wealth, as the main source of utility. This is explicit in Bentham's *Principles of the Civil Code:*

> Law does not say to man, *Work and I will reward you* but it says: *Labour, and by stopping the hand that would take them from you, I will ensure to you the fruits of your labour—its natural and sufficient reward, which without me you cannot preserve.* If industry creates, it is law which preserves; if at the first moment we owe everything to labour, at the second, and every succeeding moment, we owe everything to law.[14]

This passage reflects Bentham's view that although the rule of law is essential to the pursuit of utility, law should limit itself to ensuring that people can pursue utility for themselves. This view need not be implied by the logic of utilitarianism as we will see, but it seems clear that Bentham was committed to it.[15]

The role for government that *is* required by the logic of Bentham's theory is rooted in his egoist assumption that pleasure seeking and pain avoidance always operate at the level of individual psychology. People are individual utility-maximizers, who care nothing for the overall good of society. This view suggests that they will break their promises and steal from others if it is worth their while and they can get away with it, unless there is a criminal law to protect life, limb, and property rights and a civil code to enforce contracts and otherwise facilitate commerce. On its own this possibility is not sufficient to justify government from Bentham's premises, because a war of all against all in which the strong consume the weak might, for all we know, lead to the greatest possible net utility for the survivors. (Indeed, we will see that one of the most trenchant critiques of utilitarianism derives from the fact that it places no moral importance on who experiences utility, only that it is experienced.) Accordingly, there must be something more to motivate the need for government, from Bentham's perspective, than the mere fact that the selfish pursuit of pleasure and avoidance of pain trump all other human impulses.

The "something more" comes down to two things, the first being that selfish behavior can be self-defeating. There are various circumstances in which purely selfish individuals will not voluntarily do what is in their interest. The example Bentham gives, which may be one of the earliest accounts of the logic of free riding, concerns the financing of a war. Although each individual benefits from the security provided by the army, there is no discernible individual return to him on his tax contribution, so he has no reason to support the war voluntarily if he can get a better return on what would otherwise have been his tax contribution to the war effort.[16] Generally, if one knows that a good will be provided regardless of whether one contributes to its provision, then a purely selfish utility calculator will refuse to contribute. This problem of funding the provision of public goods is one of a class of market failures, where the market's invisible hand leads to suboptimal outcomes for all concerned.[17] Bentham saw that because "society is held together only by the sacrifices that men can be induced to make for the gratifications they demand," government would have to force them to make sacrifices in circumstances when they might get away with not doing so. To obtain these sacrifices is "the great difficulty, the great task of government."[18]

In addition to this nascent market-failure justification of government, Bentham also believed that there was a robust role for government in computing people's utilitarian interests and enacting policies to further them. Contemporary arguments that take self-interested individuals as their building blocks are usually radically anti-paternalistic in assuming, also, that the individual is sovereign over the definition of his own utility. This further assumption did not begin to work its way into the utilitarian tradition until John Stuart Mill refashioned it a generation after Bentham wrote. It did not evolve into a radically subjectivist position until Charles L. Stevenson, following in the wake of Ayer's logical positivism, rejected the idea that had been taken for granted in the utilitarian tradition at least since the time of Hume: that the sources of pleasure and pain are alike across different individuals. Hence Hume's belief that if all factual questions were resolved no moral questions would remain, and that a science of the passions could yield conclusions that would be generalizable across individuals. This is what Stevenson radically questioned. Arguing that there is no good reason to believe that "factually informed people will have approbation for the same objects," he concluded that "if there were *nothing* for which all or most informed people would have a similar approbation, people being temperamentally different in this respect—then *nothing* would be a virtue and *nothing* a vice."[19]

For Bentham, writing a century and a half before the full transformation of egoism into mere subjectivism, the whole point of the new utilitarian science was to get definitive answers that went beyond mere opinion or subjective assertion. "It is with the anatomy of the human mind as with the anatomy and physiology of the human body: the rare case is, not that of a man's being unconversant, but that of his being conversant with it."[20] Bentham's egoism thus had a strongly objectivist cast. He never doubted that utilitarian calculations could be made for everyone, and that cost-benefit calculations could then be made by government to determine the optimal course for society. He thought of pleasure and pain along four dimensions: intensity, duration, certainty or uncertainty, and "propinquity or remoteness."[21] He also thought the "extent," or number of persons to whom a given pleasurable or painful act applies, could be computed for a political community. Like many political economists since, he doubted that intensity could be accurately measured, but he was sure that all the other dimensions could be quantified.[22] He thus envisaged giant cost-benefit calculations of utility for society, ranging from the fundamentals of constitutional arrangements to the optimal punishments of particular infractions of the criminal law.[23] Indeed, much of the nitty gritty of the *Principles of Morals and Legislation* was devoted to making a start on a grand utilitarian scheme of this kind, to be refined, though not in its essentials revised, by subsequent generations. Bentham saw it as a kind of all-purpose textbook to which legislators might refer in calibrating what we might describe as their *utilitometers* as they sought to refashion society on a scientific basis.

In addition to being quantifiable, Bentham regarded the pains and pleasures relating to different activities as interchangeable. Once this move is made, the question arises: What is the metric or unit of account by reference to which they are rendered comparable to one another? Unless there is such a metric, he noted, "there is neither proportion nor disproportion between punishments and crimes."[24] More generally, there would be no way for individuals to compare different sources of pain and pleasure with one another, or to make judgments across individuals about the "extent" of utility. Intra- and inter-personal comparisons of this kind presume the existence of a single metric to which the multitude of pleasures and pains can be rendered mutually commensurable. There has to be a tangible proxy for utility.

Money was Bentham's utilitometer. Just as the thermometer is "for measuring the heat of the weather" and the barometer is "for measuring the pressure of the air," so money "is the instrument for measuring the quantity of pain and pleasure." Bentham recognized that money may not be seen as an entirely satisfactory basic unit of account. But he placed the burden of proof on the skeptic to "find out some other that shall be more accurate, or bid adieu to politics and morals."[25] Noting that "the rich man is apt to be happier, upon an average, than a poorer man," he insisted that using money as a proxy for utility is likely to get us "nearer to the truth than any other general suppositions that for the purpose in question can be made."[26] Money has the additional advantage of giving us some leverage on the difficult subject of intensity of preference, since people can sell things they want less in order to buy things that they want more. As Bentham puts it:

> If I having a crown in my pocket, and not being athirst hesitate whether I should buy a bottle of claret with it for my own drinking, or lay it out in providing for a family I see about to perish for want of any assistance, so much the worse for me in the long run: but it is plain that, so long as I continue hesitating, the two pleasures of sensuality in the one case, of sympathy in the other, were exactly worth to me five shillings, to me they were exactly equal.[27]

"So much the worse for me" refers to complexities relating to interpersonal comparisons that will be taken up shortly. The point to conclude with here is that Bentham saw money as the best proxy for utility, both to measure pleasure and pain and to calibrate systems of incentives to influence human conduct.

2.3 Interpersonal Comparisons and Consequentialism

Bentham's scheme was a cardinal system inasmuch as he supposed that units of pain and pleasure, appropriately dubbed "utils," could be added and subtracted to produce aggregate results for an individual. Thus we can in principle make judgments of the form that if someone derives three utils of pleasure from reading a book but suffers two utils of pain from earning the money to purchase it, then on balance doing the work in order to buy the book is desirable. Bentham's system also permitted interpersonal comparisons of utility, enabling a third party to judge the relative utilities derived by different people from the distribution of goods and harms throughout society. The injunction to maximize the greatest happiness of the greatest number is ambiguous among the ideas that the happiness of the majority should be maximized, that the greatest happiness of the largest possible group should be maximized, or merely that the sum total of the utility in society should be maximized. On any of these interpretations (the last is usually taken to capture Bentham's meaning best), there is no interest in *who* experiences the relevant utility. Goods and harms are distributed solely by reference to the criterion that they have the consequence of maximizing net social utility.

Classical utilitarianism is thus a radically consequentialist doctrine. Even if a policy involves grave harm, perhaps death, for some, that is no reason to object to it if the net effect is to maximize total utility. This is why links can be drawn between utilitarianism and eugenics, and why it confronts severe difficulties in dealing with the disabled. If the costs of keeping someone alive exceed the benefits to her and to the rest of society, then there is no utilitarian reason not to let her die. And if supremacist members of the Aryan race experience an increase in utility as a result of exterminating the Jews in their midst that exceeds the suffering experienced by those Jews, utilitarianism supplies no grounds for objecting. On the contrary, it would actually support such a policy, as even those who are sympathetic to consequentialist theories have been forced to concede.[28]

In addition to its interpersonal effects, Bentham's thorough-going focus on the experience of pleasure brings with it a threat to autonomy and authenticity that most will, on reflection, find troubling. Robert Nozick points out that on such a theory we should be willing to plug into "experience machines," if they could be created, that would cause us to experience no pain and a continual stream of pleasures, when in fact we were floating in vats with our brains connected to electrodes.[29] This is a logical extension of the brilliant portrayal of satiated conformism in Aldous Huxley's dystopia, *Brave New World*.[30] As with Huxley's "feelies" and "soma," reflecting on Nozick's pleasure machine reminds us that people are unlikely to abdicate control over their lives, or knowingly to trade in reality—no matter how much it often disappoints—for pleasurably soothing fiction. Avoiding pain and seeking pleasure are often important to people, but for most of us they are not always the most important things.

Ignoring the disabled, exploiting vulnerable minorities, inauthenticity, and loss of autonomy are ever-present dangers of utilitarianism, but they were not high on Bentham's list of concerns when thinking about redistribution so as to maximize net social utility. The manifestly pressing question for him, given the vast wealth owned by a tiny minority and the hordes of rural, and, increasingly, urban poor, was whether redistribution from the rich to the poor would be a net social improvement. For Bentham the answer was obviously yes, given his embrace of what has come to be known as the principle of diminishing marginal utility. Although wealth increases happiness, Bentham insists that "ten thousand times the quantity of wealth will not bring with it ten thousand times the quantity of happiness." Indeed, he is doubtful that it will even bring twice as much happiness. The reason is that "the effect of wealth in the production of happiness goes on diminishing, as the quantity by which the wealth of one man exceeds that of another: in other words, the quantity of happiness produced by a particle of wealth (each particle being of the same magnitude) will be less and less at every particle; the second will produce less than the first, the third less than the second, and so on."[31]

The principle of diminishing marginal utility has since become standard in economics and political economy. When coupled with a utilitarian scheme that permits interpersonal comparisons, it takes on a radically redistributive hue, as Bentham was well aware. Other things equal, "with the greatest happiness of the greatest number for its end in view, sufficient reason would have the place for taking the matter of wealth from the richest and transferring it to the less rich, till the fortunes of all were reduced to an equality, or a system of inequality so little different from perfect equality, that the difference would not be worth calculating."[32] The logic of classical utilitarianism was thus friendly to the idea that the state should engage in massive redistribution from England's exceedingly affluent aristocracy to the disposed poor, starting with transfers from the wealthiest to the poorest. "The larger the fortune of the individual in question, the greater the probability that, by the subtraction of a given quantity of the matter of wealth, no subtraction at all will be made from the quantity of his happiness."[33]

Bentham became an increasingly radical democrat over the course of his life. In his early years as a reformer he thought it would be sufficient to enlighten the aristocracy in order to see his ideas implemented. But later he came to see the aristocracy as a corporate body, a society within society that looks to aristocratic interests rather than those of the nation as a whole. Bentham came to understand that "the spirit of corporation," as Elie Halévy put it, "is the worst enemy of the spirit of the principle of public utility,"[34] so that radical political reform would be necessary to achieve his agenda. This led Bentham, along with James Mill, Major Cartwright, and the other radical utilitarian reformers, to embrace the universal franchise in his *Resolutions on Parliamentary Reform*, published in 1818. For "it is only in so far as the members of the House [of Commons] are in fact *chosen*, and from time to time *removable* by the free suffrages of the great body of the people, that there can be any adequate assurance, that the acts done by them, are in conformity to the sense and wishes of the people; and, therefore, that they can, in truth, and without abuse of words, be styled, or declared to be, representatives of the people."[35]

Reluctant radical democrat that he became in the first decades of the nineteenth century, Bentham was never a revolutionary.[36] Even on the matter of redistribution of wealth his view was that other considerations should temper redistributive policies. As he put it in *The Philosophy of Economic Science*, although the "first order" effect of redistributing from the wealthy to the poor would be a large increase in net social utility, once we take account of "effects of the second and those of the third order" then the result would be quite different. "To maximization of happiness would be substituted universal annihilation in the first place of happiness—in the next place of existence. Evil of the second order,—annihilation of happiness by the universality of the alarm [among the wealthy at the prospect of redistribution], and swelling of the danger into:—Evil of the third order,—annihilation of existence by the certainty of the non-enjoyment of the fruit of labour, and thence the extinction of the inducement to labour."[37] In *The Psychology of Economic Man* Bentham spells this out more explicitly:

> Suppose but a commencement made, by the power of a government of any kind, in the design of establishing it [absolute equality], the effect would be—that, instead of every one's having an equal share in the sum of the objects of general desire—and in particular the means of *subsistence*, and the matter of *abundance*, no

one would have any share of it at all. Before any division of it could be made, the whole would be destroyed: and, destroyed, along with it, those *by* whom, as well as those for the sake of whom, the division had been ordained.[38]

Accordingly, Bentham argues for the pursuit of "practical equality," where this is understood to mean "whatsoever approach to absolute equality can be made" that does not undermine subsistence, abundance, and security—which are "of superior necessity."[39]

It is not clear how Bentham expects us to know what "practical equality" requires as a practical matter. Beyond ruling out slavery,[40] he writes as if there is a threshold below which the wealthy will tolerate redistribution and above which they will balk. This is the kind of view one heard in Apartheid South Africa when it was frequently said that the minority of wealthy white farmers would burn their crops before submitting to black majority rule. The example is instructive because, in the event, virtually all of them accepted majority rule without any such drastic response.[41] Similarly, in the United Kingdom, the wealthy have lived with marginal tax rates of over ninety percent under some post–World War II Labour governments, and, even in the United States, quite high tax rates have been tolerated, particularly during wars.[42] If there is a tax threshold above which the wealthy will defect, just what it is seems to be highly elusive. It is thus far from clear how a utilitarian planner could be expected to apply the distinction between absolute and practical equality to redistributive tax policy.

Rather than deal with this problem in terms of a prohibitive threshold, contemporary economists would think of it by reference to a trade-off between tax rates and the propensity of those who are taxed to work or invest, with changing effects at the margins: as tax rates go up, people will be marginally less inclined to work or invest. Bentham himself had the tools to construct the problem in this way, given his grasp of the principle of diminishing marginal utility. More realistic and intellectually satisfying as this approach might have been, it scarcely resolves the contentious political issues. What the rate of trade-off (between rates of taxation and productive activity) actually is will have to be computed in order to find the optimal tax rate for redistribution, and this is bound to be ideologically charged and disputed. It will be ideologically charged because the wealthy have an interest in portraying the rate of trade-off to be steeper than the poor or their representatives are likely to believe is the case. It will be contentious because it is always difficult to disentangle the effects of tax rates from the other factors that influence economic performance. This has been dramatically illustrated in the debates over "supply side" economics that were ushered into the United States and Britain by the Reagan and Thatcher administrations in the early 1980s. The theory is that tax cuts will actually increase government revenues by prompting increased investment and economic growth. In reality the number of interacting variables that influence economic performance is sufficiently large that it is impossible to find data that tests the supply side hypothesis decisively, and decades later economists and politicians continue to line up on both sides of the issue.

Notice that what is at stake in debates of this kind does not turn on the logic of utilitarianism. Arguments about the dynamic effects of tax policies on the size of the pie over time turn, instead, on what Bentham referred to as second- and third-order effects. This takes us into the world of contentious empirical issues of macroeconomics where claims and counter-claims swirl, everyone has a vested interest, and evidence may be terminally inconclusive. The redistributive presumption remains at the core of the theory, but it is far from clear that anyone professing to be a Benthamite utilitarian will need to feel compelled to act on it in any given situation.

It should also be noted that no particular redistributive policy can be inferred from the principle of diminishing marginal utility. A common error is to suppose that the principle suggests that the wealthier people are, the less important money will be to them. Someone in the grip of that misconception might think it supplies grounds for thinking that the wealthy will be less likely to resist redistribution than Bentham feared. In fact the principle of diminishing marginal utility has no such implication. The principle says that the wealthier you are, the less new utility you will derive from each additional dollar. This suggests that the more money you have, the *larger* the dollar increments that will be required, at the margin, to increase your utility. The better analogy is to a heroin addict who needs increasing amounts of the drug to achieve the same "fix": the more you have, the more you want. A poor person derives more utility from a given amount of money than a wealthy person, but this does not mean that the wealthy person wants money less; on the contrary.

It would be equally misguided to draw the competing conclusion from this observation, supposing that it supplies ballast to the supply-side presumption that increasing marginal rates of taxation will make the wealthy less likely to work or invest. The principle of diminishing marginal utility tells us nothing about intensities of preference or about how steep the rate is at which utility diminishes. Moreover, precisely because money has the "the more you have, the more you want" implication just described, it may be the case that, as tax rates go up, the wealthy will actually work harder or invest more.[43] Perhaps they would stage a coup or revolution to take over and abolish the progressive tax system if they could, but, if they are not in a position to do this, perhaps they will work harder and invest more than they would have done but for the existence of the high marginal rates. Given that the principle of diminishing marginal utility actually implies an escalating marginal desire for dollars to achieve new increments of utility, increasing marginal tax rates might be like speeding up the wheel a rat is running on: he may just run faster. A point comes when he falls off, exhausted, or decides to do something else—what an economist would describe as trading off work for leisure. However, nothing in the theory of utilitarianism or the principle of diminishing marginal utility tells us where that point would be, or what the optimal tax rate is to get people to work and invest as much as possible.

In short, an initial presumption in favor of absolute equality falls effortlessly out of the logic of Bentham's system. Once prudential considerations pull us away from its radical simplicity, we enter the messy empirical world of macroeconomic policy and its effects on human behavior at the margin. Intuitions can pull in conflicting directions about these questions, and they are likely to be supplied with impetus by the interests that are served by having them move in one direction rather than another. Bentham underestimated the difficulty of resolving these questions, as well as the degree to which they would likely be contaminated by conflicts of interest, largely because of his faith in science. That is the subject we turn to next.

2.4 Scientific Neutrality and Human Freedom

Arguing for utilitarian solutions inevitably raises the questions: Who will wield the utilitometer? and what are their motivations likely to be? This is where Bentham's immense confidence in science kicked in. He was sure that, done correctly, maximizing utility could have no outcome other than to produce vast increases in happiness for a nation's entire population. Nor did he doubt that governments could be induced to maximize utility correctly once the right answer was known. Yet this confidence was problematic.

Bentham's loss of faith in the possibility of an enlightened aristocratic class scratched the surface of large difficulties associated with self-interested motivations in politics. Halévy points out that Bentham applied "not the principle of natural identity, but the principle of artificial identity of interests" to political affairs, believing that it was possible to organize a representative regime "under conditions such that the general interest, and the harmony of interests of the governors with those of the governed, would infallibly result from the legislative decisions adopted."[44] His mature view of the aristocracy as an inward-looking corporate body made it akin to what Jean-Jacques Rousseau and James Madison referred to as "partial associations" and "factions" that undermine the general interest of society.[45] Today they are called "special interests." Our examination of this subject in §7.2 will reveal that it is far more difficult than Bentham and these other writers supposed to show either that there is a general interest or, if there is, that democratic procedures will converge on it. Without getting to those issues here, it is fair to say that there is reason for skepticism from Bentham's own premises. If the aristocracy was a special interest, why might others not form under conditions of universal franchise? Redistributive politics in a democracy involves dividing up money and other goods by majority rule. It seems undeniable that some coalition can always form, under such conditions, to enrich itself at the expense of the rest. The coalition will be unstable in the sense that some of its members may always be tempted to form a new coalition with those currently excluded to the detriment of some present beneficiaries.[46] There is, however, no reason to suppose self-interested individual maximizers, of the kind Bentham insists we all are, will ever eschew private benefit in the interests of the general interest. As a result, we should expect the aristocratic corporate interest he so despised to be replaced by others that will be no less self-interested than they.

This is to say nothing of the venality of the politicians. Bentham seems to suppose that those in power can transcend the selfish impulses in whose grip he insists we are all inescapably caught. It would make more consistent sense from his perspective to assume that politicians would invariably be susceptible to pleasing special interests if the price was sufficiently high, if not straightforwardly corrupt—trading on their positions of public trust for personal profit. Bentham thought these impulses could be reined in to some extent via the threat of removal in a democracy, but, even if this is so, the same temptations would presumably afflict magistrates, bureaucrats, prison-wardens, and others to whom he would have us look to implement the utilitarian calculus throughout society. They must surely be expected to be corrupt at every turn on his account, feathering their own nests rather than building the Benthamite utopia. In fact Bentham believed that an ethos of public service would make government officials responsible, but, as Rosenblum notes, he never pointed out who would serve or why they would transcend self-interested impulses and feel constrained by the professional good government ethos he advocated.[47]

Bentham's inability to perceive this tension in his account is perhaps best explained by reference to his commitment to the early Enlightenment conception of science discussed in §1.1.2. He seems to have thought that the Cartesian force of his proposals must make them irresistible to any thinking creature. Voting citizens in a democracy and their representatives in the government and agents in the bureaucracy would transcend self-interest when it came to making and implementing public policy—acting instead on the compelling precepts of utilitarian science. Just as knowledge was power for Bacon, Bentham saw knowledge as moving us from blind and slavish adherence to the pleasure/pain calculus to conscious control of the collective rules within which it operates. Science does not enable us to transcend human nature, but it does give us the capacity to manage it rationally.

Trying to decide whether this brings Bentham down on the side of free will or of determinism involves grappling with a secular version of Locke's dilemma about God and natural law. If we focus on Bentham's view that his arguments are rationally irre-sistible, then we will see them as inescapably binding on all ra-tional creatures and so come down on the side of determinism. If, on the other hand, we see him as he was for much of his life, struggling at every turn to persuade opponents and skeptics that his was a better way to organize society than that which they currently embraced, then a different view emerges, one with a foundational place for agency and choice. Reasoned persuasion must have a purpose—namely, to persuade—and this suggests not only that persuasion is possible but also that it can fail, and that it is important to try to make it succeed.

In conclusion, then, we should note that although Bentham is justly famous as an utterly mechanistic determinist, there are two points at which individual rights and human agency figure im-portantly in his theory. The first concerns his insistence that the means to utility are privately produced. As a result, he argues that government's principal role is to create an environment in which you can enjoy "the fruits of your labour," by protecting those fruits through the rule of law. This embryonic libertarianism launched his distinction between absolute and practical equality, blunting what would otherwise have been the radically redistribu-tive implications of his theory and relegating government to a regulatory role in a highly inegalitarian world. This is among the reasons that his party eventually became known as that of the "intellectual" or "philosophical" radicals, as Halévy notes, losing its utopian and revolutionary character and becoming instead the party of "bourgeois doctrinaires."[48] The other point at which hu-man agency enters is more fundamental. By embracing the idea that science allows us to understand and shape our destinies in ways that are better than those based on religion, superstition, natural law, or blind impulse, Bentham affirms the Enlighten-ment aspiration to achieve freedom, even as he embeds it in a thoroughly determinist science.

Synthesizing Rights and Utility

CHAPTER 3

Classical utilitarianism was beset by two profound difficulties. One is that the amount of information needed to implement it is staggering. Bentham's optimism and self-confidence notwithstanding, it is far from evident that the kind of utilitometer he had in mind could ever be constructed. For any government to aspire to delve into the psyches of individuals, get the relevant data, and compare it across people seems excessively ambitious, leaving aside the troubling issues relating to the incentives facing those empowered to wield the utilitometer just discussed. The second difficulty concerns the reality that the classical utilitarian scheme is insensitive to all moral boundaries among persons.[1] Some might be reassured on this front by Bentham's libertarian impulses, and his concomitant endorsement of a regulative stance for the state geared to enabling people to produce the means of their own utility. The merits and demerits of such views are taken up in §5.3. The point to stress here is that Bentham's libertarian impulses were independent of the logic of classical utilitarian theory. Those with different impulses could deploy it in vastly more interventionist ways—ranging from aggressive redistributive programs, to draconian forms of sacrifice of the disadvantaged and chronically depressed, to euthanasia and possibly even genocide.

Had Bentham's been the mature formulation of utilitarianism, it would likely be no more than an historical relic today in light of these difficulties—contributing nothing constructive to our search for a viable principle of political legitimacy. But utilitarianism was reshaped in ways that spoke to both difficulties, contributing to its resilience as one of the major political ideologies of our time. It was a transformation that took place in a context of changed assumptions about the possibility of certainty in science, and it was reinforced by developments in economics and philosophy between the mid-nineteenth and early twentieth centuries. How that process occurred, and what its implications are for thinking about political legitimacy, are the subject of this chapter.

3.1 Changes in the Meaning and Measure of Utility

The architects of neoclassical price theory, William Jevons (1835–1882), Léon Walras (1834–1910), Alfred Marshall (1848–1924), Francis Edgeworth (1845–1926), Knut Wicksell (1851–1926), and Vilfredo Pareto (1848–1923) were principally interested in understanding the behavior of prices in market economies. In the opening paragraph to his *Manual of Political Economy*, for example, Pareto differentiates his enterprise of developing knowledge for its own sake from those of practical advice giving or promoting a particular doctrine aimed at social improvement.[2] Some of these theorists were deeply committed to social improvement, and some thought advances in economic theory would lead to it, but the activity itself was truth seeking: to understand the laws of motion of economic systems, particularly capitalism, so as to predict their future behavior. They wanted to develop their theories with a minimum of metaphysical baggage. In particular they wanted to find a way to proceed without getting involved in two debates that seemed both problematic and unnecessary. One was about the labor theory of value. It had preoccupied the classical economists, Adam Smith (1723–1790), David Ricardo (1772–1823), and Karl Marx (1818–1883), and will concern us in §4.2. The other, which we focus on here, dealt with what Pareto described as the theory of tastes. Acutely aware of the information problems confronting classical utilitarianism, he had every reason to want the new science of political economy to be as little dependent on solving them as possible.

The question, from this perspective, became: How much can we understand about the ways markets operate with a minimum of information about people's utility? Most obviously problematic was the idea of interpersonal comparisons of utility. Thus Pareto distinguished the study of "sensations of one man in different situations" to determine what choices he would make from study that involves comparing "the sensations of one man with those of another man, and determines the conditions in which the men must be placed relative to each other if we want to attain certain ends." This latter type of study, he insists, "is one of the most unsatisfactory in social science." The reason is our lack of a utilitometer to make the relevant comparisons. Just as we cannot tell whether the happiness a wolf would derive from eating a sheep would exceed the happiness the sheep derives from not being eaten, the same, Pareto insists, is true with humans.[3] Or again:

> The happiness of the Romans lay in the destruction of Carthage; the Carthaginians' happiness, perhaps in the destruction of Rome, in any case in the saving of their city. How can the happiness of the Romans and that of the Carthaginians both be realized? . . . It could be replied: the total happiness would be greater if the Romans would not destroy Carthage, nor the Carthaginians Rome, than if one of the cities were destroyed. This is an idle affirmation which cannot be supported by any proof. How can one compare these agreeable, or painful, sensations, and add them?[4]

Pareto was convinced that any greatest happiness principle that made use of interpersonal comparisons could lead to such objectionable results as support for slavery, if slaveholders could be said to gain more happiness than slaves lost, or an inability to rule out theft as immoral. "To know whether theft is moral or not," he asks rhetorically, "should we compare the painful sentiments of the robbed with the agreeable sentiments of the robbers, and look for those with the greater intensity?"[5] Instead of abandoning the goal of maximizing social utility in the face of such examples, Pareto's move was to abandon the use of interpersonal comparisons of utility. Predecessors such as Marshall, Edgeworth, and Wicksell had diminished reliance on assumptions about interpersonal comparability, but Pareto was the first to dispense with them entirely.[6] He could see no conceivable scientific basis for making them, so that any theory that deploys them must be an ethical choice that reflects "the sentiments of the one who constructs it, sentiments which, for the most part, are borrowed from the society in which he lives, and which, in very small part, are his own; sentiments which are a non-logical product which reasoning changes very little."[7]

In addition to ruling out interpersonal comparisons, Pareto advocated greater modesty in what we should aspire to know about the psychology of individuals. He wanted to avoid delving into why people want things or even whether they consume the goods they try to acquire. He thought it entirely unnecessary to enter into questions concerning whether consuming goods brings people happiness. "Morphine is not useful, in the ordinary sense of the word, since it is harmful to the morphine addict; on the other hand it is economically *useful* to him, even though it is unhealthful, because it satisfies one of his wants."[8] He even coined the term *ophelimity* to designate the idea of purely economic utility, though it never caught on and will not be used here. His point was that in order to understand the ways in which desires influence people's economic behavior, and through that, the operation of the economic system in the aggregate, we need know nothing about why they have the desires that they do, whether they are good or bad, or what mental states are produced by satisfying them or failing to satisfy them. Nor need we concern ourselves with philosophical debates about the propriety of identifying happiness with pleasure.[9] Pareto had no objection to our developing opinions about peoples' tastes from moral, psychological, or other points of view, but he thought them irrelevant to a scientific political economy:

> One is grossly mistaken then when he accuses a person who studies economic actions—or *homo oeconomicus*—of neglecting, or even of scorning moral, religious, etc., actions—that is the *homo ethicus,* the *homo religious,* etc.—; it would be the same as saying that geometry neglects and scorns the chemical properties of substances, their physical properties, etc. The same error is committed when political economy is accused of not taking morality into account. It is like accusing the theory of the game of chess of not taking culinary art into account. . . . In separating the study of political economy from that of morality, we do not intend to assert that the former matters more than the latter. In writing a tract on the game of chess one certainly does not intend to assert thereby the preeminence of the game of chess over the culinary art, or over any science or any art.[10]

This disclaimer was to some extent disingenuous. We have already seen that Pareto was profoundly skeptical of the possibility of any scientific basis for moral judgments. Fewer than thirty pages after the passage just quoted he was insisting that "ethics or morals" is a subject "which everyone believes he understands perfectly, but no one has been able to define in a rigorous way," and that they "have almost never been studied from a purely objective point of view."[11] For Pareto, objective scientific study is most emphatically not "reasoning about words." He insists that "we must get rid of that method" if we want the social sciences to progress.[12]

As a methodological matter Pareto was clear that the political economy of his day exemplified the path forward in the study of human relations. Political economists had come to recognize that

all theories are fallible because science is in perpetual development. "One we hold true today will have to be abandoned tomorrow if another one which comes closer to reality is discovered."[13]
For Pareto "it is quite obvious that any phenomenon whatsoever
can be known only through the idea it gives rise to within us."
This inevitably means that we get "only an imperfect image of the
reality." We must always compare "the subjective phenomenon,
that is, the theory, with the objective phenomenon, that is, with
the empirical fact."[14] Where experimental testing is possible, as
in most of the natural sciences, that is best; where it is not, as
in meteorology, astronomy, and political economy, we must "be
content with observation."[15] The idea that knowledge claims can
aspire to have any scientific force if they are not tested systematically against experience was anathema to him; hence his dubious-
ness about ethics and moral philosophy. This is a far cry from the
early Enlightenment view of these subjects as preeminent sciences along with logic and mathematics. Pareto's view of ethics
actually had much more in common with Stevenson's doctrine
discussed in §2.2.

Contemptuous though he generally was of normative inquiry,
for the most part the Pareto of the *Manual* saw it as superfluous.
Attention to the moral and other dimensions of human action
was unnecessary because his system did not depend on judgments about these matters. It did not even require that a person's
utility be expressed on a cardinal scale, since Pareto did not require that we perform any arithmetic functions on it. This, too,
was an important modification of the classical utilitarian doctrine,
because the idea of expressing utility in terms of cardinal units is
highly demanding even if we bracket the difficulties associated
with interpersonal comparisons. Very often, perhaps typically, it
would be impossible to know how much utility is derived from
one activity as compared with another. Trying to answer that ques-

tion was another unnecessary diversion for Pareto. All that was required was the idea of an ordered ranking in which a person declared himself to prefer one thing to another or to be indifferent between the two. Nothing needed to be known about how much things were preferred to one another, and, although Pareto embraced the assumption of diminishing marginal utility, he did not need to assume anything about the rate at which utility diminishes for a particular good for a particular person.[16]

The only other assumption he needed to make, which is generally seen as a minimal condition of rationality rather than a feature of utility, was the idea of transitivity: if I prefer a to b and b to c, then I must prefer a to c.[17] He did not need to make a judgment on whether people are selfish or altruistic. Noting that it is customary in political economy to make the egoistic assumption that "man will be guided in his choice exclusive by consideration of his own advantage, of his self-interest," Pareto points out that this assumption is unnecessary. Without loss for his system, we could just as readily assume people to be altruistic, if this could be rigorously specified, or work with any other consistent rule "which man follows in comparing his sensations." It is not even an essential characteristic of the class of acceptable theories "that a man choosing between two sensations choose the most agreeable; he could choose a different one, following a rule which could be fixed arbitrarily."[18] So long as we restrict our comparisons to a single person and require the minimal condition of rationality that preferences be transitively ordered, that is sufficient for Pareto's purposes.

Pareto's denial of the possibility of interpersonal comparisons had the effect of importing a powerful doctrine of individual autonomy into the core logic of utilitarianism. Whereas Bentham's libertarian impulse was at best contingently related to the analytics of his greatest happiness principle, it is axiomatic in Pareto's scheme that each person is sovereign over her preferences. The individual is constrained to be rational in the exceedingly minimal sense implied by transitivity, but beyond this, no third party judgments are made about what people do, or should, value. His system thus creates analytical and moral space for the Enlightenment ideal of individual rights.

Pareto was a creature of the Enlightenment also in being powerfully committed to science. Unlike Bentham, however, his was a mature Enlightenment conception of science that "deduces its results from experience, without bringing in any metaphysical entity" or relying on "reasoning about words."[19] As we are about to see, he tried to deal with the tensions between the two Enlightenment commitments through a predictive science of transactions that autonomous individuals can be expected to engage in without compromising their autonomy. As with Bentham, then, utilitarian efficiency remains the secular heir to natural law determinism for Pareto, but this is realized at a deeper level because respecting individual rights is now constitutive of utilitarianism. In place of a contingent coexistence of rights and utility, Pareto offers a synthesis.

3.2 The Market as Utilitometer

Although Pareto's is not a normative theory, it nonetheless has normative implications. These derive from the pivotal role it ascribes to free individual choice as embodied in and expressed through market transactions. To understand these implications, and distinguish them from spurious normative implications that are often wrongly attributed to the Pareto system, it is necessary to focus on his account of what market behavior tells us, and what it does not tell us, about individual and social utility.

The core notion here is that of an indifference curve. The intuition behind it is a synthesis of three ideas already discussed: that people want to maximize utility in Pareto's stripped-down sense, that their choices generally reflect the principle of diminishing marginal utility, and that they are minimally rational in that their orderings of their desires do not violate transitivity. If we think in terms of two different goods, bread and wine, diminishing marginal utility suggests that someone who has no wine but a large supply of bread will be willing to trade comparatively large amounts of bread for comparatively small amounts of wine, but that the bread "price" that they will be willing to pay for wine will decrease as their stock of wine goes up and their bread pile shrinks—and vice versa. Indifference means exactly what it says: someone is indifferent between two goods if exchanging one for the other would neither increase nor decrease his or her utility. Applying this notion to loaves of bread and bottles of wine, we can imagine that there would be an array of possible bundles of different amounts of the two among which a person would be indifferent, such as the following: forty loaves of bread and six bottles of wine, fifteen loaves of bread and eight bottles of wine, five loaves of bread and nine bottles of wine. We do not need to know what the numbers are, nor do we need to assume they would be the same for everyone, only that they increase and diminish in the directions predicted by diminishing marginal utility and that they do not violate transitivity. Indifference curves capture this idea, as shown in figure 3.1.

Each indifference curve, I_1, I_2, I_3, I_4, and so on, represents different combinations of bread and wine among which individual A is indifferent. Her utility would improve only if she could move to a higher indifference curve, for example from I_1 to I_2, or I_2 to I_3. She is assumed to want to be on as high an indifference curve as possible, so that the hyphenated arrow pq, pointing northeast from the origin, indicates the direction of change that would increase her utility. Indifference curves always have a negative slope and are generally convex from the point of origin (i.e.

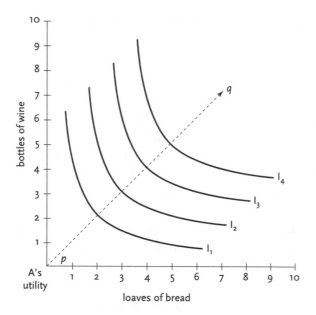

Figure 3.1. Paretian indifference curves for one individual and two commodities

the curve lies above its tangent at every point), reflecting diminishing marginal utility. They cannot intersect, since that would violate transitivity.[20]

Pareto's genius lay in seeing that this conceptual apparatus afforded predictions about how people would interact in market situations so as to improve net social utility that did not require any interpersonal comparisons of utility. The market renders the need for a utilitometer superfluous, since people can reveal their preferences to one another through their market behavior. The operation of this theory of revealed preference can be seen in figure 3.2.

Here we suppose that there is some existing distribution, denoted x, of goods between two individuals A and B, that the available supply of these goods is fixed so that it is not possible to

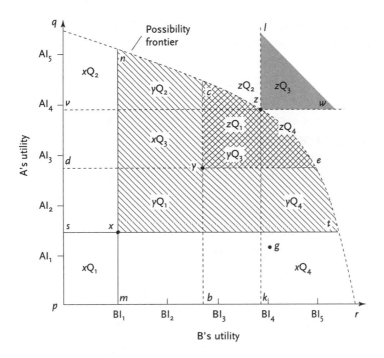

Figure 3.2. Illustration of the Pareto principle with two individuals in a fixed commodity space

move outside of the possibility frontier qr, and that each individual behaves as depicted in figure 3.1, seeking to get onto as high an indifference curve as possible. That is, person A wants to move as indicated on the arrow in the direction pq, and person B wants to move as indicated on the arrow in the direction pr. A's indifference curves might be imagined as passing through the two arrows at the points indicated by AI_1, AI_2, AI_3, and so on; B's indifference curves by BI_1, BI_2, BI_3, and so on. If we draw a vertical line mn and a horizontal line st through the status quo x, the commodity space divides into the following four quadrants: xQ_1 is to the southwest of x, xQ_2 is to the northwest, xQ_3 is to the northeast, and xQ_4 is to the southeast.

What can we say about each of these quadrants? xQ_1 is distinctive in that any move into it would be judged inferior to the status quo by A and by B. We might imagine such changes as resulting from a tax by the state imposed on both of them to fund a program from which neither benefits in proportion to the amount levied against her or him. This might be because of government waste, because the funds are sent in the form of foreign aid to a country both A and B despise, or for some other reason. Such changes make everyone in our two-person society worse off. As a result they would not be expected to occur in a market system. They are *Pareto-inferior* to x.

By contrast, any moves from x into xQ_3 would make both people better off. Perhaps A produces wine and B produces bread, and they find a mutually agreeable exchange that moves each to a higher indifference curve. These *Pareto-superior* changes will occur in a free market; both A and B derive benefit from the exchange, so both can be expected to engage in it voluntarily. Thus we might imagine an exchange of some quantity of bread for some quantity of wine that moves them from x to a new status quo y.[21] Any exchange that makes at least one person better off without making anyone worse off exhibits this property. Note that this would include a move such as from x to n, which would involve an increase in A's utility but to which B would be indifferent.[22]

We can then repeat the exercise, drawing vertical line *bc* and horizontal line *de* through the new status quo y, giving us four new quadrants yQ_1, yQ_2, yQ_3, and yQ_4, exhibiting the same properties as their predecessors did for x. Again we can say that neither party will have any interest in moves into yQ_1, but that both would benefit from moves into yQ_3. This should be expected to lead to iterated exchanges of bread for wine until A and B reach some status quo that lies on the possibility frontier *qr* such as z. Again we can draw our vertical line *kl* and our horizontal line *vw* and our four new quadrants zQ_1, zQ_2, zQ_3, and zQ_4. But the possibility of further exchanges that benefit both is exhausted, as is indicated by the fact that zQ_3 falls entirely to the northeast of the possibility frontier. This means that there is no way to improve A's utility without diminishing B's, and vice versa, and a *Pareto-optimal* point has been reached. When x was the status quo, any point on the possibility frontier between n and t might potentially have been reached, depending on their relative bargaining power, or bargaining skill, and the steepness of the slopes of A's and B's indifference curves. Once they have reached some point on the possibility frontier, however, no additional exchanges will occur between them voluntarily; an equilibrium will have been reached.

What of the northwest and southeast quadrants, xQ_2 and xQ_4, yQ_2 and yQ_4, zQ_2 and zQ_1, and so on? These are changes from the status quo where one gains at the expense of the other. As with Pareto-inferior changes, they will not occur in a free market because the potential loser will oppose them. Such *Pareto-undecidable* changes are the bread and butter of redistributive politics, as the state taxes one group and redistributes the proceeds to another. They are undecidable for Pareto in that it is not possible to determine from his premises whether or not they lead to a net improvement in social utility. A move, for example, from status quo x to distribution g may benefit B more than it harms A, but it may not. Because we are working with ordinal utilities and impersonal comparisons have been ruled out, no inference can be made from the distances on the axes about amounts of utility gained or lost by either party. All that can be said is that A loses and B gains; nothing about by how much.

Notice that the Pareto principle does not entail that Pareto-superior changes produce greater net social utility than Pareto-undecidable ones. For all anyone can know, distribution g might produce more combined utility for A and B than distribution y; there is no better reason to deny that it does than to affirm that it does. Pareto was aware that his principle would be misconstrued as implying a prescriptive argument to the effect that Pareto-superior exchanges, or market transactions, lead to greater net improvement than Pareto-undecidable nonmarket transactions, but he was adamant that his argument did not imply this, and that, in any case, he was not in the business of offering prescriptive arguments about redistribution because he could see no scientific basis for them.[23] What *can* be said is that Pareto-superior changes are unambiguous improvements on the status quo and that Pareto-inferior changes are unequivocally worse than the status quo; nothing more, nothing less.

It is possible to combine the information conveyed in figures 3.1 and 3.2 into a single figure known as an Edgeworth box diagram, as portrayed in figure 3.3. In this figure we have both A and B and the two commodities, bread and wine, which are assumed for convenience to be the only two commodities in the economy. As in figure 3.1, A seeks to move to the northeast from her southwest point of origin *p* in order to get onto the highest possible indifference curve. B's preferences are represented as the mirror image of A's, so that his indifference curves advance to the southwest from his point of origin in the northeast corner of the diagram at *p'*. The status quo *x* now lies at the tip of a football-shaped Pareto-superior zone, its curves being formed by the indifference curves of A and B that intersect at *x*. The move from *x* to *y* creates a new, smaller football representing the new Pareto-superior zone from status quo *y*, and a further move to *z* brings them to the possibility frontier as indicated by the fact that A's and B's indifference curves pass through it at points of tangency to one another. This is thus the same type of equilibrium as represented by *z* in figure 3.2; there is no way to improve the utility of either without diminishing the utility of the other. If we imagine a line from A's point of origin *p* to B's point of origin *p'* that passes through all the points of tangency between A's and B's indif-

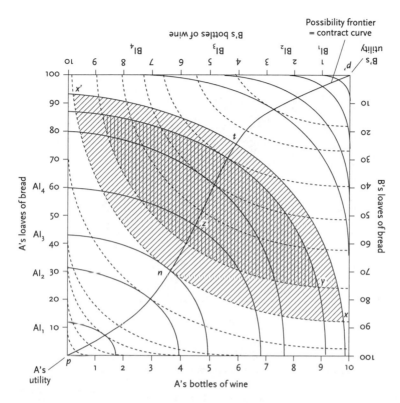

Figure 3.3. Edgeworth box with two individuals in a fixed commodity space

ference curve, that is the possibility frontier (line *qr* in figure 3.2), also known as the contract curve. The prediction is that, no matter where they start, voluntary agreements will lead A and B to make exchanges that move them toward the contract curve, and when they reach it they will be in equilibrium—meaning that no further exchanges between them will occur. Exactly where they end up on the contract curve within the football defined by *xx'* (i.e., between *n* and *t*) will depend on their relative bargaining power, or bargaining skill, and the steepness of the slopes of their indifference curves.

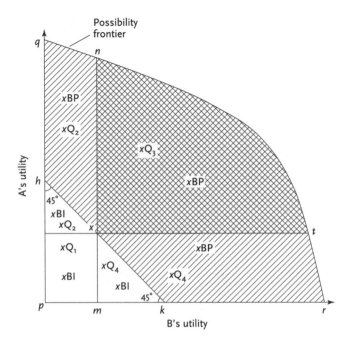

Figure 3.4. Partial comparison of the Pareto principle with Bentham's greatest happiness principle in a fixed commodity space

Before moving to an assessment of the Pareto principle from the perspective of our concern with the foundations of political legitimacy, it will be helpful to compare it with Bentham's greatest happiness principle as represented in figure 3.4. This comparison is, of necessity, partial, because the greatest happiness principle applies to cardinal interpersonally comparable utilities, whereas the Pareto principle applies to ordinal noncomparable utilities. Nonetheless, by superimposing one on the other we can underscore what is at stake in the move from classical to neoclassical utilitarianism. Supposing the status quo again to be x, if we draw a downward sloping line hk at 45 degrees from axis pq to axis pr, then everything between this line and the possibility frontier is

Bentham-superior to x, and everything between it and the origin p is Bentham-inferior to x. This follows from the fact that Bentham's principle is sensitive only to the total amount of utility in the society. Everything that is Pareto-superior to x is thus also Bentham-superior, but not vice versa because parts of the Pareto-undecidable quadrants xQ_2 and xQ_4 are Bentham-superior to x. The line hk that forms this decisive divide for the greatest happiness principle marks off parts of xQ_2 and xQ_4 as Bentham-superior to the status quo x. This reflects Bentham's willingness to discriminate among outcomes that Pareto would regard as impossible to distinguish from one another scientifically.

Part of what is at issue between these two principles for thinking about the political legitimacy of distributive arrangements can be seen by considering the limiting case depicted in figure 3.5. This Edgeworth box is identical to the one portrayed in figure 3.3, except that the initial status quo x is now in the southwest corner at p, reflecting an extreme maldistribution in which B has all of both commodities. Consequently, it also differs from the previous case in that x now falls on the possibility frontier, so that it has the same properties as z in figures 3.2 and 3.3. This status quo is thus a Pareto-optimal equilibrium, even though it is presumably one in which A starves. Since A has nothing that B wants, there will be no exchange between them.

Here we see the force of Pareto's rhetorical query concerning how can we hope to know whether the wolf's utility derived from eating exceeds the sheep's utility derived from not being eaten. This is an easy case to make Bentham's principle look good. It is obvious that small transfers from B will bring large benefits to A, and it is difficult to take seriously the notion that A's utility gain will not exceed B's utility loss. But no principle can be judged by how well it does with the easiest case. The general point that emerges from the comparison is that neither principle does well for thinking about the conditions under which it is legitimate

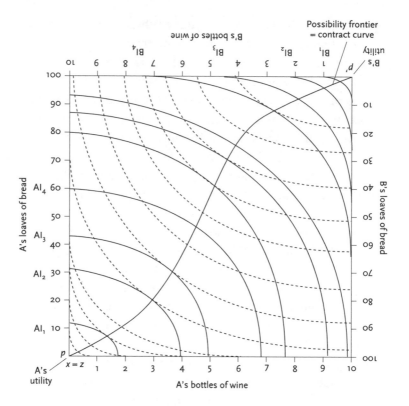

Figure 3.5.

for the state to alter distributive arrangements. Bentham's "objective" principle is too strong. He is validly criticized for being naïve about whether contentious comparisons might be avoided, and for his insufficient attention to monitoring the behavior of governments and bureaucrats charged with making and implementing policy based on those comparisons. Similar considerations come into play when evaluating the claims of contemporary objective utilitarians such as Peter Singer, when he defends infanticide and euthanasia.[24]

Pareto's "subjective" principle is, by contrast, too weak. He was right that Pareto-superior transactions differ importantly from

Pareto-undecidable ones. But those who deploy his argument to suggest that the state gains legitimacy by leaving distribution to the market overreach in at least two ways, one concerning the realm of the Pareto-superior, the other that of the Pareto-undecidable. Concerning the first, we should embellish figure 3.5 with a little more reality by noting that in the actual world bread and wine are not the only commodities. Those who own large amounts of what others need can induce them to agree "voluntarily" to become prostitutes, to work for starvation wages, to sell themselves into indentured servitude, or perhaps in some cases even into slavery. That a change would be a Pareto-superior move from the status quo may not be a reason to accord it legitimacy if it involves humiliation, exploitation, or something worse. In short, although a conception of individual rights is constitutive of the Pareto system, close inspection reveals it to be a narrow, not to say artificial, conception that is unlikely to win many adherents among the vulnerable or dispossessed.

With respect to Pareto-undecidable outcomes, we have seen from the preceding discussion that these range over vast arrays of exceedingly different possibilities, validating Bentham's impulse that we should aspire to discriminate among them in a principled fashion. If we concede that his account of how to bisect the Pareto-undecidable quadrants is less than successful, this merely underscores the compelling need to try to do better. The most serious and influential attempt over the past century and a half was put forward by John Stuart Mill (1806–1873), to which I turn next.

3.3 Preventing Harm as Legitimating State Action

Mill's father, James (1773–1836), had been a contemporary and enthusiast of Bentham's, raising his son on an uncompromising diet of utilitarianism. Although the young Mill reacted strongly

against this, much of his subsequent writing in political philosophy was devoted to reformulating utilitarianism in ways that
would render it palatable to a liberal consciousness.[25] *Utilitarianism* (1863) contains his most fully developed statement, but it is in
On Liberty (1859) that he squarely confronts the tension between
the utilitarian demands of society and the Enlightenment commitment to individual freedom. The approach he takes in that
work seems at first sight to be disarming in its simplicity, and to
come down decisively on the side of individual freedom.

> The object of this essay is to assert one very simple principle, as
> entitled to govern absolutely the dealings of society with the indi-
> vidual in the way of compulsion and control, whether the means
> used be physical force in the form of legal penalties or the moral
> coercion of public opinion. That principle is that the sole end for
> which mankind are warranted, individually or collectively, in inter-
> fering with the liberty of action of any of their number is self-
> protection. That the only purpose for which power can rightfully be
> exercised over any member of a civilized community, against his
> will, is to prevent harm to others. His own good, either physical or
> moral, is not a sufficient warrant. He cannot rightfully be com-
> pelled to do or forbear because it will be better for him to do so,
> because it will make him happier, because, in the opinions of oth-
> ers, to do so would be wise or even right. These are good reasons
> for remonstrating with him, or reasoning with him, or persuading
> him, or entreating him, but not for compelling him or visiting him
> with any evil in case he do otherwise. To justify that, the conduct
> from which it is desired to deter him must be calculated to produce
> evil to someone else. The only part of the conduct of anyone for
> which he is amenable to society is that which concerns others. In
> the part which merely concerns himself, his independence is, of
> right, absolute. Over himself, over his own body and mind, the
> individual is sovereign.[26]

Mill's motivation in defining this harm principle can be traced
to both of the core Enlightenment values I have been discussing,

but he offers an account of the relations between them that differs from any we have confronted thus far. His commitment to individual rights, manifestly embodied in the harm principle, rests partly on the idea that individual freedom is an intrinsically valuable feature of human existence. Mill worried that "individual spontaneity is hardly recognized by the common modes of thinking" of his day "as having any intrinsic worth, or deserving any regard on its own account."[27] He quoted German romantic humanist Wilhelm von Humboldt (1767–1837) approvingly to the effect that "the end of man . . . is the highest and most harmonious development of his powers to a complete and consistent whole." The development of originality requires "individual vigor and manifold diversity" that arises from "freedom, and variety of situations."[28] For Mill, "it is the privilege and proper condition of a human being, arrived at the maturity of his faculties, to use and interpret experience in his own way."[29] Mill believed individual autonomy to be insufficiently valued in democracies (of this more later), but he had no doubt about its intrinsic worth. Hence his emphatic insistence "on the importance of genius and the necessity of allowing it to unfold itself freely both in thought and practice,"[30] and his advocacy of such measures as a second vote for university graduates.[31]

Mill also thought the regime of individual rights implied by his harm principle was instrumentally valuable for the promotion of utility, not in the stipulative fashion that led Pareto to define utility as whatever voluntary exchange among rights holders generates, but as mediated by science. He regarded utility "as the ultimate appeal on all ethical questions; but it must be utility in the largest sense, grounded on the permanent interests of man as a progressive being."[32] Mill believed this meant respecting the harm principle because what is in the interests of man as a progressive being has to be discovered through science, and freedom is essential to that venture. Promoting individual freedom is the surest path to the expansion of knowledge, and that, in turn, is vital to utilitarian progress.

Mill's long second chapter on liberty of thought and discussion is devoted to establishing the first part of this claim by reference to a fallibilist conception of knowledge that has much in common with Pareto's. Opinions, for Mill, are either true, false, or—as is typically the case—partly true and partly false. If we suppress an opinion on the grounds that it is false, there is always the chance that we are mistaken. Even if we are not, and the silenced opinion is in error, "it may, and very commonly does, contain a portion of the truth; and since the general or prevailing opinion on any subject is rarely or never the whole truth, it is only by the collision of adverse opinions that the remainder of the truth has any chance of being supplied." Moreover, even if the received opinion on a subject is the complete truth, unless it is "vigorously and earnestly contested, it will, by most of those who receive it, be held in the manner of a prejudice" rather than on credible scientific grounds. As a result, the truth in question will run the risk of being "lost or enfeebled" so that it will be "a mere formal profession, inefficacious for good."[33]

Freedom of speech is thus essential to the pursuit of science, though Mill clearly thinks of this as more than a mere negative right. Unless individuality, critical thinking, and resistance to accepting arguments from authority are actively promoted through a robust individual rights regime, the danger of slavish obedience grows. This, in turn, will undermine the scientific attitude and with it, the growth of knowledge that is essential to long-run utility. Indeed, finding ways to foster and maintain individuality is all the more important, for Mill, because he expects the advance of knowledge and the egalitarian effects of widespread education to breed conformity. Important though the advance of science is for sound utilitarian decision-making by government, education "brings people under common influences and gives them access to the general stock of facts and sentiments," leading to a general social leveling so that "the very idea of resisting the will of the public, when it is positively known that they have a will, disappears more and more from the minds of practical politicians" and "there ceases to be any social support for nonconformity."[34] Even when a creed is based on valid knowledge, there is the danger that it will evolve into an "hereditary creed,"

> to be received passively, not actively—when the mind is no longer compelled, in the same degree as at first, to exercise its vital powers on the questions which its belief presents to it, there is a progressive tendency to forget all of the belief except the formularies, or to give it a dull and torpid assent, as if accepting it on trust dispensed with the necessity of realizing it in consciousness, or testing it by personal experience; until it almost ceases to connect itself at all with the inner life of the human being.[35]

Knowledge can thus be misused and the advance of science may breed undesirable forms of conformity, but at the end of the day Mill's fallibilism forces him to place his bet on the pursuit of truth. There might be other ways to preserve individuality, but betting on anything other than the pursuit of truth is too dangerous.

To understand Mill's conception of the link between truth and utility, we need to look more closely at how he intended the harm principle to operate in practice. At first sight there appears to be a tension between the principle as stated and Mill's account of its applications in chapter five of *On Liberty*. For instance, he says that "whoever succeeds in an overcrowded profession or in a competitive examination, whoever is preferred to another in any contest for an object which both desire, reaps benefit from the loss of others, from their wasted exertion and their disappointment." Yet Mill defends competitive meritocracy despite this, on the grounds that it is "by common admission, better for the general interest of mankind that persons should pursue their objects undeterred by this sort of consequences."[36] Similarly, Mill recognizes that free trade is harmful to some, yet he defends it on the grounds that "it is now recognized, though not till after a long struggle, that both the cheapness and the good quality of commodities are most effectually provided for" in a free trade regime.[37] By the same token, although sanitary regulations, workplace safety rules, and the prevention of fraud coerce people and interfere with their liberty, such policies are acceptable because the legitimacy of the ends they serve is "undeniable."[38]

The obvious question is: How can Mill in these and other cases justify interference with liberty by reference to prevailing opinion, when he inveighs so forcefully against it in defending the harm principle? Recall that he directs the harm principle against compulsion and control, whether by "physical force" or "the moral coercion of public opinion," so that the fact that a policy is widely accepted is scarcely grounds for pursuing it. Indeed, Mill is perhaps best known for endorsing Alexis de Tocqueville's (1805–1859) claim that the tyranny of the majority is "among the evils against which society requires to be on its guard," insisting, with Tocqueville, that oppression by received opinion is one of the more insidious forms that majority tyranny can take.[39] Unlike Bentham, Mill saw little reason for confidence in democracy as a stay on the oppressive hand of government. Limiting the power of government over the individual "loses none of its importance when the holders of power are regularly accountable to the community, that is, to the strongest party therein."[40] The majority, whether institutionalized or in the form of hegemonic opinion, is what must be guarded against. Mill thus seems to put the fox in charge of the hen house in the "Applications" chapter of On Liberty when he appeals to received wisdom to justify interference with liberty.

To understand how Mill resolves this apparent contradiction, think of the harm principle as operating in two steps. When evaluating a particular action or policy, the first step involves deciding whether the action causes, or has the potential to cause, harm to others. If the answer is no, then the action is in the self-regarding realm and the government would be unjustified in interfering. Indeed, in that case the government has a duty to protect the individual's freedom of action against interference from others as well. If, however, the answer to the initial query is yes, then different considerations arise. We are then in a world in which harm is being committed willy-nilly, and the question is: What, if anything, should the government do about it? In this regard, a more accurate summation of the harm principle than the more famous formulation already quoted can be found at the start of chapter four: "As soon as any part of a person's conduct affects prejudicially the interests of others, society has jurisdiction over it, and the question whether the general welfare will or will not be promoted by interfering with it becomes open to discussion. But there is no room for entertaining any such discussion when a person's conduct affects the interests of no persons besides himself."[41]

If the harm threshold is crossed, then utilitarian considerations come into play for Mill. However, the aim should not necessarily be to prevent any particular harm. Rather, the goal should be to determine the best policy for society as a whole, given that we are now in the other-regarding realm. In this respect Mill was a rule-utilitarian rather than an act-utilitarian; he thought decisions should be made about the net effects of classes of actions and policies in the aggregate, not about each action or policy taken on a case-by-case basis.[42] In making these determinations Mill did indeed think that we should appeal to the kind of state-of-the-art knowledge that he invoked in his chapter on applications, always recognizing that such knowledge claims are fallible. They might, and probably will, stand in need of revision as science and received wisdom advance.[43]

Seen from this perspective, the tension in chapter five dissolves, but Mill is scarcely out of the woods because much then turns on the determination of relevant harm. If, for Bentham, we had to worry about how to build and operate the utilitometer, the question for Mill is how to build and operate the instrument we might describe as a *tortometer*?[44]

Starting with the definition of harm, it seems clear that the Mill of *On Liberty*, at least, conceived the sphere of self-regarding action quite capaciously.[45] Despite his low opinion of religion in general and Christianity in particular, he favored wide religious toleration and extensive freedom of belief as already discussed. He was also a vigorous defender of freedom of speech, except in circumstances when it becomes a clear incitement to riot. Thus "an opinion that corn dealers are starvers of the poor, or that private property is robbery, ought to be unmolested when simply circulated through the press, but may justly incur punishment when delivered orally to an excited mob assembled before the house of a corn-dealer, or when handed about among the same mob in the form of a placard."[46]

But this is a list of examples. What is the general principle that leads Mill to declare that some actions cross the harm threshold, and that others fall short of it? Mill's answer is that actions enter the other-regarding sphere when they are "calculated to produce evil to someone else."[47] You cannot be penalized for addiction and bad habits, but you can when they harm others; drunkenness is not objectionable in itself, "but a soldier or policeman should be punished for being drunk on duty."[48] What you do, it seems, is your business; how it affects others is society's business.

Things, however, are not so simple. Uncontroversial as these particular examples of Mill's might seem, they divert attention from a profound ambiguity in Mill's definition of harm that his reliance on the term *calculated* encapsulates. That term could signify something intentional, as in "he calculates," "he is a calculating person," and so on. Alternatively, it could be given a consequentialist interpretation, as in "we calculate that his actions are harmful to others." Much turns on which interpretation we adopt. A thoroughgoing intentionalist reading would create an exceedingly robust harm principle, protecting the individual from many forms of interference that are countenanced in modern liberal democracies. It is not clear, by contrast, that a consequentialist reading would give her much protection from government interference at all. Virtually every action has some harmful consequence for someone somewhere, even before we get into the abstruse philosophical world of whether omissions count as actions. Our actions have what Arthur Pigou (1877–1959) described as externalities: consequences for third parties that may be harmful regardless of whether this is intended.[49]

Mill deployed both interpretations at different points in *On Liberty*. In his defense of Mormon polygamy, for example, although he was entirely convinced that it harms women, he felt that society must defer to the desires of the participants. If people choose it voluntarily, society has no business interfering.[50] He saw no justifiable basis for Sabbatarian legislation, which was popular in the United States when he wrote, again on the grounds that commerce on Sundays involved no harm to others, and he likewise insisted that moralizing legislation aimed at stamping out addiction and bad habits for their own sake was without legitimate warrant.[51] His discussion of prohibition is utterly contemptuous of the claim that the consumption of alcohol has deleterious effects on those who do not consume it; he dismisses this claim as an assertion of specious "social rights."[52]

Much of the time, however, Mill clearly embraces the consequentialist meaning of *calculated,* as when he says that whenever there is "a definite damage, or a definite risk of damage, either to an individual or to the public, the case is taken out of the province of liberty and placed in that of morality or law."[53] The examples concerning meritocratic competition, free trade, and industrial regulation, discussed earlier, all exhibit this hue. Interpreting the harm principle seems, then, to present us with a dilemma that parallels the Hobson's choice between objective and subjective definitions of utility. Like Bentham's objective conception, the consequentialist reading of the harm principle gives the state carte blanche to sacrifice individual freedom in the name of social utility. Like Pareto's subjective account, by contrast, the intentionalist reading leads to a libertarian stance that renders the state powerless to limit many extreme forms of exploitation. Rendering either of these readings morally satisfying is difficult, if not impossible. This is perhaps why the partisans on both sides of the issue tend to argue by pointing to the demerits of the interpretation they oppose, while overlooking the drawbacks that attend the interpretation they defend.

3.4 Contextual Variation in the Definition of Harm

Finding a single compelling interpretation of the harm principle is likely an impossible task. Perhaps it makes more sense to entertain the possibility that different definitions of harm might be appropriate in different circumstances, so that there is no one correct interpretation to be had. This pluralist course begins to look plausible if we reflect on the various ways in which harm is defined in American law. The criminal law revolves around an intentionalist standard in that the existence of *mens rea*, or a guilty mind, is one of the elements of a crime that the prosecution must prove beyond a reasonable doubt. Much civil law, by contrast, revolves around consequentialist standards of harm, the limiting case being strict liability in torts, where the tortfeasor (wrongdoer) is held liable without reference to whether he was at fault and regardless of his intentions. The difference here is explained by the fact that criminal law and tort law are motivated by different purposes. Criminal law is intended to discourage an activity, such as murder, rape, assault, or theft, that has been judged wrong, and to which moral sanctions have been deemed appropriate. Before convicting someone of such an act and making them pay the price in terms of lost liberty and social opprobrium, establishing the existence of the relevant malevolent intent is in order.[54]

Tort law is also intended, in part, to discourage such blameworthy intentional acts as battery and trespass. But tort law is mainly concerned with apportioning the harmful externalities of activities that are not themselves objectionable, such as manufacturing goods and services, producing pharmaceutical drugs, or practicing medicine. Because suppression of the activity itself is not the purpose of the exercise, there is no point in requiring a *mens rea* standard to find out whether or not the person intended to perform the act in question. Tort law is concerned, rather, with protecting us from the harmful effects of otherwise legitimate actions, with minimizing the costs of accidents plus the costs of their avoidance, to use Guido Calabresi's celebrated formulation.[55] This may be served best by strict liability, by a negligence standard that requires establishing that the tortfeasor failed to meet an appropriate standard of care, or by some other criterion. The appropriate standard may vary from activity to activity— products liability, medical malpractice, environmental damage, and other areas of torts all present distinctive issues—and the standard may change over time in response to new discoveries about how best to influence behavior.[56] This is just the kind of utilitarian calculation informed by advancing science that Mill thought should be undertaken once the harm principle has been triggered.

Recognizing that different conceptions of harm are appropriate to different provinces of the law is an important step in recalibrating expectations about what we should want general principles to deliver. It is not, however, a panacea, because it does not speak to the question: Who should wield the tortometer? or, on this more pluralist conception, who should decide which tortometer to wield in which context? We might find considerable agreement on the proposition that harm should be thought about differently in criminal law and civil law, and within civil law, that different conceptions may be appropriate for contracts, torts, products liability, medical malpractice, and so on, without getting agreement on which activities belong in these different areas. Unresolved, for example, would be the questions whether abortion, prostitution, recreational drugs, or denying medical treatment to children on religious grounds should be criminalized. True, many matters would be uncontroversial. Extortion, blackmail, assault, battery, and rape would fall within the ambit of most conceptions of what is appropriate for the criminal law, but much would remain unresolved.

When it comes to the role of the government in responding to social injustice outside the criminal law area, perhaps the larger part of the terrain must be expected to be controversial. One way of underscoring what is at stake here is to note that the criterion for identifying a relevant harm can be controversial not just for technical reasons, as when Calabresi disagrees with Richard Posner over whether negligence or strict liability maximizes efficiency in tort law,[57] but also for normative reasons. This has been illustrated in American Supreme Court jurisprudence by the ideological shifts since the Warren Court era of the 1950s and 60s. Since that time, the Burger and Rehnquist Courts have been marked by retreats in many areas of public law from consequentialist *de facto* standards for identifying the kinds of injustice that warrant the Court's remedial intervention to the considerably higher hurdle of intentionalist *de jure* standards.[58]

In the area of school desegregation, for instance, *Green v. County School Board* (1968) and *Swann v. Charlotte Mecklenburg Board of Education* (1971) had established that if *de jure* segregation had ever been shown in a school district in the past, then continuing patterns of discrimination would be presumed *de facto* to be a consequence of it. Remedies would be ordered so long as schools continued to exhibit a racially identifiable character.[59] This standard has been effectively eroded, however, by such cases as *Freeman v. Pitts* (1992) and *Missouri v. Jenkins II* (1990). The Court now places the burden on the plaintiff (who goes to court seeking a remedy) to establish that every instance of apparent discrimination is the result of an intention to discriminate on the part of a public official.[60] In the area of employment discrimination, *Griggs v. Duke Power* (1971) permitted plaintiffs to recover on a claim of "disparate impact," but the Court has since steered shy of inferring discrimination from effects.[61] With respect to voting rights, *Rogers v. Lodge* (1982) rejected earlier suggestions in *Mobile v. Bolden* (1980) and *Rome v. United States* (1980) that discriminatory effects were sufficient for a remedy, and required, instead, a showing of discriminatory intent. *Rogers v. Lodge* was effectively overturned by Congress in an amendment to the Voting Rights Act in 1982, once more validating a standard that permits "effects" to prove violations.[62]

At issue in such cases is considerably more than technical disagreement. Rather, we have two contending views of injustice: one rooted in particular malevolent acts that stand in need of individual redress, the other in patterns of structural disadvantage requiring sustained action by government if they are to be addressed effectively. Which of these is the more plausible view will concern us in subsequent chapters. The point to stress here is that Mill's harm principle offers us no assistance in choosing between them. Mill may be right that preventing harm is an important criterion in determining the legitimacy of state action, but his principle does not tell us which harms are relevant to which sorts of state action, how disagreements about such matters are to be resolved, or how far-reaching the state's remedial actions should be. The harm principle is better thought of as part of the skeleton of a theory of legitimate government rather than anything like the whole beast.

Before leaving Mill we should take note of an inertial conservative bias to the harm principle on both the interpretations we have been considering. On the intentionalist reading Mill's principle is analogous to the Pareto principle in making mutual consent the only justification for change. We can remonstrate, reason, persuade, or entreat, but never compel people if these other approaches are ineffective—at least so long as those who harm do not specifically intend to do so. We can argue in the newspapers or in peaceful demonstrations that corn-dealers are starvers of the poor, or that private property is robbery, but if corn-dealers and property owners resist the force of our reasoning, there is no recourse beyond the soap box on Hyde Park corner. Requiring the agreement of all parties to alter the status quo inevitably privileges it, as critics of unanimity rule have long since established.[63] The status quo may be suffused with injustice, facilitating the implausible identification of voluntary transactions with the rights part of the rights-utility synthesis identified in §3.2.

The consequentialist reading of the harm principle might seem potentially more radical, but the requirement that the consequentialist calculus be informed by received opinion is a major practical constraint. As Mill was well aware in his own life, received opinion can be dogmatic and profoundly regressive.[64] He believed that as knowledge advanced and education became more widespread, superstition and irrationality would gradually be displaced by a scientific attitude that would inform public opinion and, with it, the utilitarian calculations of policy makers in the other-regarding realm. In this sense Mill had his own variant of replacing the government with administration. Ambivalent as he might have been about this development on other grounds, his anticipation of it suggests that Mill's attitude was a bit like that of American Progressives such as John Dewey (1859–1952). In practice, however, this is no more than a bet, and from the vantage point of the twenty-first century it does not look like a particularly good one. This was dramatically underscored by the attacks on the World Trade Center and the Pentagon on September 11, 2001. Trusting the scientific attitude to domesticate dogmatism and irrationality in politics seems naïve in the wake of fascism and communist totalitarianism, not to mention the various religious fundamentalisms and tribalisms that threaten to dominate politics, if they do not dominate it already, in so many countries today. Even in liberal democracies such as Britain and the United States, Mill would likely be surprised by the power of anti-scientific attitudes in politics and the persistence of pervasive ideological disagreements almost a century and a half after he wrote *On Liberty*.

This suggests that the solution to the tension between the Enlightenment views of science and rights that flows from the consequentialist reading of the harm principle is as problematic as the solution that flows from the intentionalist reading, if for different reasons. The intentionalist reading trades, we saw, on a conception of choice that ignores, as it preserves, inherited oppressive contexts of individual choice. The intentionalist reading may thus render the harm principle perverse as a device for preserving individual rights. The consequentialist reading avoids this difficulty, but at the price of embracing a groundless faith in the idea that scientific understanding will, increasingly, shape the utilitarian decisions made by governments in deciding both when the harm principle has been violated and how to intervene.

There is a double difficulty here. First, there is the one already alluded to, that scientific attitudes may not, in fact, replace prejudice and dogmatism in the public mind and, *eo ipso*, in the actions of public officials who are charged with reading the tortometer in light of received wisdom. Second, it is far from clear that good science will lead to rights-protecting policies once the threshold of harm has been crossed, triggering government's legitimate intervention. Recall that Mill does not say that when harm occurs, government should enact policies designed to minimize it, or protect those who are most vulnerable to it, but rather that government should act in "the general interest of mankind." The accepted scientific wisdom of the day may hold that the general interest of mankind is best served by anti-miscegenation laws, eugenics policies, or worse. So long as those wielding the tortometer decide that they are acting in an area where harm of some kind can occur to someone, there is nothing in Mill's argument in *On Liberty* to stop them from pursuing these coercive policies in response to it.[65]

CHAPTER 4 | Marxism

What if corn-dealers really are starvers of the poor and private property really is robbery? Enter Karl Marx, for whom both propositions must be taken with deadly seriousness. Marx would take the view that, far from legitimating the political order, the Pareto principle and Mill's harm principle provide ideological smoke that obscure its lack of legitimacy. This derives from the fundamental injustice of the status quo that they protect. As Marx's view is so diametrically opposed to theirs, one might think that they share nothing in common. Reflecting this, some commentators contend that Marx and Mill worked from fundamentally opposed paradigms or world views.[1] Here I make the contrary case that, like all those examined thus far, Marx was a creature of the Enlightenment, and, as such, profoundly committed to the tension-ridden task of marrying a scientific view of human social arrangements to a robust conception of individual rights. There were differences between his and liberal understandings of both ideas, but dissimilarities are exaggerated, and points of commonality overlooked, more often than they should be.

It might reasonably be asked: Why should we bother with Marxism from the vantage point of the twenty-first century? For one thing, virtually every prediction Marx made turned out to be wrong. He thought communist revolutions would occur in the advanced capitalist countries, as radicalized and increasingly cosmopolitan urban proletariats banded together to overthrow capitalist systems he thought were tottering on the edge of collapse in the mid-nineteenth century. Marx believed that the communist party was the vanguard of the proletariat that would lead the revolution, replacing the bourgeoisie as the ruling class and thereby winning "the battle of democracy." According to Marx, this vanguard would "push forward" working-class parties of all other countries; they would "point out and bring to the front the common interests of the entire proletariat" in order to achieve their objective: "formation of the proletariat into a class, overthrow of the bourgeois supremacy, [and] conquest of political power by the proletariat."[2] V. I. Lenin (1870–1924) reiterates this idea in *State and Revolution* when he insists that by "educating the workers' party, Marxism educates the vanguard of the proletariat, capable of assuming power and leading the whole people to socialism, of directing and organizing the new system, of being the teacher, the guide, the leader of all the working and exploited people in organizing their social life without the bourgeoisie and against the bourgeoisie."[3]

In fact, where communist revolutions did occur, the dictatorship of the proletariat turned out to be a dictatorship over the proletariat by the vanguard party, suggesting that Marx had been right to worry, in his third thesis on Feuerbach, that "the educator himself needs educating."[4] Moreover, the working classes of advanced capitalism turned out to be enduringly nationalistic and decidedly nonrevolutionary, and Marxist scholars writing about "late" capitalism even a century after Marx turned out to be engaging in statements of hope rather than statements of fact.[5] Revolutions whose leaders pledged allegiance to Marx's ideas either occurred in peasant societies like Russia and China, or they were imposed from outside by force or the threat of it—as was the case in much of Eastern Europe after World War II. These regimes have, in any case, now collapsed, with the exception of lingering outposts like Cuba and North Korea, or they are embracing capitalism with the zeal of converts—as is the case in

China. Marx would doubtless have been appalled by the various uses made of his doctrines in the real world, but those who are waiting for the genuine article seem, increasingly, to be waiting for Godot.

Another reason for the "why bother?" question is that Marx's theoretical edifice scarcely looks better, today, than his political prognostications. It has been dealt waves of devastating criticism, much of the most penetrating from scholars with egalitarian predispositions and who are not well disposed toward capitalism. Whether one focuses on the economic determinism at the core of his materialist theory of history, the labor theory of value that supplies the basis for his analysis of exploitation, his theory of the declining tendency in the rate of profit and the inevitability of capitalist crises, or the accounts of how socialism and communism would work, Marx's arguments have not stood the test of time. This combination of political and theoretical failure suggests that any attempt to salvage Marxism, whether as an explanatory or normative system, is doomed to failure.

This catalog of failure is striking, though it scarcely distinguishes Marxism from the other major theoretical systems of the modern West considered here. Predictive theory has fared poorly in all precincts of political science, whether in the realm of forecasting elections and other features of everyday politics or in the realm of forecasting regime type that has characteristically engaged Marx and his successors. As for the failure of Marx's overall theory, here he also shares much in common with the variants of utilitarianism already considered and with theories that will engage us subsequently. The question is not whether Marx was wrong about a great many things, but whether he was illuminatingly right about some things.

There is the additional consideration that for all its weaknesses, Marxism has supplied the most enduring alternative to liberal and conservative political thinking since the early Enlightenment.

It has been endlessly reformulated—by Lenin and Leon Trotsky (1879–1940) in Russia, by Rosa Luxembourg (1871–1919) and Karl Kautsky (1854–1938) in Germany, and by Mao Zedong (1893–1976) in China, not to mention the Latin American variant of Che Guevara (1928–1967). Marxism has spawned the critical theory of the Frankfurt School,[6] much contemporary feminist theory, various brands of critical legal studies and other forms of anti-establishment theory in American law schools. The so-called structuralist, post-structuralist, and deconstructionist intellectual movements also contain Marxism centrally in their pedigrees, and figures such as Max Weber (1864–1920) and the elite theorists Gaetano Mosca (1858–1941), Robert Michels (1876–1936) and C. Wright Mills (1916–1962) bear the indelible stamp of the Marxism against which they were reacting. This is not to mention the decisive impact Marxists and Marxist ideas had on the emergence and evolution of modern social democracy.[7] In short, Marxism persists in the intellectual consciousness of the West, partly because of the dearth of alternatives and partly because, for all its failures, it articulates criticisms of the present and aspirations for the future that have never been entirely driven from the field.

4.1 Historical Materialism and Individual Agency

Marx's historical view of social science was thoroughly Cartesian in the sense discussed in §1.1. His was a deductive view, held to be valid for internal theoretical reasons, and he had not the slightest interest in fallibilism or empirical tests of his claims. Indeed, he thought the phenomenal world would be profoundly misunderstood if we relied on "appearances" or the world of empirical data.[8] Like Bentham, Marx believed that the laws governing human society were not generally understood, and that they could be grasped only by comprehending his theoretical system as a whole. This would make sense of the phenomenal realm, making it possible for people to understand themselves, and their place in the evolution of society, for the first time in human history. Once they did, the tension between deterministic science and a conception of individual rights that embodies free will would finally disappear because people would be in a position self-consciously to make their own history.

Marx was also like Bentham in grounding his theory in an account of the underlying interests of the human organism; in this respect they both fall into the naturalist tradition that stretches backward to Hume and Aristotle, and forward to Darwin, Stevenson, and the emotivists. Naturalist theories derive their injunctions for action from theories of human nature or human psychology, theories that are, we might say, endogenous to the human creature and its needs. They are generally contrasted with anti-naturalist theories that look in the first instance to something exogenous—be it Plato's theory of the forms, the will of God, eternally given natural laws, or other extrinsic standards to which humans must in some sense live up. Like other naturalists, Marx based his account on what he took to be distinctive about the human animal. For him this was not the pleasure seeking of utilitarianism, the power seeking of Hobbes, the imperatives for species reproduction that would motivate Darwin, or the capacity for consciousness that motivated G. W. F. Hegel (1730–1831) and the German idealists against whom Marx reacted most directly and immediately. Rather, Marx contended that although humans "can be distinguished from animals by consciousness, by religion, or anything else you like," they distinguish themselves from animals "as soon as they begin to *produce* their means of subsistence."[9]

4.1.1 Dialectical Determinism

If Marx is reminiscent of Bentham in developing an inclusive architectonic from which the laws of human interaction could be derived, he differs by adding a dynamic element. The young

Marx's principal formative antagonist was Hegel, who also had an inclusive architectonic theory with a dynamic element. Hegel's theory revolved around the displacement of systems of ideas by one another throughout human history in a dialectical process in which the imperfections of ideas bred reactions, and were then replaced by new ideas incorporating elements of the original ideas and the reactive alternative. Hence the famous labels of Hegelian dialectical logic: *thesis, antithesis, synthesis.*[10] The thesis is displaced by the antithesis, both of which are subsumed in the new synthesis; then the process begins anew with the synthesis becoming the next thesis. There can be no end to this process so long as humans live in the world of imperfect ideas, but Hegel believed it could and would end in his own lifetime with the Prussian state of his day being recognized as the perfect form of political association, literally bringing about an end to history.

Marx took over this structure of thinking about historical change, but jettisoned its content. His dialectical theory was a materialist one revolving around the ways in which human beings organize production. Like Hegel, he had a view of short-run disequilibrium and long-run equilibrium in the sense that every hitherto existing mode of production contained internal tensions or "contradictions" that must inevitably breed a reaction and replacement by another internally contradictory system, to be replaced again and again until a stable system could be reached. For Marx rather than the Prussian state of nineteenth-century Europe, the stable equilibrium would be a communist utopia ushered in by a socialist state following the overthrow of capitalism. Until that point was reached, history would be a series of unsatisfactory reactions to unworkable tensions, always marked by a contradiction between the relations of production and the forces of production. What he meant by this was that the productive process divided people up into classes, generally those who owned or controlled the means of production, and those who worked for them in order to produce the surplus that people consume. When Marx and Engels open *The Communist Manifesto* with "The history of all hitherto existing societies is the history of class struggles,"[11] they mean that in every mode of production throughout history the class that has owned or controlled the means of production has exploited the class that worked on it by appropriating the fruits of their labor. As they put it more fully in *The German Ideology*, history is thus "nothing but the succession of the separate generations, each of which exploits the materials, the capital funds, the productive forces handed down to it by all preceding generations, and thus, on one hand, continues the traditional activity in completely changed circumstances, and, on the other, modifies the old circumstances with a completely changed activity."[12]

This was typically an unconscious process on Marx's account. Thus when the serf worked a certain number of days on the lord's land in return for protection from attack by the armies of other feudal lords plus the right to engage in subsistence farming for his family, he might see this as an advantageous exchange even if he had no hope of escaping poverty throughout his lifetime. Although there might be intermittent expressions of rage, perhaps even occasional collective rebellion, neither serf nor lord fully comprehends the dynamics of the feudal mode of production, or, therefore, what would be needed to displace it with a system that did not revolve around exploitation of one class by another. Rather, feudalism is displaced by a different dynamic.

For Marx, every mode of production contains the seeds of its own destruction. Feudalism differs from primitive subsistence agriculture in that, instead of every family producing what its members consume, there is a productive peasant class and an unproductive class of landowners, whose interests diverge over time. Under capitalism, the "rule of the bourgeois democrats will from the outset bear within it the seeds of their downfall." Or, as

he and Engels say more fully in the *Manifesto*, "The development
of modern industry, therefore, cuts from under its feet the very
foundation on which the bourgeoisie produces and appropriates
products. What the bourgeoisie, therefore, produces, above all, is
its own grave-diggers. Its fall and the victory of the proletariat are
equally inevitable."[13]

Perhaps the most important force shaping the evolution of
modes of production, for Marx, is the division of labor.[14] Two
aspects of it are of central importance here. The first, as Adam
Smith (1723–1790) had pointed out in *The Wealth of Nations*, was
that it led to vast increases in productivity noted in his celebrated
analysis of pin-making:

> One man draws out the wire, another straights it, a third cuts it, a
> fourth points it, a fifth grinds it at the top for receiving, the head; to
> make the head requires two or three distinct operations; to put it
> on is a peculiar business, to whiten the pins is another; it is even a
> trade by itself to put them into the paper; and the important busi-
> ness of making a pin is, in this manner, divided into about eighteen
> distinct operations.

As a result of this division of labor Smith calculated that ten
workers could make "upwards of forty-eight thousand pins in a
day," but "if they had all wrought separately and independently,
and without any of them having been educated to this peculiar
business, they certainly could not each of them have made twenty,
perhaps not one pin in a day; that is, certainly, not the two hundred and fortieth, perhaps not the four thousand eight hundredth
part of what they are at present capable of performing, in consequence of a proper division and combination of their different
operations."[15]

The other significant feature of the division of labor, also underscored by Smith's example, is that there is no stopping it once
it gets underway. Yet if the multiplication of tasks promotes efficiency, it is manifestly at odds with a productive order marked by

a single division of labor between lord and peasant. As a result, feudalism atrophies; it is inevitably, if gradually, replaced as a new class emerges whose members understand the massive potential inherent in the division of labor and see how to take advantage of it. This bourgeois, or capitalist, class displaces the landed aristocracy and calls the modern working class or proletariat into being by making wage labor available—the magnet that attracts peasants to new urban centers where factory production takes place.

Although the landed aristocracy and the peasantry were in an objective sense the principal antagonists under feudalism, they did not see themselves as such and the feudal order does not dissipate as a result of conflicts between them. Like the antagonists in all previous modes of production, they constitute classes "in themselves" but not classes "for themselves" in Marx's terminology.[16] They are bearers of historical relations, acting out a script which they do not understand and are therefore powerless to influence.[17] Capitalism differs from all previous modes of production in that this is not the case. For the first time in history those in the exploited class come to understand the dialectical process of history and their own place in it, so that the proletariat is not only a class "in-itself," but a class "for- itself" as well.

Working-class consciousness grows, on Marx's account, as capitalism evolves from its radically innovative productive phases to a problem-ridden maturity, marked by the surfacing of contradictions that are explained in §4.2. The result is that a genuinely self-conscious revolution on the part of the proletariat becomes possible because its members understand the dynamics and problems of capitalism, and such a self-conscious revolution becomes necessary because the socialism championed by the proletariat offers the only viable solution to capitalism's travails. "The proletarian movement is the self-conscious, independent movement of the immense majority, in the interest of the immense majority."[18] This leads to a socialist world, in which the distributive principle is: from each according to his ability to each according to his work.[19] The socialist world also contains contradictions because it continues to be a realm of rights in which some do better than others. A worker who has children to support, for example, is worse off than a similar worker who does not, if both are paid on the basis of their work. As Marx says more generally:

> Right, by its very nature, can consist only in the application of an equal standard; but unequal individuals (and they would not be different individuals if they were not unequal) are measurable only by an equal standard insofar as they are brought under an equal point of view, are taken from one *definite* side only—for instance, in the present case, are regarded *only as workers* and nothing more is seen in them, everything else being ignored. Further, one worker is married, another is not; one has more children than another, and so on and so forth. Thus, with an equal output, and hence an equal in the social consumption fund, one will in fact receive more than another, one will be richer than another, and so on. To avoid all these defects, right, instead of being equal, would have to be unequal.[20]

Marx treats these inevitable inequalities as resulting from the new order's being marked by the society from which it emerges, because "right can never be higher than the economic structure of society and its cultural development conditioned thereby." Socialism is an improvement on capitalism because "the individual producer receives back from society—after the deductions [for public goods provision and future investment] have been made—exactly what he gives to it." Nonetheless, "what we have to deal with here is a communist society, not as it has *developed* on its own foundations, but, on the contrary, just as it *emerges* from capitalist society; which is thus in every respect, economically, morally, and intellectually, still stamped with the birthmarks of the old society from whose womb it emerges."[21] Only later, by a process that is not entirely clear, is it followed by the withering away of the socialist state and the emergence of the communist utopia that the superabundance of wealth produced by capitalism makes possible. There the distributive principle is: "from each according to his ability to each according to his needs."[22] It is Marx's equivalent of Hegel's end of history.

4.1.2 Agency and Individual Autonomy

What place is there for individual agency in this sweepingly determinist view of historical change? Interpreted as a causal question, it depends on which Marx one reads. Some formulations of the materialist conception of history suggest an utterly mechanistic determinism in which what goes on in the material "base" of society, to wit, the dynamic contradiction between the forces and relations of production, determines what goes on in the "superstructure" of politics, ideology, culture, and all self-conscious human action. In these formulations Marx insists that "in the social production of their existence, men inevitably enter into definite relations, which are independent of their will, namely relations of production appropriate to a given stage in the development of their material forces of production." These relations constitute "the economic structure of society, the real foundation, on which arises a legal and political superstructure and to which correspond definite forms of social consciousness." The economic base "conditions the general process of social, political, and intellectual life," so that "it is not the consciousness of men that determines their existence, but their social existence that determines their consciousness."

The science of historical materialism is concerned with the material base. In studying its transformations "it is always necessary to distinguish between the material transformation of the economic conditions of production, which can be determined with the precision of natural science, and the legal, political, religious, artistic, or philosophic—in short, ideological forms in which men become conscious of this conflict and fight it out."[23]

Individuals are destined to play out their class-determined roles, usually unwittingly, in the grand historical narrative. Indeed, even in the proletarian revolution, when the "class in-itself" becomes a "class for-itself," there is not obviously much room for agency or choice. Because the proletarian revolution leads inexorably to the end of history, it seems even the revolutionary proletariat acting in its true interests lacks the freedom to do otherwise than it does.

Some of Marx's other formulations suggest a significant place for human agency, however, as in the *Eighteenth Brumaire of Louis Bonaparte,* where Marx says that man makes his own history, but not within limits of his own choosing.[24] It seems clear, if only from the urgency with which Marx in his polemical writings urged intellectuals to work to raise working-class consciousness, that his settled view was that there are choices to be made in politics and bad choices can lead to bad outcomes. Since his time there have been various attempts to make rigorous sense of a materialist conception in which the economic realm is determinative "in the last instance," but in which there is "relative autonomy" of the political and ideological realms.[25] In the terms of contemporary social science, such interpretations of the Marxian intuition are best reformulated as the claim that material interests and conflicts account for most, but not all, of the variance in explaining different social and political outcomes, and that free human agency is a significant independent variable as well. Whether the relative weights of the different variables can be specified in general terms then becomes a question for empirical research rather than armchair speculation.

Sometimes it is said that once free choice is acknowledged as a causal factor in explaining social outcomes, this undermines the aspiration for any deterministic social science, including Marx's.[26] This is not compelling partly for the reason just mentioned: even if free choice accounts for some of what happens in social life, this does not mean it accounts for all of what happens. But the critique also fails for another reason that I take up more fully in §6.4: granting that free choice is causally significant, social scientists might nonetheless reasonably aspire to make probabilistic predictions about what people will generally choose in certain types of circumstances.[27] In any event, it seems clear that if the Marxian causal theory is to be plausibly entertained in light of its predictive failures to date, it will have to be as part of a multivariate explanation. Whether any single causal theory of all social and political phenomena can be sustained, even as part of a multivariate model of this kind, remains to be seen.[28]

The issue of what place there is for human agency in Marx's account can also be interpreted as a normative question. Even if people have the capacity to act differently than they do, if the theory dictates that there is only one right choice for them to make, in what sense is agency really being validated? Viewed from this perspective, Marx's claim that communism is the only acceptable choice is reminiscent of Rousseau's famous—and no less enigmatic—declaration to the effect that mankind should be "forced to be free."[29] In fact, it is similar in logical structure to arguments in the social contract tradition taken up in chapter 5, where a particular type of social arrangement is deemed legitimate on the grounds that freely choosing people would choose it if they were thinking clearly about their interests, as well as the utilitarian arguments already discussed. At some level all these arguments maintain that there is a right answer to the question "what are the best social and political arrangements for human beings?" and that it is the right answer partly by virtue of the alleged fact that uncoerced people, thinking clearly about their interests, would choose it. These formulations all embody secular variants of the tension we first encountered in Locke's wrestling with the tension between God's omnipotence and timeless natural law in §1.1.1. In Marx's case there is the additional claim for freedom that it is only, in fact, realizable in a communist order because every other mode of production involves exploitation.

What sense, if any, can be made of this last claim is taken up next in the course of my examination of the idea of Marxian exploitation. First it is necessary to deal with another sense in which Marxism is sometimes said to be hostile to authentic human agency. If, for Marx, communism is legitimate and capitalism illegitimate on the grounds that a freely acting revolutionary proletariat would reject capitalism and embrace communism, it might be said this is a doctrine about classes that leaves little room for individual rights or freedom. This critique misses the mark for two reasons. One is that Marx's logic is ultimately individualist, both because classes are defined by reference to the relations in which *individuals* stand to the means of production, and because Marx believed that the obstacles to realizing individual freedom result from the dependencies inherent in the division of labor.[30] Communism, which makes possible abolition of the division of labor, is a highly individualist utopia in which people are free to "hunt in the morning, fish in the afternoon, rear cattle in the evening, criticize after dinner, just as I have a mind, without ever becoming hunter, fisherman, shepherd, or critic,"[31] and "the free development of each is the condition for the free development of all."[32] Collective action is necessary, in short, so long as the obstacles to individual freedom are collectively sustained, but it is individual freedom, not collective action, that is the normative ideal. As I elaborate more fully in §4.2.3, this makes Marx a theorist of strongly conceived individual rights notwithstanding the fact that he would dismiss rights-talk as bourgeois verbiage.

This is not to say, however, that Marx's understanding of freedom is identical to the liberal one. His is what Isaiah Berlin once described as a "positive" conception of freedom in that his focus is on freedom to do, achieve, and become certain things, as distinct from a "negative" conception where the focus is on a zone of activity within which the individual is left alone.[33] What is at stake between the two views can be overstated, in that all accounts of freedom make reference (however implicitly) to both restraining conditions and actions.[34] Nonetheless, Marx and those he influenced are more likely to focus attention on what people are able to do with the freedoms that they have rather than on merely what cannot be done to them. Hence Anatole France's sardonic quip to the effect that under the French law of his day the poor were prevented no more than the rich from sleeping under the bridges of Paris, begging in the streets, and stealing bread.[35]

Objecting to class analysis on the grounds that it is inimical to individual rights also misses the mark because Marx holds the standpoint of the proletariat to be the universal standpoint, defined as one in which no exploitation takes place. In *The Discourses*, Niccolò Machiavelli (1469–1527) endorsed the Roman argument in favor of republicanism that the common people should be made the guardians of freedom because, unlike the aristocracy whose desire is to dominate, their desire is not to be dominated.[36] In a like spirit, Marx thought the interests of the proletariat universal human interests. Vindicating those interests would lead not only to the expropriation of the expropriators, but the end of expropriation as such. Marx's identification of the interests of the proletariat with universal human interests is analogous to John Rawls's identification of the standpoint of justice with the standpoint of the least-advantaged representative individual (taken up in §5.3.1). How plausible Marx's variant is turns on the defensibility of his account of exploitation and the possibility of its abolition, to which subject I turn next.

4.2 The Labor Theory of Value, Workmanship, and Exploitation

Like the Pareto principle, Marx's labor theory of value was offered as a technical theory designed to explain the behavior of prices in a competitive market economy. English thinkers since at least the time of Hobbes and Sir William Petty (1623–1687) had been flirting with the notion that human work, rather than trade (as their

English predecessors believed) or the land (as the French Physio-
crats would insist for some time to come), determines the price
that is paid for exchangeable goods in a market economy.[37] By the
time Marx came to write volume one of his magnum opus *Das
Kapital* in 1867, labor theories had been systematized by Adam
Smith in *The Wealth of Nations* and improved upon by David
Ricardo (1772–1823) in his *Principles of Political Economy and Taxation* (1821). These and the other classical economists were all
seeking to discover the laws of motion of market economies,
which they understood as the search for a theory of wages, prices,
rents, and profits. Like the neoclassical economists who would
follow them, they wanted to account for the ways in which these
elements varied in competitive markets. Unlike their successors,
however, they thought the way to do this was develop a theory of
natural wages, prices, rents, and profits around which market
wages, prices, rents, and profits were thought to fluctuate.[38]

Marx fell squarely into this classical tradition, developing a
labor theory that he believed could account for natural values,
market values, and the relations between the two. He also thought
his theory could explain the dynamic and innovative character of
capitalism as well as its inevitable decay over the long run as
contradictions inherent in the system played themselves out. The
normative critique of capitalist exploitation was presented as a byproduct of this technical analysis. This is true in part, but we will
see that by presenting his normative critique as a purely technical
argument Marx engaged in some disingenuous subterfuge to
disguise a commitment to surprisingly individualist assumptions
about rights. To see why this is so, it is necessary first to lay out the
theories of value and exploitation.

4.2.1 *Value, Surplus Value, and the Analytics of Exploitation*

Marx's analytical goal in *Capital* was to explain the value of commodities, which he defined as goods (and one could add services

without damage to his argument) that are produced for exchange. Commodities were conceived of as exhibiting two types of value that stood in need of explanation: "use-value," which is best thought of as utility, and "exchange-value" or "Value," by which Marx meant price. Use-value for Marx was dealt with as a neo-classical economist would, by reference to supply and demand. Nothing can be a commodity unless there is demand for it, and the existence of demand calls forth supply of the good or service in question. But whereas a neoclassical economist would deploy the same tools of supply and demand to explain variations in prices, the classical economists, including Marx, thought there must be more to be said about prices than that they increase with demand and decrease with supply. There must be a point, they thought, around which the prices of a given commodity fluctuate, and they conceived of the need for a theory of natural prices as the need for a theory to explain why that point is what it is.

Marx conceptualized this by thinking of fluctuations of supply and demand as shaping short-run prices and long-run output. In classical terminology, any theory of what determines those fluctuations would be a theory of market prices. The labor theory of value was, by contrast, a theory of natural prices. Translated into contemporary terminology, we might call it a theory of long-run equilibrium prices: it was meant to explain why the prices of commodities are what they are when supply and demand are in equilibrium. Those who complain that the labor theory of value makes no sense on the grounds that it cannot deal with the reality that supply and demand influence prices thus misconstrue the project of classical political economy and Marx's orthodox under-standing of that project.[39]

To come up with a theory of natural prices, the classical econo-mists looked for a common denominator. What is it, they asked, that is needed to produce all commodities? The answer they came up with was labor, or, as Marx put it more precisely than his

predecessors, socially necessary labor time: "What exclusively determines the magnitude of the value of any article is the amount
of labour socially necessary, or the labour-time socially necessary
for its production. . . . The value of a commodity, therefore, varies
directly as the quantity, and inversely as the productivity, of the
labour which finds its realization in the commodity."[40]

This focus on socially necessary labor time was intended to
reflect and incorporate the imperative for efficiency that lies at the
core of competitive capitalism. Suppose you and I are the only two
cotton manufacturers in the economy. You invent a Spinning
Jenny that enables you to produce the same amount of cotton as
we both did previously, but now in a tenth of the time. Marx's
labor theory of value does not say that my cotton will exchange for
ten times the price for your cotton, an obviously problematic
implication of labor theories that had relied on actual amounts of
labor expended in accounting for a commodity's value. Rather,
the advent of the Spinning Jenny in effect means that ninety
percent of the labor I am expending has become socially unnecessary. As a result, my additional work will not be reflected in the
value. The price of a unit of cotton will fall to that dictated by the
amount of labor time that must be expended to produce it using
the new technology.

The classical economists also believed that an adequate theory
of value must account for the existence of profits in a market
economy. Marx believed his theory could do this, while at the
same time explaining the determinants of wages and uncovering
the nature of exploitation. His first innovation here was to conceive of a commodity quite generally as literally anything that is
produced for exchange. Thus money is a commodity like any
other for Marx; its use-value is that it functions as a means of
exchange and its exchange-value is determined by the amount of
labor time socially necessary for its production. There is nothing
special about gold (which served as the basis for money in his

day). Any commodity that is both durable and divisible could serve as a medium of exchange. It provides a convenient measure for expressing the amounts of socially necessary labor time embodied in different commodities in terms of one another.

Most importantly for Marx, labor-power is also a commodity in a market economy. Its use-value is that it can be utilized for the creation of new exchange-value. Its exchange-value, like that of any other commodity, is determined by the labor-power socially necessary for its production. Short-run wages should be expected to fluctuate with supply and demand, but long-run wages will reflect the costs of producing workers. Where there are long-run wage differentials, this does not reflect the value of what the different workers produce, but rather the costs of producing different workers. It takes more socially necessary labor time to produce a skilled technician than a manual laborer; this will be reflected in wage differentials. Even extreme differentials can be explained in this way: in calculating the value of a highly paid baseball player, we must take account of all the costs of producing him—maintaining a minor league system, all the investments made in players who do not work out, and so on. The worker is thus a commodity like any other for Marx. His value is determined by the costs of producing him.

There is, however, a unique feature of labor-power that explains the source of profit on Marx's account. This he explained by reference to the labor theory of surplus value. A conundrum the classical economists had faced was: How could there be profits in a market economy if equivalents always exchange for equivalents? Marx's answer was that equivalents do indeed exchange for equivalents, measured in terms of socially necessary labor time, but that labor-power is a unique commodity because its consumption as a use-value leads to the creation of fresh exchange-value. Put differently, consumption of labor-power is productive while other forms of consumption are not. Intuitively, if I buy a book, which I consume by reading, or a meal, which I consume by eating, no new value is created by these acts of consumption. If, however, I buy your capacity to work for ten hours a day, and consume what I have bought by putting you to work on my Spinning Jenny, once the labor-power I have bought has been consumed I have something new that you have produced: the cotton that can be sold. Once I have covered my wage bill and other costs—raw materials, rent, machinery, marketing costs, etc.—what remains of the surplus is my profit. The capitalist is distinctive because whereas others in a market system produce commodities, exchange them for money, and use the proceeds to buy other commodities purely for consumption, he is interested in something different. Capitalists start with money, buy the particular commodity labor-power, consume it, and sell the product for more money than they started with. So we get profits and the possibility of capital accumulation.

The worker is distinctive in needing to sell his labor-power to someone else in order to live. Anyone in these circumstances is working class for Marx in the "in-itself" sense, regardless of whether he realizes it. If you are unable to buy the means of production but must instead work on those owned by others, your objective interests lie with others who are similarly situated. It is sometimes asked what Marx would say about contemporary workers, millions of whom own stocks in mutual funds. Such an example need not unsettle him. The key point is not ownership, but necessity: if a worker owned enough stocks that he could choose not to work for someone else, living from the dividends instead, then he would no longer be a member of the working class—even if he continued in wage-employment. Until that threshold is crossed he belongs to the working class. Workers must sell their labor-power to others in order to live, capitalists need not do so. Increasingly, Marx argued, under capitalism people would fall into one group or the other—the vast majority into the working class.

Marx distinguished *variable* from *constant* capital. The former denoted the wage bill, the latter all other investments in the
productive process—raw materials, rent, machinery, marketing
costs, etc. He also distinguished *necessary* from *surplus* labor time.
Necessary labor time was the quantity of time the worker must
work to produce goods which, once sold, would cover the cost of
the wage. Surplus labor time was the balance of time the worker
worked, producing goods which, when sold, would cover the capitalist's constant capital costs and provide profit. Marx assumed
that labor is in permanent over-supply. This existence of a permanent reserve army of the proletariat meant that wages would
always tend toward subsistence.[41] The unemployed would always be willing to work at subsistence if some of the employed
were not.

This raises the question what *subsistence* means. Marx was famously imprecise about this, eschewing a definition by reference
to mere physical survival in favor of one that includes a "historical
and moral element."[42] He sought to capture the notion that what
counts as subsistence may change over time with accepted norms
and technological conditions. Thus, in a suburbanized economy
like the contemporary United States, Marx might not be at all
surprised that having the resources for car-ownership becomes
an accepted part of the definition of subsistence. As we will see
shortly, there are reasons in Marx's argument to suppose that
some capitalist dynamics will put upward pressure on the accepted definition of subsistence.

Given these assumptions and definitions, *exploitation* is defined as the ratio of surplus to necessary labor time, or surplus
value to variable capital. In principle it can be calculated precisely,
as illustrated in figure 4.1. In situation A, the working day is
assumed to be ten hours long, the first four hours of which are
necessary labor time. The rate of exploitation is then 6/4 or 1.5. In
situation B the working day is increased to eleven hours, so that

$$\text{rate of surplus value} = \frac{\text{surplus value}}{\text{variable capital}} = \frac{s}{v} = \frac{\text{surplus labor time}}{\text{necessary labor time}} = \text{rate of exploitation}$$

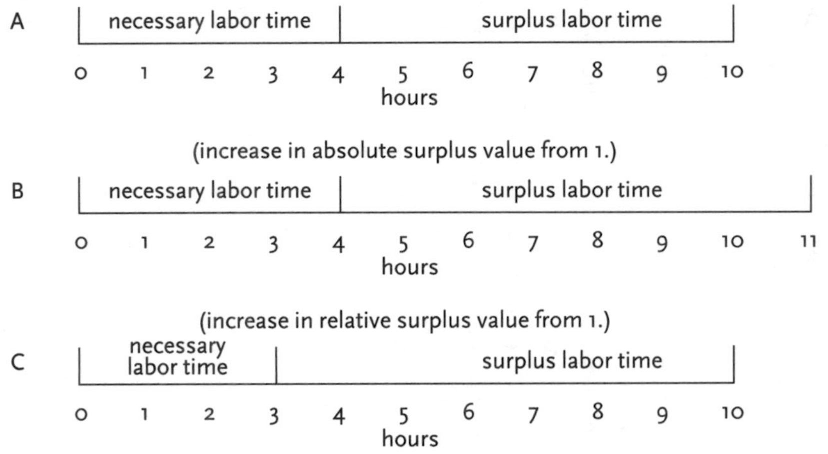

rate of exploitation

A

necessary labor time	surplus labor time
0 1 2 3 4 5 6 7 8 9 10
hours

$$\frac{6 \text{ hrs. surplus labor time}}{4 \text{ hrs. necessary labor time}} = 1.5$$

(increase in absolute surplus value from 1.)

B

necessary labor time	surplus labor time
0 1 2 3 4 5 6 7 8 9 10 11
hours

$$\frac{7 \text{ hrs. surplus labor time}}{4 \text{ hrs. necessary labor time}} = 1.75$$

(increase in relative surplus value from 1.)

C

necessary labor time	surplus labor time
0 1 2 3 4 5 6 7 8 9 10
hours

$$\frac{7 \text{ hrs. surplus labor time}}{3 \text{ hrs. necessary labor time}} = 2.33$$

Figure 4.1. Relative and absolute surplus value and the rate of exploitation

the rate of exploitation increases to 7/4 or 1.75. In situation C we suppose that a technological innovation is introduced that increases the laborer's productivity so that he can now cover the cost of his wage bill in three hours' necessary labor time. With a ten hour working day the rate of exploitation increases to 7/3 or 2.33. Marx called changes of the kind from A to B increases in "absolute" surplus value and changes of the kind from A to C increases in "relative" surplus value. In either case we can compute the rate at which the capitalist exploits the worker—while nonetheless paying him for the full value of his labor power.

4.2.2 Implications for Understanding Capitalism

In developing his variants of the labor theories of value and surplus-value, Marx believed he had formulated a consistent theory of natural values, market values, and the relations between the two. He also thought he had provided the basis for showing why in its innovative phases capitalism was the most dynamic and productive system ever devised, but that it must become increasingly dysfunctional as it matured. Although we are not principally interested here in his macroeconomic predictions, it will be helpful to attend to them briefly as a prelude to examining the normative properties of his theory of exploitation.

One apparent phenomenon the classical political economists believed stood in need of explanation was a long-term declining tendency in the rate of profit. Marx's theory predicts this outcome by assuming that only living human labor power creates fresh surplus value and that variable capital, which pays for labor power, will be a declining proportion of total capital expenditures. Why? The answer has to do with the dynamics of competition. Every capitalist is assumed to be minimizing costs so as to undercut the competition. If wages are already at subsistence, by assumption, then the only way in which to do this is to get more out of laborers, either by making them work longer hours (increases in absolute surplus value) or making them work more productively (increases in relative surplus value). There are obvious physiological limits to forcing them to work longer hours, not to mention political limits once trade unions begin to form and workers otherwise organize politically. Indeed, it is not in the least surprising, from this perspective, that agitation for measures like the Ten Hours Bill—limiting the working day as its name implies—is characteristic of early capitalism.[43]

Because of these limits in the era that Marx describes as that of primitive accumulation, the real action in capitalist competition over the long haul is going to be with technological innovation to increase labor's productivity—increases in relative surplus value. You increase your workers' productivity by putting them to work on Spinning Jennies. This gives you a competitive edge in the cotton business: you can undercut my prices while increasing your profits; in the short run you have every incentive to do it. But then I must also put my workers to work on the Jennies and respond to your price cuts or go out of business, and there's the rub. Once the Jennies have been deployed throughout the cotton industry, the rate of profit in it will be lower than before they were introduced anywhere, because every capitalist is now spending relatively more on constant capital—Spinning Jennies—and only variable capital is a source of new surplus value and hence profit. Marx thought of machinery as containing "congealed" labor that is transferred to the product as the machine is deployed, not as a source of new value. As the ratio of constant to variable capital increases and production becomes more capital intensive in sector after sector (in his terminology the "organic composition of capital" rises), the rate of profit falls.

From the vantage point of the twenty-first century, it is empirically questionable that there is a long-term tendency for the rate of profit to decline. Marxists, who have thought this alleged tendency an important source of capitalism's eventual infirmity, have tended to look, as Marx, Smith, Lenin, and others did, to offsetting countertendencies such as imperialism, which could stave off the declining tendency in the rate of profit for a while.[44] It is worth noting, however, that even on Marx's reasoning it is far from obvious that profits must fall over time. Even in one industry, if the rate of productivity growth from technological innovation exceeds the rate at which constant capital displaces variable capital in the productive process, then the rate of profit can remain constant or increase. Moreover, one could grant Marx's argument for a single industry, yet still remain unconvinced that the rate of profit must fall economy-wide. There may always be new lines of production into which capital can flow in search of new profits, as profits in a given industry fall in relation to the amount of capital invested. Railways, cars, airplanes, spaceships, computers, gene banks, bottled water and designer coffee for yuppies, and so on; why should the list ever run out? Marx seems to have thought in terms of a limited number of lines of production that did not begin to take account of the possibilities.

The other reasons Marx gives for the inevitably worsening crises of capitalism are likewise vulnerable. He thought that dependence on money created the possibility of liquidity crises as the result of "hoarding" capital.[45] So it does, but this can be forestalled by actions of governments to facilitate liquidity at critical moments—as we saw dramatically when the Clinton administration underwrote the Mexican peso with $20 billion in 1995. Marx thought there was an endemic problem of weak effective demand in capitalist economies (he liked to think of it as "overproduction") deriving from the fact that the workers, collectively, cannot afford to buy what they produce, so that the "conditions of bourgeois society" become "too narrow to comprise the wealth created by them."[46] Perhaps capitalism is beset by endemic weak demand, but we have already seen that Marx conceded the possibility of upward flexibility in the definition of subsistence, and

he agreed with Smith that the search for new markets was another source of the impetus behind imperialism. In any case,
Marx did not begin to see, as John Maynard Keynes (1883–1946)
did after him, that governments can do things to manage weak
demand such as engage in deficit spending during recessions or
straightforward redistribution, through taxation, from the non-
consuming to the consuming.

Marx also thought capitalism would become decreasingly competitive. Competition would tend to eliminate competitors, not
least because the entry costs for new competitors must rise due to
the increasingly capital-intensive nature of production.[47] Here
again, Marx ignored what might be done by governments, in this
case by way of antitrust legislation. He also missed the fact that
there might be great economies of smallness in some industries,
as Apple's transformation of the computer industry in the 1980s
and the dot.com transformation of retail sales in the 1990s both
showed so dramatically.

A surprisingly time-bound and mechanical view of economic
processes informs Marx's economic arguments about the sources
of capitalist crisis, but an institutional naïveté permeates them as
well. In discussing why the political rights characteristic of democratic systems would do little to advance the interests of workers
under capitalism, Marx was quick to dismiss democratic government under capitalism as "but a committee for managing
the common affairs of the whole bourgeoisie."[48] Yet he underestimated just how effective governments operating in that role
might become in creating and maintaining what contemporary
theorists describe as "social structures of accumulation" to avoid
and manage crises, and to assist in capitalism's mutation into
forms that would defeat its internal tensions.[49] In short, Marx was
hoodwinked by his base and superstructure metaphor into ignoring the importance of elements of the superstructure, such as
institutions, in forestalling economic crises.[50]

This is not to say that Marx ignored politics entirely in his discussion of capitalist crises. He thought that growing revolutionary working class consciousness was essential to achieving a socialist transformation. Although he never offered a precise account of the sequencing and relative importance of the different sources of crisis, his picture seems to have been that the worsening economic problems would exacerbate one another, leading to a dysfunctional monopoly system that had lost its innovative dynamic and was ripe for takeover by the revolutionary working class. Close inspection reveals, however, that his argument about working class consciousness is as vulnerable as his claims about the economic sources of crisis. His picture is of capitalist competition leading to an increasingly emiserated proletariat whose members eventually see that they have "nothing to lose but their chains."[51] The difficulty is that nothing in the theory of exploitation explains why this will actually occur.

Marx conflates increasing absolute emiseration, which might indeed reasonably be expected to persuade people that they have nothing to lose but their chains, with the increasing relative emiseration that is entailed by his theory. Returning to figure 4.1, if we were to suppose A to be the status quo and give the worker the choice of moving to either B (an eleven-hour working day with a rate of exploitation of 1.75) or C (a ten-hour working day with a rate of exploitation of 2.33), it is far from obvious that she would pick B. The example highlights the fact that Marx's is an other-referential theory of human valuation. It assumes that people evaluate their well-being by reference to what they get in relation to what others get, and that the relevant other, for the worker, is her capitalist employer. But people may often be self-referential in their valuations, as the Pareto principle assumes them to be, indifferent to what others get unless it affects their own basket of goods. This was the assumption behind Ronald Reagan's 1984 reelection slogan: "Are you better off now than you were four years ago?" Working class people can answer this in the affirmative (as enough arguably did to reelect him) if there has been a small improvement in their welfare, even though that of the wealthy has increased much more—perhaps due to an across the board tax cut. In terms of Marx's discussion of exploitation, it is quite possible for wages to remain constant or even rise somewhat as the rate of exploitation goes up. Indeed, this might be judged likely given my earlier discussion of upward pressure on the "historical and moral" component of the definition of subsistence. To the extent that people are self-referential, they will not become exercised by what Marx describes as their increasing exploitation; they will cling to their proverbial chains.

In fact, the evidence suggests that although other-referential comparisons motivate people a good deal of the time, they are not made with the comparators Marx had in mind. People make relatively local comparisons, measured by class, status, and physical proximity, when evaluating their circumstances. The research from sociology and social psychology shows that workers do not compare themselves to their employers in assessing their circumstances. They do not even compare themselves to the wealthy classes, but rather to similarly situated workers. This is true up and down the occupational scale. A professor will be much more troubled to learn that his salary is $10,000 less than that of a peer down the corridor than that it is $200,000 less than that of the cardiologist down the street.[52]

The reasons for this are much debated; no doubt more than one dynamic is often at play. Cognitive limitations, the need for recognition from peers, what Tversky and Kahneman have described as "availability heuristics" (frames of reference in which to interpret information about inequality and distribution), and physical proximity are all implicated in perceptions of relative well-being.[53] In different ways they all lend credence to W. G. Runciman's view that deprivation relative to a salient group of

comparatively local others is more important than global economic position in influencing the demands that people are likely
to make. Runciman's relative deprivation thesis has had a mixed
empirical record in predicting collective mobilization for political
change, but it does better than objective class position, and in any
case its failures may have more to do with a lack of organizational
resources, or to the requirements of spatial proximity, than with
the thesis itself.[54] As an account of how people see their entitlements in relation to others, it seems to do reasonably well a good
deal of the time.[55] It may also help account for the phenomenon
that in contemporary Western countries the overwhelming majority conceives of itself as middle class. People tend to see the
world as an enlarged version of their—comparatively homoge-
nous—local reference groups, pushing those very different from
themselves into the background.[56]

4.2.3 Normative Analytics of Exploitation

Whether people are self- or other-referential, then, Marx's theory
of exploitation is a poor instrument for predicting working class
militancy in the actual world. But this does not speak to its co-
gency as a normative argument: a theory of what people are justly
entitled to, but deprived of, under capitalism and its predecessor
modes of production. This is important for our purposes because
a political system that underwrites unjust appropriation of people's just entitlements can scarcely be judged legitimate. Even if
the working classes are unlikely to overthrow capitalism, does a
political order that sustains it deserve their allegiance?

Marx avoided explicit normative argument, preferring that normative injunctions appear to flow from his "scientific" theory. In
fact the theory of exploitation is normative at its core, though this
is obscured by Marx's claim that living human labor-power is
selected as the basic unit of value on the grounds that it is the only
element of production that is involved, directly or indirectly, in

the production of all other commodities. There are two difficulties with this claim, one concerning the productive consumption of labor power as distinct from the unproductive consumptions of other goods discussed in §4.2.1, the other deriving from the reality that although labor-power may be *a* common denominator of all commodities it is not the *only* common denominator.

With respect to the first, how persuasive is my earlier example that consumption of books and food is not productive in the way that consumption of labor-power is? True, if the labor power I have bought is consumed on my Spinning Jenny, then I own valuable cotton at the end of the exercise. But if I eat food, the calories I consume replenish my energy levels enabling me to do new work that I could not otherwise have done. Surely this is productive consumption just as the consumption of labor-power is. The case of reading is arguably more dubious, though time spent reading might be a form of relaxation that enhances the capacity to work. The food example is sufficient, however, to undermine Marx's claim that the consumption of labor-power is uniquely productive.

This brings us to the second difficulty, noted by Pierro Sraffa and others: labor-power is not the only common denominator of commodity production.[57] To illustrate, imagine a three commodity economy in which corn, books, and labor-power are all that is produced, and we can stipulate that corn is needed to produce labor-power and books, that labor-power is necessary to produce corn and books, but that books are not needed to produce corn or labor-power. As several commentators have noted, under such assumptions there is no analytical difference between corn and labor-power in the system, so that it would be quite possible to produce a corn theory of value and compute the rate of exploitation of corn by capital just as Marx did for labor-power.[58]

The upshot is that if we are to say that the exploitation of the worker should prompt moral disapprobation, an additional argument must be supplied to the effect that people are entitled to the fruits of their labor in a way that corn is not entitled to the surplus it generates in the productive process. This brings us to claims of right of the sort Marx sought to dismiss. It seems undeniable that whatever normative pull the theory of exploitation has comes from an implicit commitment to a secular variant of Locke's workmanship ideal discussed in §1.2: people have a right to what they make, and they are exploited to the extent that they are denied it. To drive the point home, consider an intermediate case between workers and corn. A horse down a mine shaft works for ten hours a day pulling coal from the mining frontier to the bottom of the shaft, covering the cost of its feed and maintenance in one hour per day. Is the horse exploited? Intuitions will likely divide over this question depending on whether one takes the idea of animal rights seriously, those who do being more likely to countenance the exploitation claim than those who do not. Reflecting on the example suggests that the lowest common denominator idea may not even be necessary for a normatively compelling notion of exploitation, let alone sufficient.

Marx seems to have resisted the idea of talking about workers' rights partly out of his antipathy for entering the terrain of bourgeois discourse, but also partly because he saw that any realm of rights is inevitably a realm of legitimated inequality. Recall his discussion of rights under socialism in *The Critique of the Gotha Program*. The existence of rights to what one produces is characterized as a transitional mark of the old order, unsatisfactory because such rights breed inequality in view of the different needs of different workers deriving from the number of children they have, and so on. Communism is superior to socialism, on his telling, precisely because the superabundance of wealth that the development of the productive forces has generated under capitalism makes possible a distributive system based on need rather than right. Hence the Marxian conviction that under communism the government of persons is replaced by the administration of things, finally dissolving the Enlightenment tension between rights and science.[59]

But how plausible is this? The idea of superabundance is not defined by Marx. If it is to mean that rights are no longer necessary, it must mean that scarcity has been transcended. For scarcity to be transcended, human desires must be judged finite; otherwise no matter how much abundance there is, there will be scarcity by definition. It is sometimes thought that the reluctance to place limits on what wants are regarded as legitimate results from the neoclassical avoidance of interpersonal judgments of utility. Arguably, neoclassical economists are wrong to conflate wants with needs into the general category of preferences or desires. Wants might be infinite, on this account, but needs are not, and, if there were no macroeconomic imperatives to induce demand for unnecessary goods, then one could in principle arrive at a list of basic human needs that could be satisfied for all after some threshold of abundance had been passed.

Without getting to the interpersonal measurement difficulties any such project must encounter, it is bound to fail. Even on the sparest definition of human needs as those things necessary to sustain human life, needs will always outstrip available resources. The examples of dialysis machines, artificial hearts, AIDS and cancer research, or their very possibility, suggest that there will always be a scarcity of resources that could be deployed to sustain people's lives, and hence there will always be opportunity costs to deploying them in one way rather than another. No matter what the level of abundance, scarcity is therefore endemic to human society. This means that adjudication of competing claims is inescapable, and so, therefore, is some regime of rights. In sum, Marx seems to have assumed that technological advance can outstrip the demands generated by human needs, but there is no reason to suppose that this will ever be the case.

Rejecting as unsustainable Marx's belief that scarcity, and hence the realm of rights, can be transcended means rejecting as incoherent his conception of communism. The question then becomes, what, if anything, remains of his critique of capitalism and argument for the superiority of socialism? Given the twentieth-century experience of centrally planned economies, one might readily be persuaded that there are serious practical obstacles to a centrally planned state directing all investment and distribution in the economy as Marx envisaged under socialism. Because the information problems alone are likely to produce massive inefficiencies, contemporary neo-Marxists such as John Roemer have concluded that the market system is essential.[60]

But what of the claim that the market system is exploitative? Raising this issue takes us beyond the technical features of the labor theory of value into the workmanship ideal that gives the theory of exploitation its normative edge. Locke saw human productive capacities as God-given, as discussed in §1.2, so for him the question of why people might be said to own what flows from the use of their productive capacities never arose. Locke was explicit in denying that people can ever own one another, relying on the claim that God makes children, using parents for that purpose. To give life "is to frame and make a living Creature, fashion the parts, and mould and suit them to their uses, and having proportion'd and fitted them together, to put into them a living Soul." Parents are "but occasions" for their children's being. When they "design and wish to beget them, [they] do little more toward their making, than *Ducalion* and his Wife in the Fable did toward the making of Mankind, by throwing Pebbles over their heads."[61] Human beings are God's workmanship, not one another's. This was the nub of Locke's attacks both on slavery and on Filmer's patriarchal authority. People are bound to respect one another's rights, on this account, because God requires this of them.

It is a small step from this to the proposition that human beings are self-owning. Indeed, Locke had all but taken it himself by insisting that no secular authority is empowered to settle disagreements among individuals over the meaning of natural law. We can never aspire to own another person, Locke thought, because she is God's property. For all practical purposes, however, it might just as well be because she is her own property, since each individual is obliged to recognize every other individual as free to veto disagreeable interpretations of what natural law, which is, after all, nothing more than God's will, requires. And this is so even before we add in the substance of natural law, which surely reinforces the commitment to self-ownership. Natural law, it will be recalled, commands each person first to preserve himself and then to preserve mankind.[62]

Self-ownership of humans vis-à-vis one another turns each individual into a miniature God, enjoying dominion over the product of her creation; this is the core of Locke's strong conception of individual rights. Locke's conception depended for its coherence on his theology, and, once this is removed, the way is open to pose the radical question: Why embrace self-ownership at all? The implications of that question are taken up in §5.5. The point to notice here is that the Marxian idea of exploitation takes the workmanship ideal, and with it the idea of self-ownership, for granted. It is a Lockean idea of individual rights, rooted in workmanship and violated under capitalism, that gives the Marxian critique its moral force. The wage-labor relationship is presented as facilitating the illegitimate appropriation of the product of the worker's labor-power by the capitalist. This compromises the worker's entitlement to the product of his own work. Marx's deployment of such terms as the "commodification" of the worker, and his "alienation" from the products of his work, make his reliance on the workmanship ideal obvious.[63] But the appeal goes beyond semantics to the structure of the theory itself. People are exploited to the extent that their status as owners of the products of their work is compromised.

Unfortunately, the labor theory of value is not a promising exploitometer—even if we take the workmanship ideal for granted. Leaving to one side, for the moment, the conventional objection that Marx takes no account of the work done by the capitalist, it is otherwise problematic. For one thing, Marx ignores the exploitation of prior employees by prior employers that is embedded in the labor-power "congealed" in the machinery deployed by current workers. In effect this exaggerates the rate of exploitation of current workers at the expense of their predecessors, and it underestimates the computational problem involved in measuring exploitation—which would be much more complex than that depicted in figure 4.1 if we sought to take account of the past exploitation embodied in machinery.[64]

For another thing, people are more or less productive partly as a result of work that others do for them. In recent decades American courts have begun to recognize how complex this can be in divorce settlements. The domestic labor performed in support of a spouse attaining a professional qualification can be seen as part of the relevant work in creating the capacity to generate the income that the qualification brings. For this reason, a divorcing spouse who has performed such labor can be thought of as having a property interest in the stream of future income that the other (now qualified) divorcing spouse is newly capable of generating.[65] Feminist theorists have generalized the intuition behind such examples to show that it was arbitrary for Marx to measure the rate of exploitation by exclusive reference to the relation between the surplus produced and the wage paid to the worker. Any such calculation ignores the contributions of the worker's spouse to what he produces, which Marx arbitrarily takes to be the worker's "own." From this standpoint Marx's argument can be turned on the worker's relationship with his spouse to reveal *it* in certain circumstances to be exploitative.[66]

And this is the tip of the iceberg, because the feminist critique of Marx can be generalized. The productive capacities a stay-at-home wife expends on her husband's attainment of a professional qualification no doubt partly incorporate the work of others: parents, perhaps children, Sunday school teachers who drummed a particular mix of the work ethic and family values into her, and so on. If one pushes the idea of productive work as supplying the normative basis for entitlements to the limit, it seems to lead inexorably to a tangled and indecipherable web of overdetermined entitlements. For Marx to make the buck stop with the wage-laborer, as far as measuring exploitation is concerned, is arbitrary.

4.3 Enduring Insights

Unsatisfying as the labor theory of value is for theorizing about rights, Marx was correct that there is no reason to think that the market system, which rewards people by reference to agreements they negotiate, does any better—even though it does indeed revolve around Pareto-superior exchanges. True, capitalists often bring creative skill to the productive process, but why suppose that the market system gives them their proportionate due, assuming this could be calculated? Performing the calculation would be a formidable task, since the questions we have been considering in relation to the worker could obviously be asked about the capitalist's contribution to the value of the product—not to mention upstream and downstream contributions by parents, children, and spouses. In short, the difficulties that are involved in figuring out whether or not the worker gets his just deserts in

terms of workmanship would plague any similar attempt with
respect to the capitalist.

Who gets what out of a market transaction reflects, among
other things, the relative power of the players. Neo-Marxists such
as G. A. Cohen have sought to capture this reality by recasting
Marx's theory of exploitation as a theory about the class monopoly
of the means of production. Jettisoning the labor theory of value,
Cohen argues that it is the "structure of proletarian unfreedom"
that puts workers in a position that they must work for some
capitalist in order to survive. This is not a claim about a right
to some proportion of the value of the produced product. Rather,
it is an argument about freedom that calls to mind the ironic
quip often attributed to Cambridge economist Joan Robinson to
the effect that the one thing worse than being exploited is not
being exploited.[67] Those who are compelled by their relative lack
of resources to work for others in a market system enjoy what
we might describe as *transactional freedom* to engage in Pareto-
improving exchanges of their labor power for wages, but they lack
a type of *structural freedom* that those not in this constraining
situation enjoy.

Reconceptualizing the Marxian critique of capitalism in this
way turns it into an argument about power and freedom rather
than one about labor-power and value. It suggests that, for all
Marx's conceptual and predictive failures, his intuition that some
under capitalism lack a basic freedom that others enjoy at their
expense merits our continuing attention. Indeed, it underscores
the limitations of transactional conceptions of freedom such
as the one embodied in the Pareto-system. This realization has
prompted some subsequent theorists of freedom to conceive of it
as the capacity to shape the conditions within which people act
and make choices, rather than by exclusive focus on the acts and
the choices themselves.[68] Marx himself hints at such an under-

standing of freedom when he declares in *The Eighteenth Brumaire of Louis Bonaparte* and elsewhere that human beings make their own history, but not within limits of their own choosing.[69] The implication is that people will be genuinely free only when they influence the circumstances that limit their actions. Indeed, Marx conceives of a proletarian revolution as differing from all previous ones on the grounds that it is transformative in just this sense.

From the perspective of our present concerns, this discussion suggests that if the legitimacy of states is tied to the degree that they preserve or undermine freedom, structural as well as transactional freedom should figure in our analyses. This does not tell us how structural freedom should be taken into account, or that market systems will necessarily be judged wanting when compared to the feasible alternatives in a world that has been cut loose from Marx's unrealistic assumptions about the possibility of transcending scarcity and distributive conflict. It is to say, however, that we still lack compelling answers to the questions mentioned at the start of this chapter. Our analysis of the difficulties with Marx's concept of exploitation suggests that any claim to the effect that private property is robbery has yet to be sustained, but this by no means suggests that private ownership of the means of production can be justified either. And if corn-dealers *are* starvers of the poor, this contributes to the structural unfreedom of the poor in Cohen's sense, which, in turn, raises questions about the legitimacy of regimes that sustain this state of affairs. Marx's most important legacy is to remind us of the enduring importance of these questions, and to show why conventional answers to them are unsatisfactory.

CHAPTER 5

The Social Contract

We can recast the structural critique of transactional views of freedom by saying that they are myopic: procedural conceptions that lack attention to the contexts within which transactions, such as the exchange of labor-power for a wage, occur. One reason why there has been a revival of interest in the social contract tradition in recent decades is that it seems more satisfying on this front. As one influential theorist in this tradition, Robert Nozick, puts it, any fully adequate theory of justice must comprise a theory of justice in acquisition, a theory of justice in transfer, and a theory of the rectification of past injustices.[1] In developing his theory of justice, John Rawls insists that the focus of the social contract should be on the major institutions that make up the "basic structure" of society. He defines these expansively to include fundamental constitutional protections of political, religious, and personal freedoms, the systems of economic organization and property ownership, including ownership of the means of production, and such major social institutions as the family. Rawls conceives of the basic structure as the primary subject of justice, "because its effects are so profound and present from the start."[2] Whatever their other shortcomings, expansive conceptions of this sort cannot be faulted for myopia.

The social contract tradition is older than any we have considered thus far. Elements of social contract arguments can be traced to well before the conventional identification of their founding in mid-seventeenth century English political thought.[3] Here our focus is on the Lockean social contract tradition, and its revival since the 1960s by Rawls, his followers, and many of his critics. In some respects this revival was a response to the inadequacies of utilitarianism, which seemed to many by the 1960s to be locked in an unwinnable battle between objective and subjective utilitarianism. The latter, which had evolved out of the neoclassical tradition as we saw in §3.1, denied the possibility of interpersonal judgments and was silent, as a result, on the great moral issues of the day: coming to grips with the full horrors of Nazism and fascism and the contentious issues surrounding the Vietnam war. The classical utilitarianism that permits interpersonal judgments seemed to err in an opposite direction, permitting the exploitation—or worse—of some for the utilitarian benefit of the rest, prompting Rawls's insistence that utilitarianism must be rejected for its failure to take seriously the differences among persons.[4] Attempts to find middle ground between the two had been unsuccessful. The most formidable and enduring was Mill's harm principle, but, as we saw in §§3.3 and 3.4, making sense of and measuring harm confronts difficulties that are analogues of making sense of and measuring utility. The revival of interest in the idea of politics as a social contract was a response both to the moral urgency of the time and to the failure of these exhausted disputes to resolve themselves.

5.1 Classical and Contemporary Social Contracts

For there to be a contract there must be contractors, so the first question for any theory of politics as a social contract is: Who are the parties to it? The seventeenth- and twentieth-century theorists gave very different answers. Hobbes and Locke both thought of it as an actual agreement. Hobbes believed that England had been plunged into a state of nature during the civil war, and he conceived of his argument in *Leviathan* as a recipe for avoiding that result in the future.[5] Locke thought that much of the world of his day existed in a state of nature, and that returning to it was sometimes to be preferred over living under political tyranny.[6] By the time the late twentieth-century theorists wrote, by contrast, anthropologists had been waging war on the idea of pre-political man for generations. The implication was that Aristotle had been right all along to insist that man is naturally a political animal.[7] There never was a social contract, and those who appeal to some notion of natural or pre-political man as the authors of political institutions invariably commit some version of the fallacy Rousseau attributed to Hobbes: reifying aspects of the conventional behavior and institutions of his day by attributing them to "natural" man.[8]

As a normative matter, the idea of politics as rooted in a social contract has also seemed to many to be built on quicksand. Perhaps the closest thing to such an agreement historically was the American founding, to which Nozick makes oblique reference when setting up his argument.[9] But the parties to this agreement notoriously excluded women, blacks, and native Americans, and the result preserved slavery. This is scarcely an encouraging contractual basis for political legitimacy, even if we ignore the fact that ratification of the American Constitution violated the procedures of the Confederation, or the reality that millions of Americans were subsequently forced to accept it as a result of losing the civil war. This raises the further issue that even if an agreement is judged to have been valid and binding on all parties when originally made, why should subsequent generations, who played no part in the original agreement, be similarly bound? In the law of trusts and estates we enact significant constraints on the degree to which we can be ruled from the grave by those who have passed on. Why should politics be different? Answers like Locke's, that by continuing to remain, people demonstrate their tacit consent to what has been established, are underwhelming.[10] In practice the costs of exit will be insurmountably high for all but a tiny minority, and in any case there will likely be nowhere available for them to go in order to create the kind of regime they find congenial.

Mindful of these difficulties, twentieth-century social contract theorists appeal to the idea of a hypothetical contract. Their concern is not with what was or was not agreed to at some historical juncture, but rather what would be agreed on were people given the choice. It is the claimed rationality of what would be agreed to, not the fact of agreement, that gives these theories their normative edge. It is the calculus, rather than the consent, in James Buchanan and Gordon Tullock's *Calculus of Consent* that suggests the decision rules they propose should be adopted.[11] For Nozick, the aim is to persuade the reader that the minimal state he advocates would emerge if people acted rationally in a "non-state situation." Because this requires no explicit agreement, it is in fact more reminiscent of Locke's idea of tacit consent than his theory of the social contract.[12] And Rawls's notion of reflective equilibrium is intended to persuade the reader of the desirability of his principles of justice by convincing her that rational people would opt for them in the specified choice situation.[13]

Although these writers all deploy much of the social contract idiom, then, at the end of the day their arguments rest on accounts of what it makes sense for people to accept, not what anyone accepts in fact. At bottom, contemporary social contract theory is thus a rationalist scientific enterprise just as much as Bentham's was. People are conceived of as acting collectively in the initial or constitution-making situation, but their function as the ultimate repository of political legitimacy does not derive from any decisions taken or interactions among them. This is one reason I have described Rawls's enterprise as solipsistic, in contrast to those of theorists who emphasize deliberation in the democratic tradition. Rawls's contractor reasons alone.[14]

Partial exceptions to the preceding observation are Jürgen Habermas and Bruce Ackerman. Habermas places heavy emphasis on what would be selected in an "ideal speech situation," Ackerman on principles that are hammered out as legitimate in structured "dialogic" exchanges among inhabitants of an imaginary planet.[15] On closer inspection, however, even these seemingly more deliberative theories have a strongly rationalist flavor. Habermas believes certain political institutions are necessary for his ideal speech situation to pertain, and Ackerman reaches determinate conclusions about the political institutions he thinks would be selected in his dialogic interchanges. As a result, if either of their preferred political arrangements were instituted tomorrow there would be nothing left for ideal speech or deliberation to accomplish. This suggests that, as with the other theorists just mentioned, claims about the political legitimacy of the chosen institutions depend on the rational desirability of the institutions, not the deliberation that is instrumental in getting people to agree on them. This should be kept in mind so as not to confuse mere expositional devices, such as Ackerman's dialogic forms, Rawls's "original position," or Nozick's evolutionary story about the minimal state's evolution with the arguments these authors advance in support of their preferred political arrangements.

The answer to "who agrees?" is thus that the rational person thinking clearly allegedly does. This is not to deny that the seventeenth-century theories also exhibit a rationalist strain. For Hobbes it was explicit that the agreement at the foundation of the *Leviathan* is one that people would make were they not distracted by their overpowering fear of death, or hoodwinked by the proponents of various ideologies, leading them to act against their interests.[16] For Locke, too, we saw in §1.3 that the agreement to leave the state of nature was held to be rational, guided by the laws of nature. True, there is a radical populist element in Locke's argument that is lacking in Hobbes's and those of the contemporary social contract theorists, because Locke makes living individuals sovereign in deciding what natural law requires in practice. Locke's right to resist the sovereign would thus be valid even if others judged it plainly irrational, but, for all that, it is a rather restricted right because in order to have practical effect, it must coincide with a similar judgment by many others. The lone dissenter does have an inalienable right to resist, but he must look for his reward in the next life.[17] In any event, Locke is the outlier here. Generally in the social contract tradition from Hobbes to Rawls, the alleged rationality of the choice trumps its reality. Indeed, for Nozick, "independents" who refuse are forced to join his minimal state. They are expected to accept this result as rational on the grounds that society could compensate them for their suffering and still be better off—even though it does not compensate them in fact.[18]

One frequently misunderstood facet of social contract arguments concerns the relationship between contracting agents and the state. This varies from formulation to formulation, but the underlying agreement is almost never between the ruler and the people. Rather, it is a mutual agreement among the people to forswear unilateral action in defense of one's rights provided all others forswear such action as well. That the fundamental agreement is not between ruler and people is most obvious in Hobbes's formulation. Rational individuals would agree mutually to submit to an absolute sovereign, on his account, because the alternative is perpetual civil war involving "continual fear, and danger of violent death" where life is "solitary, poor, nasty, brutish, and short."[19] In other formulations an agency relation exists between the people, whether acting individually or collectively, and the state, but it is subordinate to the fundamental mutual agreement to forswear self-help in the state of nature. This is why, for Locke, a revolution need not mean a return to the state of nature.[20] It is also why writers in the social contract tradition affirm different institutional arrangements from one another. Indeed, Hobbes, Locke, and Rousseau all thought that optimal governmental arrangements might vary, depending on the size of the population and other historical accidents.[21] But these matters of institutional form were seen as subordinate to the underlying social contract among the people. It is from this that they were held to derive their ultimate legitimacy.

What are the hypothetical thought experiments of contemporary social contract theory expected to deliver? The answer is exactly what we are seeking in this book: a yardstick for assessing the legitimacy of actual political regimes. If there were a definite answer to the question "what political institutions would rational people, given the chance, agree to?" then we would have a standard for assessing the legitimacy of existing regimes as well as possible reforms to them. This would be true despite the fact that no regime has ever come into existence as the result of such an agreement. Any regime that more closely resembles what would have been agreed to could be judged superior to one that resembles the ideal standard less closely, and reforms that move a regime toward that standard could be judged preferable to those that move it away from the consensual ideal. Despite the fact that hypothetical social contract arguments are exercises in ideal theory, then, their proponents anticipate that they will produce tangible payoffs for arguments about politics in the real world.

5.2 Rawls's Underlying Contentions

Rawls has been the most consequential social contract theorist of our generation. He developed a framework of principles for assessing the justice of political arrangements and a set of institutional and distributive arrangements which, he contended, could be shown by his principles to be superior to the going alternatives. Most expositions of his argument, including Rawls's own, start with the thought experiment of a veil of ignorance. We are asked to imagine what principles of governance people would choose if kept in ignorance of particular facts about themselves such as their race, gender, intelligence, disabilities or lack of them, their particular life plan and proclivities, and all other particular facts about their aspirations and circumstances. In this original position people would be permitted to have knowledge only of "general facts" about their societies, such as that a condition of moderate scarcity obtains, and widely accepted laws of psychology and economics. The suggestion is not, as some commentators have said, that we should suppose people could exist independently of their particular attributes and interests. Rather it is like being asked to agree on the rules for playing a game before you know whether they will work to your advantage, or a Congressman being bound in advance by the findings of a military base–closing commission before knowing whether the commission will recommend closing the base in his district. The idea is to rule out "rigged definite descriptions" that permit people to bias outcomes in their own favor, forcing deliberations to focus on what is desirable for society as a whole.[22]

Questions can be raised about this device, and about whether the principles Rawls advocates in fact flow from it. But focusing too quickly on them can divert attention from Rawls's most innovative contentions, which stand or fall independently of both his expository device and his principles of justice. These contentions deal with the political consequences of ineradicable moral disagreement, and Rawls's insistence that the differences among human beings are morally arbitrary and that, as a result, they should have no bearing on the distribution of benefits and burdens in society.

5.2.1 Enduring Pluralism

Recognizing that moral disagreement is endemic to human social arrangements is scarcely innovative in itself. We saw in §2.2

that Stevenson's critique of Hume revolved around exactly that possibility. In fact so did Hobbes's critique of Aristotle, for failing to see that what is good for one person may not be good for the next.[23] Sometimes it is said that persistent moral disagreement is a product of modernity's secularism. On this diagnosis, abandoning the theological commitments in the natural law tradition got us onto the slippery slope toward moral relativism. This is often summed up in Ivan Karamazov's dictum that if God is dead, then everything is permitted.[24] Arguments of this kind display considerable ignorance of the deep disagreements that have always permeated the natural law tradition. The theological differences between Locke and his contemporaries discussed in §1.1.1, for example, were part of a vast series of disagreements ranging over almost every conceivable question about politics and the good life that has been ably portrayed by James Tully.[25] It is difficult to read this work or other recent scholarship on medieval natural law theory by Richard Tuck, Quentin Skinner, and J. G. A. Pocock, not to mention work by earlier scholars such as Otto von Gierke, without being struck by the depth of the moral disagreements that permeated it, or by what were taken to be the political implications of these disagreements.[26] Natural law has been pressed into the service of political ideologies from anarchism to absolutism and everything in between. In every generation there are those who appeal to the good old days when there was agreement on basic values that has since been eroded by some allegedly nefarious development. Bemoaning the eclipse of natural law is but one more instance of this phenomenon. It does not withstand historical scrutiny.

Rawls's novelty, then, lies not in his recognition of enduring moral disagreement, but rather in his account of how to think about its political implications. In particular he concluded that we must be even less demanding than earlier theorists in what we can reasonably expect people to agree on. For example, Hobbes recognized differences in individual conceptions of the good life, but he thought that every rational person must nonetheless accept his account of human beings as motivated by fear of death.[27] He deployed the alleged existence of this overpowering fear to justify obedience to an absolute power whose job is to enforce a *modus vivendi* among subjects—preventing what would otherwise be their irresistible impulse to attack one another. That is quite a lot of contentious political psychology to swallow. Locke demurred, assuming people instead to be naturally benign creatures who can generally be counted on to keep their promises. On his account government is therefore needed only to diminish inconvenience and promote efficiency.[28] As a result, returning to the state of nature may be preferable to enduring political tyranny for Locke. (Nozick adapts this argument to suggest that a minimal state, which gets the efficiency advantages of government while resembling a "non-state situation" as much as possible, is best.)[29] Like the Hobbesian account, the Lockean one will seem plausible only to those who find its underlying political psychology convincing.

Rawls recognized that to expect people to assent to any such demanding political psychology as a precondition to getting their assent to political arrangements is to expect too much. In his early writings, particularly *A Theory of Justice,* he thus made it his goal to develop principles that are neutral—not only among competing individual conceptions of the good life but also among comprehensive world views and metaphysical systems. This endeavor met with considerable criticism, and it seems likely that there are no principles of social organization that do not privilege some conceptions of the good and that disprivilege others.[30] Partly in response to this criticism, Rawls shifted his ground in subsequent writings to the idea of a conception of justice that is "political, not metaphysical." His appeal is to an "overlapping consensus" on principles that are likely to "persist over generations and to gain a sizable body of adherents in a more or less just constitutional regime, a regime in which the criterion of justice is that political conception itself."[31]

Rawls's "political, not metaphysical" intuition is that people might agree on a set of principles without agreeing on the reasons for their agreement. Instead of the idea that it is easiest to get people to agree on general principles and that the devil is in the details, Rawls proceeds from the notion that it is generally impossible, and, more important, politically unnecessary, to get people to agree on general principles, comprehensive doctrines, or metaphysical commitments. Just as university appointment committees, legislators, and judges routinely agree on outcomes when they could never agree on the reasons for their agreement, so we should not expect citizens to agree on fundamentals as a condition for their acceptance of particular political arrangements. Rather, it is the fact of overlapping consensus that supplies the basis for political legitimacy.[32] It is this stripped-down conception of the enterprise of political legitimation that distinguishes the "political, not metaphysical" approach. It involves a considerably chastened view of the Enlightenment aspiration to ground politics on science, since views that are included in the overlapping consensus might be based on superstition while some scientifically justified views might be excluded. Rawls tries to diminish this difficulty by maintaining that only "reasonable" views be part of the overlapping consensus.[33] But it is evident that, if the idea of overlapping consensus is to do the real work here, Rawls is bound to countenance the disquieting possibility just suggested. Otherwise overlapping consensus would have been defined by reference to the doctrines that Rawls had previously decided pass the test of reasonableness.

Nonetheless, Rawls does not give up entirely on the Enlightenment aspiration to come up with right answers to questions about politics, answers that depend on a dispassionate assessment of the human condition rather than this or that theology or contentious metaphysics. In this connection it should be noted that although Rawls is sometimes faulted for the abstract character of his reasoning about justice (and we will see below that a version of this critique is persuasive), his basic method is comparative, not deductive. True, he describes his principles as procedural expressions of the categorical imperative.[34] This formulation suggests that they are supposed to enjoy the status of moral laws in Kant's sense, meaning that they are universally applicable and are not derived from experience. In fact Rawls constrains the conditions under which he thinks they apply (for example, to polities where moderate scarcity obtains), and he proceeds by comparing his proposed principles to the going alternatives—such as utilitarianism and perfectionism. His claim is that his principles do better than the alternatives when assessed by the standards that he thinks it would be rational for people behind the veil of ignorance to deploy, but if someone showed that he was wrong, or came up with a different principle that did better still, then he would be bound to change his judgment. For these reasons, despite Rawls's occasional Kantian flourishes, his actual modus operandi is very much in the fallibilist spirit of the mature Enlightenment.

One might thus be unpersuaded by Rawls's particular application of his "political, not metaphysical" approach, yet still find the approach itself appealing. The implications of taking up that course are explored below. Notice, for now, that there are two senses in which the "political, not metaphysical" approach is democratic. First, Rawls's claim is that principles are legitimate when they flow from the overlapping consensus among views that are likely to develop and persist in a just constitutional regime. This suggests that being compatible with views held in a society is a significant element in judging the political reasonableness of a life plan or set of values there. Second, and implicit in what has already been said, there is no expectation that the proponent of a plan of life or set of values be willing or able to justify it to others in terms that they will find persuasive. Just as the secret ballot shields people in a democracy from having to justify their votes to others, so Rawls's "political, not metaphysical" device places the reasons why one is committed to one's views off limits as far as both fellow citizens and the government are concerned. Democracy requires representatives and officials to be publicly accountable, but not the voters who elect them. By not requiring citizens to give reasons for their political choices that others will accept, in his "political, not metaphysical" mode Rawls adopts an analogous stance.

5.2.2 Moral Arbitrariness

Moving from the mode to the substance of Rawls's argument, his most fundamental innovation concerns the way in which he deals with the differences among people. The self-ownership scheme as we have considered it from Locke to Marx is strongly egalitarian in one sense: everyone is equally a locus of moral autonomy and creative agency, whether because God is said to have made us that way in Locke's formulation or by assumption in secular renditions such as Marx's or Mill's. The egalitarian dimension of this postulate is obvious when we reflect on what Locke counterposed it to in the *First Treatise,* namely Filmer's view that God gave the world to Adam and his heirs. That view underwrites an inegalitarian structure based on patriarchal primogeniture. Locke's insistence, by contrast, that God gave the world to mankind in common and the equal right to use it as miniature gods (so long as they neither waste it nor exclude others), manifestly does not.

There is another sense, however, in which the self-ownership postulate is inegalitarian. Locke himself had no objection to inequalities deriving from human work so long as the provisos against waste and exclusion of others from the common were not violated, and our discussion of the inevitable inequalities attending a work-based distributive principle in *The Critique of the Gotha Program* in §4.2.3 made it clear that Marx understood that a regime based on self-ownership would also breed inequalities. But Marx's focus in his discussion of distribution under socialism concerned inequality of circumstance (as when one worker has children and the next does not). He did not confront inequalities that might result from differences in the capacities of different workers, or between workers and managers. Inequalities resulting from these sources would not have presented difficulties for Locke. Because God created us on Locke's account, if it turns out that we have unequal abilities and disabilities, this must have been part of the divine plan. But in secular formulations, the question has to be confronted: What if some people are more able than others?

For much of the twentieth century, debates about this question have been caught up in the nature/nurture controversy. Egalitarians have tended to point to environmental factors in accounting for variations in income and achievement, inegalitarians to differences that are said to be innate. To be reminded how politically charged these debates can be, one has only to recall the firestorm of controversy that erupted in the late 1990s over Richard Herrnstein and Charles Murray's contention in *The Bell Curve* that there is a genetic basis to intelligence that partly accounts for variations in achievement among different racial and ethnic groups in the United States.[35]

Rawls argues powerfully, however, that from the standpoint of justice these debates are beside the point. Whether the result of nature *or* nurture, differences in ability are morally arbitrary: they depend either on luck in the genetic pool or in the milieu into which one happens to have been born.

> [T]he initial distribution of assets for any period of time is strongly influenced by natural and social contingencies. The existing distribution of income and wealth, say, is the cumulative effect of

prior distributions of natural assets—that is, natural talents and abilities—as these have been developed or left unrealized, and their use favored or disfavored over time by social circumstances and such chance contingencies as accident and good fortune. Intuitively, the most obvious injustice of the system of natural liberty is that it permits distributive shares to be improperly influenced by these factors so arbitrary from a moral point of view.[36]

Whether the differences among people stem from their genes or their upbringing, or—as is likely—some combination of the two, on Rawls's account they do not supply defensible grounds for distributive outcomes. Perhaps a justification can be supplied for the gains and losses that result from differences in ability to "lie where they fall," to use Judge Learned Hand's memorable phrase from a different context.[37] But Rawls's point is that we cannot start by assuming that people are entitled to what they get as a result of their moral luck in the genetic pool or cultural milieu and then worry only about the justification for redistribution. First we must concern ourselves with the justice of initial endowments. Self-ownership and its inegalitarian implications might be defensible, but Rawls's point is that for any satisfying account the defense must be supplied. Claims like those of John Harsanyi, that we own ourselves and our abilities as matters of "sheer natural fact" are assertions, not arguments.[38]

5.3 Justice with Uncertainty about the Future

Now we are in a position to see why Rawls structures the choice in the original position as he does. His assumptions about enduring pluralism suggest that principles of justice must be acceptable to people who have fundamentally different conceptions of the good. Indeed, they might well be unable to agree on what counts as a justification for adhering to one conception rather than another—as when those whose fundamental convictions are rooted in a religious faith confront unbridgeable gulfs between themselves and adherents to other religions or nonbelievers. The assumption of enduring pluralism leads Rawls to affirm what he describes as a deontological over a teleological approach to thinking about justice. A teleological conception, he explains, is one in which the good is specified independently of the right, and then rights are distributed so as to maximize the good. In a deontological conception, by contrast, rights are distributed independently of any particular conception of the good.[39] His solution is to ask us to consider what we would choose if forced to do so in ignorance of our particular conceptions of the good. Not knowing whether we would be adherents to some religion, agnostics, or atheists; whether we would be single-minded workaholics or couch potatoes; whether we would value the arts, sports, or the preservation of wildlife; and so on. If there is a conception of justice that it makes sense to accept when we assume ourselves to be ignorant of information of this sort, then, Rawls thinks, it has a certain moral attractiveness.

5.3.1 Minimizing Controversial Assumptions and Maximizing Inclusiveness

Now a deontological conception must make *some* assumptions about the good, as I noted when pointing out that the overlapping consensus argument loads the dice in favor of conceptions that are likely to arise and "gain a sizable body of adherents in a more or less just constitutional regime." Notwithstanding his overblown claims for the neutrality of his view already mentioned, it is clear that some accounts of justice load the dice in favor of a particular conception more than others, and there are two respects in which Rawls is convincing that one can reasonably aspire to be more rather than less inclusive in this regard. One concerns his idea of a "thin" conception of the good.[40] Here the thought is that a conception that makes fewer assumptions about the good is to be preferred over a conception that makes more assumptions. Because the goal is to appeal to people with widely differing conceptions of the good, it makes sense to work with as thin a conception as possible.

The other dimension of inclusiveness has to do with expansiveness. Consider the question whether there ought to be a single established religion or the kind of toleration regime built into the First Amendment to the U.S. Constitution that prohibits both establishment of religion by government and its interference with the free exercise of religion. Fundamentalists often claim, correctly, that the American scheme disprivileges their view relative to those of nonbelievers and adherents of religions who believe it is right that religion should be pursued only in private life. For that reason, if no other, it is decidedly not neutral. But a Rawlsian would ask you to evaluate the choice by considering whether you would rather be a fundamentalist in a regime governed by the Establishment and Free Exercise clauses of the U.S. First Amendment, or a dissenter from the established religion in a theocratic state. The argument for rejecting the theocracy for the American approach rests, then, on the idea that it gives the religiously disadvantaged person or group in each case relatively greater religious freedom. If some other principle could be shown to do better for the religiously disadvantaged, then it would be superior to the American regime on a Rawlsian account.

This style of thinking exemplifies Rawls's comparative approach. His initial formulation of his "general conception" of distributive justice is that social goods should always be distributed so as to work to everyone's advantage, but, as he develops and refines it in the first half of *A Theory of Justice,* he comes to the formulation that they should be distributed so as to work to the greatest benefit of the least advantaged in society.[41] Rawls's shift to identifying the standpoint of justice as the standpoint of the least advantaged reflects his Kantian impulse to come up with universalizable principles. The intuition here is that if you would agree to a principle when you were the person most adversely affected by it, then it is reasonable to suppose that you would agree to it in every other circumstance as well.

This notion that the standpoint of the least advantaged incorporates every other conceivable standpoint by a kind of implicit proxy is not unassailable, particularly if one considers divisible goods, such as income, and multiple social strata. As several commentators have noted, it implies that it would be rational for the middle classes to be willing to forgo vast amounts of income for the sake of a negligible increase for those at the bottom.[42] But one of the "general facts" Rawls thinks we should take into account in the original position is that there is no necessary relationship between the level of economic development and the distribution of income and wealth, so that it is quite possible that, even when a society has developed to the level of moderate scarcity, the condition of the poorest segment may be dire. It therefore makes sense to assume that there are "grave risks" to being the least advantaged, even if the probability of one's ending up in this position is low. Hence the risk-aversion that is built into his identification of the standpoint of justice with the standpoint of least advantaged.[43]

5.3.2 Historical Versus Patterned Conceptions of Justice

Rawls's argument about moral arbitrariness suggests that all bets are off as far as just initial distribution of social goods are concerned, because there is no good reason to privilege any particular distribution *ex ante*. To see just how far-reaching his argument is on this point, it is helpfully contrasted with Nozick's treatment of the same subject. Nozick also begins by recognizing that initial distributions stand in need of justification, but he is unpersuaded that this has the implications that conventional left critics of market-based distribution suppose. That critique is a variant of the attack on transactional notions of freedom discussed in §4.3.

Its proponents argue that any purely procedural distributive principle must take some set of starting points for granted, and as a
result it will both embody and replicate any injustices that are
built into the status quo.

Nozick calls the left critic's bluff with an ingenious example.
Suppose a famous basketball player like Wilt Chamberlain agrees
as part of his contract with a certain team that, in addition to his
payment from the team for playing, there will be an additional 25
cent charge to spectators when he is playing that will go directly to
him.[44] Over time this surcharge leads to a transfer of hundreds of
thousands, perhaps even millions of dollars from the basketball
fans to Chamberlain. Nozick's point here is that "liberty upsets
patterns." No matter what the initial distribution of income and
wealth, allowing people to trade freely in markets will change it.
His response to the left critic who complains that the unjust
initial distribution taints all subsequent market transactions is:
pick your own initial distribution—whatever you think is just. If
you are a strict egalitarian, fine, start with strict equality. If you
then allow voluntary transactions, you will have to accept the
resulting inequalities. We have seen this type of development in
some of the post-communist countries such as Poland and the
Czech Republic after 1989, where state-owned enterprises were
often privatized by giving away vouchers on an egalitarian basis.
Banks and entrepreneurs then bought up the shares, often quite
cheaply. Some of them became exceedingly wealthy as a result.[45]

Nozick's justice syllogism is thus that if initial conditions are
just and subsequent transactions are voluntary, the outcome must
be accepted as just. It calls the left critic's bluff in the sense that it
makes clear that the gravamen of his objection is not really to
unjust initial conditions at all, but rather the inequalities wrought
by markets. It puts him on the defensive, in Nozick's terms, because it puts him in opposition to liberty, for the only way in which
a particular patterned conception of justice—be it strict egalitarian

or any other—can be maintained is by constant redistribution from government through the tax code. But taxation, for Nozick, amounts to "forced labor" once the justice of initial conditions has been established. On his "historical" conception of justice, redistribution to achieve some particular pattern of distribution or "end state" can never be justified. The only circumstances in which the state rightfully takes from Peter to give to Paul is in compensation for the rectification of past injustices.[46]

Nozick's discussion assumes that compensation is less demanding than redistribution as a criterion for the government involvement in the reallocation of assets. The idea of compensation is an equitable one that comes from torts: if I damage your property, I must compensate you in order to make you whole, leaving you on as high an indifference curve as you would have been but for my harmful act. This is what makes it a backward-looking or, as he says, "historical" criterion. There may be issues about how to determine and measure a relevant rights infringement, but, like Mill's harm principle, a compensatory model of justice has the advantage of requiring only an individual-regarding standard. Deploying it does not require the justification of any particular distribution of income or wealth in the society. This is why Nozick describes his rights as mere "side-constraints" on the actions of others.[47]

Appearances can be deceptive however. As we have seen since the revolutions of 1989, backward-looking compensation-based models of justice can be massively demanding, not to mention politically explosive. To see this, one only has to think of the claims of the descendants of the Russian Czars that the land taken from them in 1917 should be returned, or those of Zulu King Zwelintini about his forefathers' lands appropriated first by the British in the nineteenth century, not to mention the more recent claims of the millions displaced by the forced removals under Apartheid, demands for restitution that are surfacing from Australian Aborigines, and the ongoing claims of Native Americans. This is to say nothing of the conflicting claims about unjust appropriation that ought to be undone that have led to civil war or near-civil war in the former Yugoslavia, Northern Ireland, Israel / Palestine, and Zimbabwe over the past several decades.

These examples and the dozens more that could be mentioned underscore the fact that, if you go back far enough, you can virtually always find a displaced or expropriated group with a legitimate grievance. This is a byproduct of the reality that the present division of the world into nation-states is largely the result of wars, civil wars, and revolutions, which have had a massive impact on the division and re-division of assets over multiple generations. This is one reason why Nozick's syllogistic invitation, "You decide on just initial conditions," should be resisted as a polemical trap. If one takes his backward-looking compensatory idea seriously, it is far from clear that it could be consistently applied all the way back to a just beginning. But if it is not going to be applied all the way back to the beginning, why apply it at all? Wherever you stop, some group will fairly claim that you have not gone far enough.

More fundamentally, my discussion of the weakness of Marx's historical conception of entitlements in §4.3 positions us well to see the defects in Nozick's account. Suppose we modify his Wilt Chamberlain example to say that Wilt's team plays in a one-company town, and that he uses the accumulated proceeds of his ticket surcharge to buy the plant where his fans all work. He then threatens to close the plant and shift production to Thailand, where wages are a fraction of U.S. wages, unless they accept massive wage cuts and agree to give up company-funded health insurance and retirement benefits. Wilt's fans thus become vastly worse off as a result of the fully voluntary Pareto-superior transactions in which they participated, starting from initial conditions that no one faulted as unjust. What has changed dramatically in the modified example is the power context in which Chamberlain and the fans operate. Whereas previously he exercised no particular power in their lives, now he has the power to destroy their livelihood. He uses it to limit their structural freedom, taking advantage of the transactional freedom Nozick prizes.

Nozick and Marx come from opposite ends of the ideological spectrum, but the difficulties with their "historical" conceptions of entitlement are similar. Both embrace secular variants of Locke's workmanship ideal that lead them to treat self-ownership as sacrosanct. For Marx this creates difficulties deriving from the failure of an exploitation theory that incorporates self-ownership to line up plausibly with what he wants to say about exploitation. Nozick trades in a polemical way on the Marxist embrace of self-ownership, but, as my discussion of the modified Wilt Chamberlain example revealed, the difficulty with embracing transactional conceptions of freedom go beyond immunizing them from unjust starting points.[48] Rawls's identification of the standpoint of justice with that of the least advantaged invites attention to the effects of transactional freedom on the condition of those at the bottom, and his moral arbitrariness argument leads us to question whether Chamberlain justly derives advantage from his unusual talent in the first place. That is, Rawls is the first author we have encountered who is willing seriously to question the workmanship ideal's legitimacy.

5.3.3 Resourcism and Primary Goods

Rawls locates the matter of differences in skills and capacities in a broader discussion of the distribution of social goods. One way to assess his contribution here is to see that he offers a way out of the stalemated debate between objective and subjective utilitarians, both of whom were concerned with the measurement of welfare.[49] Rather than argue over which utilitometer will get their welfare temperatures right, Rawls contends that it makes better sense to focus on a few basic resources that are likely to be important to people regardless of their particular conceptions of the good. In addition to the formidable technical and normative difficulties associated with assigning governments the task of measuring and adjusting the distribution of welfare, it is well to remember that governments notoriously act with blunt instruments. One reason to focus on a few basic resources that will be valuable to people regardless of their particular conceptions of the good, then, is that it is realistic to imagine governments influencing their distribution. Rawls has in mind such goods as basic political and civil liberties, the legal structure of opportunities for advancement in the society, income and wealth, and other goods that contribute to the "social bases of self-respect."[50] With the possible exception of the last (which is less than fully explored in Rawls's writing), these are all things that we can imagine governments regularly influencing. This, when combined with the fact that Rawls sidesteps the intractable philosophical debate about welfare measurement, accounts for why numerous theorists who were unpersuaded by his particular account of primary goods have developed resourcist theories of their own.[51]

But Rawls's principal reason for focusing on primary goods is normative, not practical. Wanting not to bias the distribution of goods in favor of particular conceptions of the good life more than necessary leads him to focus on the multipurpose instrumental goods just mentioned. Whatever your particular conception of the good life turns out to be, the reasoning goes, you are likely to want more rather than fewer in the way of political and civil liberties, opportunities, income and wealth, and the social bases for self-respect. As soon as this is stated one can hear the objection that it loads the dice in favor of some conceptions of the good. The ascetic will insist, for instance, that having more rather than less income and wealth is an evil not a good. A Rawlsian would presumably handle this type of objection along the lines discussed in connection with religious freedom in §5.3.1.

Without disputing the ascetic's claim, the Rawlsian would ask: Would you rather turn out to be a nonascetic in a world in which denial of inessential income and wealth was the reigning principle, or an ascetic in a world in which it was assumed that people generally want more rather than less income and wealth? The latter regime would be preferred because the ascetic would always be free to give away her assets in the income and wealth-friendly regime, but there is no corresponding freedom for the nonascetic in the ascetic regime. The example again underscores that the early Rawls was wrong to claim his view is neutral among rational conceptions of the good life. The operative notion is the most attractive conception when viewed from the standpoint of the worst off under the relevant conditions of ignorance. A corollary of the fact that Rawls's deontological conception of justice rests on a conception of the good, albeit a thin one, is thus that his resourcism resets on some assumptions about welfare, however minimal.[52] Conceding this should not obscure the distinctive Rawlsian aspiration to have these assumptions be as friendly as possible to the disadvantaged in every conceivable regime.

The bulk of Rawls's attention in *A Theory of Justice* is devoted to developing and exploring the implications of appropriate principles for the distribution of different primary goods. Thus liberties are distributed according to the principle: "each person is to have an equal right to the most extensive total system of equal liberties compatible with a similar system of liberty for all."[53] This is a direct application of the thinking behind religious freedom that we have already discussed to most of the other freedoms protected by the Bill of Rights that makes up the first ten Amendments to the U.S. Constitution. Generally they should be distributed as widely as possible compatible with a like liberty for all.

Opportunities are thought about differently in the Rawlsian scheme. Ignorant of their religion, race, ethnicity, gender, or social status behind the veil of ignorance, people would resist any caste, apartheid, or gender-biased regimes, as well as systems with religious tests for office. Assuming that they would always be in the group disadvantaged by the denial of equality of access to advancement, they would instead embrace a principle of equality of opportunity. As Rawls puts it: "social and economic inequalities are to be arranged so that they are both (a) to the greatest benefit of the least advantaged . . . and (b) attached to offices and positions open to all under conditions of fair equality of opportunity."[54] This would presumably be a sufficiently robust principle to support equal pay for equal work, and rule out the kinds of systematic gender inequalities we see on this front in the contemporary United States.[55]

Rawls's most discussed principle, for the distribution of income and wealth, is called the difference principle, though he in fact re-christened an older principle of welfare economics called maximin—short for "maximize the minimum share." In line with the general conception of distributive justice, it requires inequalities to operate in the interests of the least advantaged. This can be shown graphically with the "L" shaped indifference curves in figure 5.1. From a status quo x we can imagine a line extending due north to l on the possibility frontier and south to m and then due east to n on the possibility frontier. m falls on the line of perfect equality vw, which intersects the origin at 45 degrees. At any point on vw A and B have identical shares of primary goods. Anything in the shaded area above lmn is superior, according to the difference principle, to the status quo x. Thus a move to y would be an improvement on x, generating a new Rawlsian indifference curve hjk, and a move to z would be an improvement on y, generating a new Rawlsian indifference curve bcd. A move to r would be an improvement on z, which could not itself be improved upon. The corner of the L shaped indifference curve always lies on the perfect equality line vw, reflecting the fact that the difference principle's goal is to increase the share of the person at

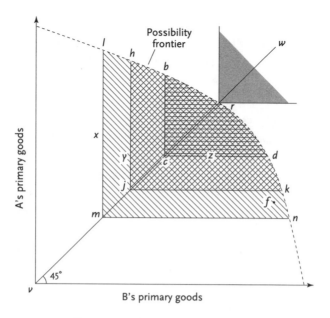

Figure 5.1. Illustration of the difference (maximin) principle with two individuals in a fixed commodity space

the bottom without reference to who that person is. Thus a move
from x to f would be Rawls-preferred regardless of the fact that
when x was the status quo A was better off than B, whereas at f B
has more primary goods than A. This captures the notion that
behind the veil of ignorance one does not know whether one will
turn out to be A or B, so the logical choice is to prefer f to x, given
those options, ensuring the larger bundle of primary goods for
whoever ends up least advantaged.

The difference principle can permit massive redistribution, but
this need not be egalitarian. Moves toward greater inequality,
such as that from x to f, will be justifiable so long as they work to
the advantage of the least well off. Moreover, in a world of perfect
equality, such as that represented at m, j, or c, the difference
principle becomes identical to the Pareto principle, permitting

market transactions (perhaps of the Wilt Chamberlain sort) that lead to increased inequality. Other types of regressive redistribution are also consistent with the difference principle, such as a tax cut that gives millions of dollars to top income earners at the relative expense of the middle classes with a nominal increase for those at the bottom. So long as the middle classes do not actually become worse off than those at the bottom, the difference principle will be satisfied. This is not, strictly, a fair way to evaluate the principle because Rawls insists that it is intended for thinking about the basic structure rather than the evaluation of particular policies such as a tax cut. But the examples indicate that it is an underdetermined principle, compatible with a wide array of distributive possibilities.

This can be seen more generally from partial comparison of the difference principle and both the Pareto principle and Bentham's greatest happiness principle as depicted in figure 5.2. The comparison is partial because we are superimposing principles on one another that refer to different underlying metrics: primary goods and Bentham's cardinal utilities, both of which permit interpersonal comparisons, and Pareto's ordinal utilities, which do not. Although the comparison reveals something about the structures of the different principles, one should not be misled by the figure into thinking that we have exact comparisons.

That said, it is clear that the difference principle allows for a vast range of distributive possibilities. Assuming x in figure 5.2 to be the status quo, we can see that all Pareto-superior changes (which fall into the area *lxh*) are also Rawls-preferred. But so are many Pareto-undecidable redistributions that Bentham would approve (such as those in the area *xgnh*), as well as some that he would not (in the area *xmg*). On the other hand, there are some redistributions that would contribute to the greatest happiness on Bentham's measure (in the areas *caxl* and *gbdn*) that would not improve the condition of the least advantaged and would be abjured by the difference principle.

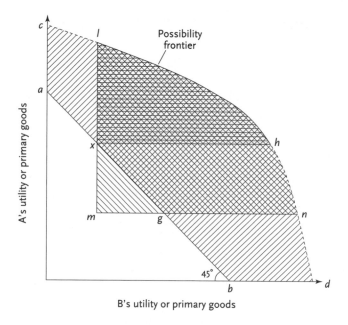

Figure 5.2. Partial comparison of the difference (maximin) principle with the Pareto principle and Bentham's greatest happiness principle with two individuals in a fixed commodity space

Rawls has sometimes been criticized for advocating such an underdetermined principle, which is compatible, for instance, with a heavily interventionist state, a pure market system, or some version of a mixed economy. I criticized him myself some time ago for his professed agnosticism in *A Theory of Justice* between capitalism and socialism.[56] But Rawls has a double-barreled response. His concern, first, is with fundamental principles—we might think of them as entrenched constitutional constraints—governing economic policy-making in the society. They set the outer limits on what can be done by insisting that the basic requirement is that distributive arrangements work to benefit those at the bottom. There are concededly many other distributive choices to make, but it is not clear that, behind the veil of ignorance, they would be accorded this kind of constitutional status.

Second, Rawls might reasonably respond that the choices among different mixes of market and nonmarket institutions are issues of political economy, not political philosophy. If laissez-faire really did, as its proponents claim, lead more benefits to trickle down to the poor than any other workable system, then Rawls would say we should endorse it. If, on the other hand, a command or mixed economy would do a better job, then we should support that. We saw in earlier chapters that these are invariably contentious questions. Rawls might reasonably say that philosophy cannot be expected to resolve them. Rather, they should be argued over in the public arena. Perhaps different possibilities should be tried out to see how well they do. Command systems look less promising in the wake of 1989 than they may have done in the 1930s, but perhaps more effective forms of state direction of economies will be made possible as a result of the information revolution, or made necessary to manage problems such as global warming. Rawls's point would be that the difference principle expresses the basic normative standard that should be deployed in debates and experiments over the various possibilities, but that it is to expect the wrong kind of thing from such a principle to expect it to resolve them. This is plausible so far as it goes, though some will remain dissatisfied with an account that abdicates on all but the most basic distributive questions.

5.3.4 Plural Commitments and Priorities

Any political scheme that affirms multiple commitments risks the possibility of internal tension if their injunctions turn out to be mutually incompatible. To deal with this, decisions have to be made about what trumps what in the event of a conflict. For instance, Locke's second proviso on the rule that everyone is entitled to use the common land is that "enough, and as good" be left available to others in common.[57] I cannot exercise my use-right in a way that forecloses your ability to exercise yours. Yet Locke also favored the enclosure of land on efficiency grounds, believing that in general the productivity gains would be so great so as to render the second proviso obsolete. So much more would be produced that everyone would be better off than they could be when living from the common.[58] If, however, the productivity argument turned out not to be true, or the benefits did not trickle down to some individual, it is clear from Locke's scheme that the proviso would kick in, entitling her to at least as much as she could have gotten by working the unenclosed common. The second proviso has lexicographical (or, as Rawls dubs it for short, lexical) priority over the efficiency provision. Locke favors both, but, in the event of a conflict, the proviso trumps.

Rawls's requirement that distributive arrangements work to the benefit of the least advantaged enjoys an analogous lexical priority to Locke's proviso. No doubt there are efficiency gains to leaving things to the market and Rawls is not opposed to society's realizing those gains, but not at the price of violating the constraint that the system operate to the advantage of those at the bottom. He also develops explicit lexical priorities among the principles governing the different primary goods. The first principle, distributing liberties, is lexically prior to the second principle, and, within the second principle, the principle of fair equality of opportunity is lexically prior to the difference principle.

By way of illustration, if affirmative action were conceded to be necessary to achieve fair equality of opportunity in a country, such as the United States, which has entrenched gender- and race-based inequalities of opportunity, this would be acceptable if it violated the difference principle but not if it contravened a liberty protected by the first principle. In a world in which Rawls's principles had been adopted as the constitution, then, supporters of gender and race-based affirmative action could admit that it might operate to the detriment of some of the worst off—such as men and poor whites, but they would argue that its only costs are economic. Opponents, by contrast, would claim that the policy undermines a liberty, such as freedom of association, protected by the first principle. Courts would have to develop rules akin to the tiers of review developed in the American system to decide who should bear the burden of proof and how heavy it should be in litigation of this sort. As they moved up the lexical ranking, courts would load the dice more heavily in favor of protecting rights and liberties, just as American courts do when they deem "fundamental" liberties to be at stake.[59]

5.4 Limits of Hypothetical Contracts

Rawls's ranking and application of his principles suggest that he is uncomfortable with some of the more radical implications of his argument. It has been pointed out, for example, that if his "grave risks" assumption is sufficiently powerful to get people to reject utilitarianism in the original position in favor of the difference principle, then surely it is also sufficiently strong to justify assigning the economic protections of the worst off a higher lexical ranking than Rawls assigns them. What good is the protection of freedom of speech to someone on the verge of starvation?[60]

This difficulty could be addressed by rearranging his lexical rankings to assign economic guarantees for the worst off a better protection in his overall scheme, but raising the issue brings up the more general question: Who is Rawls's argument really intended to persuade? His answer is that "reflective equilibrium" is intended to be a process in which the reader moves back and forth between her moral intuitions and the choice problem as Rawls depicts it in the original position.

140

THE SOCIAL CONTRACT

By going back and forth, sometimes altering the conditions of the
contractual circumstances, at others withdrawing our judgments
and conforming to them in principle, I assume that eventually we
shall find a description of the initial situation that both expresses
reasonable conditions and yields principles which match our considered judgments duly pruned and adjusted. This state of affairs I
refer to as reflective equilibrium. It is an equilibrium because at
last our principles and judgments coincide; it is reflective since we
know to what principles our judgments conform and the premises
of their derivation.[61]

It is not unimaginable that someone might revise at least some
of her initial moral intuitions as a result of such a process, so that
it would be too strong a criticism to say of Rawls that in his
substantive judgments he is merely preaching to the choir. However, the appeal to reflective equilibrium does not get him entirely
off the hook from the perspective of asking whether he escapes a
version of Rousseau's critique of Hobbes mentioned in §5.1. Reflective equilibrium is aimed at getting us to rethink our moral
intuitions and the opinions based on them. It does not extend to
the characterization of the original position and the assumptions
about human psychology and the causal operation of the world
embodied in it. The "laws of psychology and economics" and the
"general facts" about society as Rawls stipulates them—moderate
scarcity, grave risks, and so on,—which are not meant to be objects of revision through the process of reflective equilibrium. On
the contrary, Rawls deploys the assumptions about them to get
people to rethink their moral intuitions. As a result, if John Harsanyi believes people to be more risk-embracing than Rawls does,
there is nothing in the process of reflective equilibrium, no matter how sincerely entered into, to persuade him differently.[62]

Every political theory rests on assumptions about human psychology and about how the world operates causally, and it is clear
that these assumptions do a great deal of the controversial work in

hypothetical social contract arguments. Even restricting our attention to the neo-Kantian tradition in which choosers in the initial situation are assumed to place overwhelming weight on the preservation of individual autonomy, there is a dizzying array of theories depending on the assumptions about these matters that are fed into the initial situations. Robert Paul Wolff concludes that people would opt for anarchy, Nozick the minimal state, Harsanyi utilitarianism, Buchanan and Tullock a hierarchy of more and less demanding decision rules depending on the importance of the issue, Ronald Dworkin substantial health and social insurance, and Rawls a regime fixated on the condition of people at the bottom as we have seen. What drives these differences is not the contractual method or the commitment to individual autonomy, on which they all agreed, but their differing assumptions about human psychology and about how the social world operates causally.[63] In this sense Rousseau's critique of Hobbes does carry over into the contemporary contractarian literature with considerable critical bite. You cannot derive something from nothing. The abstract commitments do considerably less work, and the controversial empirical ones do considerably more work, than theorists in this camp are generally willing to acknowledge.

5.5 Revisiting Moral Arbitrariness

I noted in §5.2 that Rawls's most enduring contributions have to do with his handling of ineradicable pluralism and his discussion of the moral arbitrariness of differences among people, and that these stand independently of his argument from the original position or his theory of justice. Ineradicable pluralism, and his legacy in thinking about it, will concern us in more detail in chapter 7. Here I conclude with a closer examination of the implications of his discussion of moral arbitrariness. It is an unusual argument in that it is exceedingly difficult, if not impossible, to dispute, yet it has implications that are so radical that not only does Rawls evade them, but few of the rest of us would be willing to live with them either.

Rawls recognizes that human capacities, like other resources, should be regarded as social goods for certain purposes. We might describe this as a socialization of capacities strategy, thinking of it as a mirror image of the classical Marxian one. For Marx, non-human resources are of no independent moral interest, reducible to the capacities necessarily expended in their creation or their separation from nature. On the socialization of capacities view, by contrast, human capacities cease to be of independent moral interest; they are treated as social resources like any other. This follows naturally from Rawls's moral arbitrariness argument; as such it is subversive of the workmanship ideal in all its forms.

Rawls is not alone in realizing that, once the moral arbitrariness argument is granted, the burden of justification falls to those who would deny that human capacities are potentially up for grabs as objects of distributive justice. In a like spirit, Ronald Dworkin treats human capacities and external material resources as moral equivalents. He argues that there may be good reasons for resisting the redistribution of physical and mental resources (insofar as this is technologically feasible), but that a case might nonetheless be made for compensating those with inferior physical and mental resources for their relative incapacities.[64] If different people are differently endowed through no action or fault of their own, why should the losses lie with those who happen to be disadvantaged?

Yet both theorists are evidently uncomfortable with the full implications of this line of thinking, as many of us would be. Our reluctance has, I think, to do with the psychological side of the workmanship ideal, with the sense of subjective satisfaction that attaches to the idea of making something that one can subsequently call one's own. We all know the feeling, and it is not easily argued that we can either give it up or apply it to a generalized notion that there is a sense in which I, along with everyone else, own everything that everyone appears at a given time and place to make. And for a species so critically reliant as is ours on work for its survival, it seems perverse to deny the legitimacy of so powerful a spur as the psychic boost that producing something that one can own brings. This is perhaps why Chief Seattle's aphorism to the effect that "the earth does not belong to us, we belong to the earth" has never achieved much historical traction, and why no one has ever taken seriously Nozick's critique of workmanship when he asks, "why isn't mixing what I own with what I don't own a way of losing what I own rather than a way of gaining what I don't?"[65]

The strength of psychological attachments to workmanship may also account for why Rawls and Dworkin both evade the implications of the moral arbitrariness argument. Rawls does this when he holds that the effectiveness with which people are able to use resources, or choose to use them, is not a relevant consideration in deciding how those resources should be distributed. There are two different issues here, both of which raise tensions internal to the Rawlsian account. One derives from Amartya Sen's point that if we really want justly to distribute what people of greatly different capacities are enabled to do, then we cannot use Rawlsian primary goods; we need a different metric that takes account of how different people employ capacities and resources, as basic. In thinking, for example, about justice in the distribution of food, Sen thinks we should be interested neither in how much food a person has or how much utility she derives from eating it, but rather how well nourished she is.[66] Second, there is the point made by G. A. Cohen, Thomas Nagel, Richard Arneson, and others, that different people have different preferences and goals, some more expensive and more difficult to satisfy than others. Rawls's attempt to sidestep this problem, by arguing that these are not afflictions but are chosen, scarcely meets the objection because, as Thomas Scanlon and others have noted, often they are not.[67]

Dworkin also balks at the implications of the moral arbitrariness argument that he otherwise endorses. He invites us to speculate on how resources might in principle be equalized by use of a hypothetical auction in which all parties begin with the same finite number of bargaining chips.[68] As part of this he assumes that human capacities should be thought of as resources, yet there are two ways in which he dodges the full implications of this. He claims, first, that although capacities (his term is "physical and mental powers") are resources and therefore legitimate objects of a theory of distributive justice, they should nonetheless be treated differently from "independent material resources." With physical and mental powers, the goal should not be to strive to distribute them justly (which, for Dworkin, means equally). Instead the problem is construed as one of discovering "how far the ownership of independent external resources should be affected by differences that exist in physical and mental powers, and the response of our theory should speak in that vocabulary."[69] For this reason he argues that people should be compensated by reference to a standard arrived at by our speculations concerning whether and to what extent they would, on average, have insured against the particular handicap or disability or lack of talent *ex ante*, assuming that insurance rates would be set in a competitive market. Insuring against the possibility of not having an extremely rare skill would be far more expensive than insuring against the possibility of not having a widely shared capacity such as sight. In this way Dworkin hopes to come up with a theory of equality of resources that does not itself make implicit judgments about welfare and avoids the "slavery of the talented" problem which any theory that permits compensation for differences in capacities must confront.[70]

Notice that Dworkin supplies no principled argument for why physical and mental powers should be treated differently from material resources. The assertion that they "cannot be manipulated or transferred, even so far as technology permits" is not further explained or justified, but since Dworkin agrees that they are resources an explanation is surely in order.[71] This is so not least because compensation in any amount will sometimes be inadequate to equalize a power—or capacity—deficiency (as in the case of blindness). In such circumstances compensation based on a standard set in a hypothetical insurance auction cannot be said to equalize the resources of two persons, one blind, one sighted.[72] Moreover, it is not always true, *pace* Dworkin, that their powers of sight could not be equalized.[73] The state might forcibly transplant one eye from a sighted person to the blind one in order to equalize their resources, or, for that matter, simply blind the sighted person. Less callously and more interestingly, it might invest billions of dollars on research on and development of artificial eyes, financed by a tax on the sighted. In order to avoid such unpalatable results, Dworkin would have to supply an argument for why we might be said to be entitled to our powers and capacities (and in some sense responsible for having or lacking them) in different (and trumping) ways than we might be said to be entitled to material resources, given his equation of the two. In the absence of such an argument it is difficult to see how he can adopt the socialization of capacities strategy in principle, yet simply assert that people are entitled to, and responsible for, their capacities and incapacities in fact.

The second way in which Dworkin refuses to live with the implications of embracing the moral arbitrariness argument concerns his discussion of how our conception of a person should be distinguished from our conception of her circumstances. Dworkin argues that we need a view of distributive justice that is "ambition sensitive." It requires a view of equality by reference to which people "decide what sorts of lives to pursue against a back-ground of information about the actual costs that their choices impose on other people and hence on the total stock of resources that may fairly be used by them." This he tries to achieve by assigning "tastes and ambitions" to the person, and "physical and mental powers" to his "circumstances," arguing that tastes and ambitions are not relevant considerations in deciding how re-sources should be distributed.[74] In this way he hopes to retain an idea of individual rights and responsibilities within the socializa-tion of capacities framework. Dworkin wants to rescue the kernel of what is intuitively attractive in the workmanship ideal, the idea that when people conceive of and put into practice productive plans, the benefits from the resulting actions should flow back to them. Yet he wants to do this without being swamped by the difficulties of overdetermination that flow from the Rawlsian claim that the distribution of physical and mental powers is mor-ally arbitrary.[75]

Dworkin's strategy fails. The volitions we are able to form and the ambitions it occurs to us to develop are greatly influenced, perhaps even determined, by our powers and capacities. To "think big," to "resolve to go for broke," to steel oneself through self-control to perform demanding acts—do these reflect ambition or capacity? When we describe someone as ambitious, are we not describing something more basic to her psychology and constitu-tion than her tastes? There are certainly circumstances in which we would say that lack of confidence is an incapacity that pre-vents the formation (not just the attainment) of particular am-bitions. Different people have different capacities to form differ-ent ambitions, and those different capacities must be as morally tainted from Dworkin's point of view as any other capacities. Donald Trump is able to develop more far-reaching ambitions than Archie Bunker due at least partly to luck in the genetic pool and in the circumstances of his upbringing.[76]

Similar arguments can be made about the different abilities to form (or refrain from forming) different kinds of tastes, whether expensive, compulsive, or both as Dworkin is aware. The case he considers is where someone has an incapacitating obsession that he wishes he did not have. Dworkin argues that such cravings may be thought of as handicaps and thus handled via his hypothetical insurance scheme.[77] But this is to sidestep the point being made here, which is that the obsession may itself incapacitate a person from forming the relevant second-order desire to make Dworkin's hypothetical insurance solution work. Are we to say of an alcoholic whose affliction is so severe that he cannot even form the desire not to be an alcoholic that his preference for alcohol results from his *taste* rather than his *incapacity*? I think not.[78]

With all acquired tastes (not just the expensive), experiencing the taste is by definition conditional on the exercise of pertinent capacities. A taste for good beer, or even just for beer, a taste for a particular kind of music, perhaps even for any music—these can be developed only through the exercise of relevant capacities. We would not say of a deaf person that she could have a taste for music of a particular sort, or even a taste for music of any sort (although of course we could intelligibly say that such a person might perhaps wish that she was able to have such a taste). Likewise with beer and someone who has no functioning taste buds or sense of smell. The idea that we form our tastes and ambitions in some way that is independent of our resources and capacities is too whiggish, as would be revealed to anyone who tried to perform a thought experiment in which she was required to decide on her future tastes and ambitions while kept in ignorance of her powers and capacities. Dworkin's intuition here seems driven by the notion that people should be held responsible only for the choices they make in life, not for things over which they have no control. Yet his replacement of the resources *versus* capacities distinction with the ambitions and tastes *versus* physical and mental powers distinction fails to rescue the Lockean notion of an autonomous choosing agent, of whom rights and responsibilities may legitimately be predicated.

Some may object that the line of reasoning I have been developing leads too quickly to pure determinism. Surely we should be open to the possibility that *some* aspects of human action are subject to autonomous choice, and that people might reasonably be held to account for the aspects that fall into that category. This is implicit in G. A. Cohen's argument that "we should compensate for disadvantage beyond a person's control."[79] Granting that the category autonomous choice might not be empty, at least for many people, it is difficult to see how it can supply the basis for a serviceable account of distributive justice. How is the state to determine which part of a person's decisions are genuinely volitional, as opposed to determined, and how is it to measure differences in capacities for volitional behavior across persons? The difficulties we have encountered in attempts to build utilitometers, tortometers, and exploitometers pale by comparison with what would be required to construct an accurate "voluntometer." Beyond this, the focus on free will suggests that exotic compulsions—such as an addiction to the best available malt liquor—should trump important needs for food and shelter which people might be able to secure for themselves through voluntary action, but only at significant cost. This is to say nothing of the acute moral hazards that should be expected to arise in a regime governed by Cohen's principle. Parents would face incentives, for instance, to avoid developing capacities for individual responsibility and autonomous choice in their children, lest they be deprived of compensation to which they would otherwise be entitled.[80]

To sum up: like Rawls, Dworkin is unable to live with the implications of the socialization of capacities strategy that flow from the moral arbitrariness argument. This is at least partly because, when taken to its logical conclusion, this strategy undermines what is attractive in the workmanship ideal. This is the notion of the sovereign agent that lies at the core of the Enlightenment conception of individual rights. Yet reluctant as Rawls and Dworkin both are to abandon their intuitive commitments to the idea of moral agency that informs the workmanship ideal, neither has supplied an account of how this can be rendered consistent with the moral arbitrariness argument that both feel compelled to endorse. This reflects deep tensions within the secular variant of the workmanship ideal itself: it presses relentlessly toward a kind of moral determinism that its very terms suggest we ought to be able to deny.

One might take the view that Rawls's "political, not metaphysical" argument opens up a possible way out of this tension. If there is overlapping consensus that the workmanship ideal should be endorsed up to a point so that individuals should be held responsible for certain types of choices, but not for others, then we need not get into the question why people hold this belief or whether their reasons for holding it make any sense. Making this case would, however, take us more deeply into democratic theory than is achieved by Rawls's brief remarks about overlapping consensus. For one thing, although a wide consensus might be possible on the principle that there should be *a* zone of individual responsibility in which gains and losses lie where they fall, it seems inevitable that there would be an equally wide dissensus over what this entails in practice. At a minimum, mechanisms would be needed to settle disagreements over what should be included and excluded from the zone. One only has to think of debates in the United States about the obligation to provide health insurance for all, the right to abortion, or the extent of criminal responsibility among adolescents, battered spouses, and the retarded to be reminded that there are stark limits to the overlapping consensus about the appropriate scope of individual rights and responsibilities.

Moreover, if a variant of the workmanship ideal is embraced on "political, not metaphysical" grounds, questions are bound to arise concerning its inevitable conflict with other justice values. If the rights of human workmanship have no natural status or special trumping moral power, then there is bound to be controversy about where they fit into governing distributive schemes that must cope with multiple demands on scarce resources—from redressing the effects of historical disadvantage, to caring for the sick and elderly, to supporting just causes in other countries. It seems even less likely that an "overlapping consensus" could be developed about these tradeoffs than about what to include in the zone of individual rights and responsibilities. Once it is conceded, in a world of endemic scarcity, that there is neither an uncontroversial theological model nor a calculus of contribution from which correct distributive injunctions can be scientifically "read off," we are bound to come to grips with the primacy of politics to arguments about distributive justice. That subject will be the central focus of chapter 7. First I turn to a consideration of authors who suggest that, rather than try to reconcile and deliver on the twin Enlightenment goals of science and individual rights, we should abandon them.

CHAPTER 6

Anti-Enlightenment Politics

Every current has its undertow, and it would be surprising had the political projects of the Enlightenment not bred trenchant opposition. From the various antediluvian movements Christopher Hill describes in *The World Turned Upside Down*, to the Luddite machine-breakers and the anarcho-syndicalist followers of Pierre-Joseph Proudhon in the nineteenth century, to the critics of the American Progressives such as Reinhold Niebuhr whose story has most fully been told by Christopher Lasch, to the Greens and other environmentalist groups of our own day, the Enlightenment political undertaking has always had its detractors. Sometimes religiously motivated, sometimes secular, these detractors do not believe that progress based on science will lead to greater human betterment and individual freedom. To them, the Enlightenment faith in scientific progress is a dangerous delusion. Against it they have affirmed the need to accept preexisting limits and embrace political arrangements and patterns of conduct that have been inherited over generations, even centuries.[1]

6.1 The Burkean Outlook

The philosophical giant of the anti-Enlightenment was the Irishman Edmund Burke (1729–1797). Although he was raised as a Protestant, his mother was a Catholic and his father may have been one as well.[2] In any event, he was of a Catholic sensibility in believing that the authority of tradition lies at the core of Christian practice. This stands in stark contrast to Locke's workmanship ideal, with its emphasis on the sovereignty of each individual's subjective relationship with God and his conception of humans as miniature gods so long as they do not violate the strictures of natural law. Such a conception differed fundamentally from Burke's contempt for all forms of egalitarianism, which struck him as a doctrine that is profoundly at odds with all the evidence of nature and history. Moreover, the idea that human beings could conceive and create a social world from whole cloth seemed to him dangerous hubris that reached its apotheosis in the most traumatic event of his lifetime: the French Revolution. His prediction, well before the Jacobin terror began to unfold after 1790, that the revolution would have appalling consequences brought him out of the political wilderness, making him something of a celebrity as a political commentator for the rest of his life.

For Burke, enterprises of human perfectibility are bound to fail, probably disastrously. Embracing the doctrine of the fall meant recognizing and accepting the world's imperfections. It also meant realizing that although inherited institutions contain much that is evil, there is no reason to think that abolishing them would lead to less evil institutions. Hostile to architectonic thinking in all its forms, Burke believed that conserving an imperfect inherited world from the worse imperfections that human beings are capable of contriving is the business of political leadership; hence his emphasis on preserving tradition. He was an antipopulist to the core, contemptuous of the notion that "the constitution of a kingdom be a problem of arithmetic."[3] He is famous for propounding the doctrine that a Member of Parliament—which he was for a good part of his life—owes it to his constituents not to sacrifice his judgment to conform to their opinions. He was unimpressed by the human capacity for reason to understand much, let alone to reshape the world in accordance with the particular wills of any generation. He thought the human condition inherently opaque, and never doubted that the clarity and distinctness of understanding sought by the rationalist and neoclassical thinkers of his day was chimerical.

The Burkean outlook is often described as reactionary, but this is a mistake. Burke opposed the French Revolution because its leaders aspired to wipe the slate clean and start over. He believed that such projects were bound to fail, and he was utterly dismissive of abstract doctrines of the rights of man to which they looked for legitimation. But he was committed to the importance of protecting inherited rights and liberties from encroachment. He insisted that

> From Magna Carta to the Declaration of Right, it has been the uniform policy of our constitution to claim and assert our abilities, as an *entailed inheritance* derived from our forefathers, and to be transmitted to our posterity; as an estate specially belonging to the people of this kingdom without any reference whatever to any more general or prior right. . . . We have an inheritable crown; an inheritable peerage; and an house of commons and a people inheriting privileges, franchises, and liberties, from a long line of ancestors.[4]

Burke was quite willing to endorse political action, even revolutionary political action, to preserve these inherited rights and liberties when he judged them to be threatened, as he agreed they had been in 1688. He endorsed the American Revolution and supported Catholic emancipation and other political reform in Ireland, where he believed that the Protestant political elite had oppressed the Catholic majority and violated their traditional liberties. Nor was he against the idea that politics is rooted in a social contract, but he famously described it as a "partnership not only between those who are living, but between those who are living, those who are dead, and those who are to be born." The contract prevailing in any state at any time "is but a clause in the great primeval contract of eternal society."[5]

Burke believed morals to be rooted in the timeless universals of the Christian faith, but saw political rights and liberties as fragile civil creations, the work of many generations. He perceived them to be under constant threat from many forces, not least articulate intellectuals who are convinced that they hold the key to social improvement. Burke would have been especially wary of the Marxian idea of an ideological vanguard committed to the project of human liberation. He believed ability unencumbered by property to be particularly threatening, necessitating massive over-representation of the propertied classes in Parliament. "As ability is a vigorous and active principle," he contended, "and as property is sluggish, inert, and timid, it can never be safe from the invasions of ability, unless it be, out of all proportion predominant in the representation."[6] He would have viewed Stalinist totalitarianism as the predictable consummation of Marxist revolution, not a perversion of it as many neo-Marxists since Leon Trotsky (1879–1940) have claimed. But it would not have been their propensity for revolution that would trouble Burke so much as their belief in their capacity to demolish inherited social and political arrangements and fashion superior replacements. Since he believed the requisite knowledge to be unavailable, those who claim to have it must be charlatans, delusional, or both.

6.2 Against Enlightenment Science

The Burkean outlook is just that: an outlook not a theory. What its proponents share in common, however, is not Burke's, nor any, particular politics. As with natural law and Enlightenment thinkers, critics of the Enlightenment can be found all over the political spectrum from anarchists, to feminists, to pragmatists, to liberals, to social democrats, to traditionalist conservatives like Burke himself. Some are backward-looking, such as Rousseau in Burke's time and Alasdair MacIntyre in ours, in that they would undo the Enlightenment if they could.[7] Some are future-oriented, such as Friedrich Wilhelm Nietzsche, Richard Rorty, and Jean-François Lyotard. In different ways they all urge us to get beyond the concerns and, as they see them, the constraints of the Enlightenment. Whether antimodern or postmodern, left or right, these thinkers share with Burke a profound antipathy for its scientific pretensions.

For our purposes here it is worth recalling the distinction between the early and the mature Enlightenment discussed in §1.1.2, because most versions of the anti-Enlightenment attack on science make considerably better sense as critiques of the early Enlightenment than of the mature one. For instance, Rorty's brilliant assault on that project in *Philosophy and the Mirror of Nature* takes as its central target the Cartesian-Kantian project that revolved around achieving indubitable certainty. On Rorty's account, to think of knowledge as presenting a "problem" about which we ought to have a "theory" is fundamentally misconceived. The obsession with foundational questions, he contends, begins with Descartes's "invention" of the mind, his "coalescence of beliefs and sensations into Lockean ideas" that provided a field of inquiry that seemed more fundamental than that which had concerned the ancients, a field "within which certainty, as opposed to mere opinion, was possible." This project, eventually christened "epistemology," revolved around Kant's goal to place philosophy on the secure path of a science. Kant went further on Rorty's telling, embracing the idea that philosophy should be queen of the sciences. He turned the study of the foundations of knowledge into a nonempirical project, a matter for "armchair reflection, independent of physiological discoveries and capable of producing necessary truths." In this way he sought to reconcile the Cartesian claim that we can have certainty only about our ideas with the reality that we seemed not to doubt many things outside of that realm.[8]

6.3 Rejecting the Early or Mature Enlightenment?

Rorty and other postmodernists move too quickly from this compelling critique of the early Enlightenment obsession with foundational certainty to the wholesale abandonment of the idea that science can and should aspire to get at the truth more reliably than opinion, convention, superstition, or tradition. Under the strong influence of the later writings of Ludwig Wittgenstein, Rorty embraces his idea that truth is nothing more than adherence to the rules of a language game—the norms and conventions we have come to accept.[9] So Rorty defines truth in terms of social consensus and "solidarity" and rationality as "civility"—the result of conversational agreement. He thinks we should replace philosophy with hermeneutics and be satisfied with an interpretive discourse that "keeps the conversation going."[10] His outlook has produced predictable charges of relativism which Rorty tends to deflect playfully without engaging seriously. He intimates that the skeptic's request for criteria by which we say that one answer is better than another reveals his inability to get beyond the expectations built into the Enlightenment project. Yet Rorty glosses over questions about deep disagreements within cultures that defy appeals to ground truth in consensus and "solidarity," and he offers no responsive answer to the question how, on his account, we can say anything critical of obnoxious alien practices, from foot-binding to genocide, other than that they conflict with our world view.[11] Instead he quips, at a sufficient altitude to avoid engaging contentious issues, that we need not worry about "the grounds of normativity, the impossibility of justice, or the infinite distance which separates us from the other." In order to "achieve our country" we can "give both religion and philosophy a pass. We can just get on with trying to solve what Dewey called 'the problems of men.'"[12]

For present purposes it suffices to note that Rorty conflates the abandonment of the search for foundational certainty with the abandonment of the scientific outlook *tout court*. There are many credible fallibilist views of science that fill the space between claiming indubitable certainty for what the science produces and treating it as merely the set of conventional understandings that we happen to have inherited, no better or worse than any other. Indeed, as we saw in earlier chapters, embracing fallibilism is the hallmark of the mature Enlightenment scientific consciousness. This rests on an inherently critical stance toward all putative knowledge claims. It involves recognizing that although the best evidence may suggest that x is the case, there is always the chance that we are wrong, and that, if future research proves that we are, then this will be because the world operates differently from how we think presently. Science advances, on this view, not by making knowledge more certain but by producing more knowledge. That knowledge-claims are recognized always to be corrigible is a mark of science's superiority to opinion, convention, superstition, and tradition, not its equivalence to them. Indeed, as Max Weber (1864–1920) noted, part of what differentiates scientists from practitioners of other forms of intellectual activity is that even the best scientists expect their work eventually to be superseded.[13]

Rorty's inability to perceive this middle ground between the early and mature Enlightenment views of science is well illustrated in his attempt to capture pragmatist thinkers like Dewey for the postmodernist camp. To be sure, Dewey was dismissive of the search for foundational certainty, and he agreed completely with Rorty's view that an inward-looking armchair reflection discipline of epistemology would not yield an understanding of the foundations of knowledge that its proponents from Descartes to Kant had sought. But his outlook differed from Rorty's in two pertinent respects. First, he was not averse to thinking about foundational questions, but he thought this should always take place in the context of trying to understand particular concrete problems. "Better it is for philosophy to err in active participation in the living struggles and issues of its own age and times to maintain an immune monastic impeccability."[14] Nothing in this view involves abjuring concern with second-order questions. For instance, an argument that begins about whether or not someone is unaware of her interests in a particular situation might well become an argument about what it means to know an interest and then an argument about what knowledge is. Like Rorty, Dewey was all for resisting the idea that we had better develop a cast-iron theory of what knowledge is before getting to these issues. Unlike Rorty, however, Dewey thought we should be willing to rethink our most basic commitments critically when this is necessary to resolve particular problems.

Second, Dewey thought progress is possible, in science and in politics, as knowledge advances. His view was an evolutionary one, in terms of which less adequate views are disregarded as those more adequate to human experience are developed. Indeed, with hindsight, one is bound to say that Dewey's faith in the possibilities for scientific progress in politics was naïve. Consider his lament in 1929 that the then prevalent attitude toward such social problems as crime was still "reminiscent of the way in which diseases were once thought of and dealt with" when they were believed to have moral causes. Just as the possibility of "effective treatment" began when diseases came to be seen as having "an intrinsic origin in the interactions of the organism and its natural environment," so we should now be seeking technical solutions to the causes of crime:

> We are only just beginning to think of criminality as an equally intrinsic manifestation [as with disease] of interactions between an individual and the social environment. With respect to it, and with respect to many other evils, we persist in thinking and acting in prescientific "moral" terms. This prescientific conception of "evil" is probably the greatest barrier that exists to real reform.[15]

Contemporary debates about the politicization of crime and punishment suggest that Dewey's was a forlorn hope. The recurring hostility to rehabilitation as a goal of the penal system in favor of the more morally charged idea of retribution, the lobbying of interest groups who stand to benefit from the expansion of the prison industry, the role of criminalizing drugs disproportionately used by minorities in demonizing and controlling them, and the other political benefits of being "tough on crime" for politicians combine to suggest that Dewey's hope for an equation of the causes of crime with disease is not in the cards any time soon.[16] Indeed, the example of the AIDS debate in the United States during the 1980s and 1990s revealed all too clearly that we can scarcely be said even to have put behind us the idea that disease has moral causes.

However pollyannaish, Dewey's view of the likely impact of science on public policy, it is evident that, fallibilist though he certainly was, he thought scientific knowledge could and would lead to improvements in human affairs, as it displaced moralism and blind superstition as the basis for human interaction. In these respects he is unquestionably an Enlightenment thinker whose aspirations exhibit more in common with the utilitarian and Marxist impulses to displace politics with "the administration of things" than with the postmodernist rejection of the Enlightenment project in favor of a hermeneutic enterprise based on the acceptance of the norms contingently prevailing in a culture. As was the case with Mill, Dewey expected the scientific mindset to diffuse itself throughout society, and he showed none of Mill's ambivalence about its likely effects. He shared the Burkean view that achieving social change presents the challenges of rebuilding a ship at sea, but, unlike Burke, he did not believe that preventing the ship from sinking was the only goal worth worrying about. He thought we should aspire to improve our existing ships and build better ones that could take us to new destinations more quickly and commodiously, and that science was essential to such improvement.

The right overall verdict on the postmodern rejection of foundationalism, then, is that it is an over-reaction to the excessive hubris of the early Enlightenment that may have lingering influences in academic philosophy, but has not had much to do with the conduct of science for over a century. We should, indeed, instantly be suspicious of the claim that appeals to context offer an alternative to developing adequate foundations for our beliefs and institutions when we find one of its more lucid defenders asserting, without appearing to sense the irony, that he wants to "clear the ground" for an anti-foundational view.[17] Architects and engineers cannot design one type of physical foundation that will support every type of building, no matter what its size, its intended purpose, the material out of which it is to be constructed, or the terrain on which it is to be built. But this scarcely implies that builders should henceforth construct buildings without foundations—then they would all fall over. Foundations vary, but they share in common the structural property of providing the best available support given the terrain and the building's intended purpose.

6.4 Other Objections to the Possibility of Social Science

Many who do not embrace postmodernism are nonetheless skeptical that science should be expected to deliver significant knowledge about politics. Objections here are of various sorts. Some argue that social science is impossible because, unlike the natural sciences, the object of study is, at least in substantial part, an artifact of human language.[18] For instance, the mid-twentieth-century Oxford philosopher J. L. Austin noted that language exhibits what he described as a *performative* dimension such that saying things actually creates social reality. When a duly empowered official says, "I now pronounce you husband and wife" in the appropriate circumstances, for example, he thereby creates a new social fact. Similar observations can be made about acts like promising, conferring degrees, and many other activities where to say is to do.[19] Opinions vary on whether only some or all language exhibits a performative dimension, but in any event the performative dimension of language is not by itself an obstacle to studying human action scientifically. The question is not whether the social world is at least partly an artifact of linguistic convention (obviously it is), but rather whether the human practices that produce and reproduce the conventions are sufficiently enduring that we can aspire to make valid generalizations about them—for example, concerning which sorts of people marry which others, whether moving to no-fault divorce increases its likelihood, and so on. The extent to which we can develop such generalizations successfully is unrelated to the fact that marriage is a product of linguistic convention. Nor is it a subject for armchair reflection. If these questions can be answered, it will be as a result of empirical investigation.[20]

Another variant of skepticism about the possibility of social science might be called "voluntarist." It concerns the fact that the relevant object of study includes actions and institutions that depend on beings that have free will. MacIntyre argues, for instance, that this makes prediction impossible—if we really have free will, our actions should be expected to defy predictive models.[21] (This is an inversion of the seventeenth-century view discussed in §1.1, which held that will-dependence increased the reliability of knowledge, reflecting the mature Enlightenment move from an introspective to an experimental view of the human sciences.) Because prediction is now thought to be one of the principal ways of testing hypotheses scientifically, the possibility of a social science seems permanently threatened by the reality of free will. MacIntyre's account is no more persuasive, however, than the claim that the social world cannot be studied scientifically because much of the object of study involves institutions and practices that are artifacts of linguistic convention. Whether human beings have free will is at the end of the day an empirical question, but, assuming for present purposes that they do, this does not mean that probabilistic generalizations cannot be developed about the conditions under which they are more likely to behave in one way rather than another. This assumes that people are likely to behave in similar ways in similar circumstances which may or may not be true, but the possibility of its being true does not depend on denying the existence of free will. To say that someone will probably make choice x in circumstance q does not mean that they cannot choose not-x, or, that, if they do choose not-x, it was not nonetheless more likely *ex ante* that they would have chosen x. In any event, most successful science does not proceed by making point predictions. It predicts patterns of outcomes. There will always be outliers and error terms; the best theory minimizes them vis-à-vis the going alternatives.

Where does this leave us? On the one hand the various postmodernist, conventionalist, and voluntarist critiques have been oversold as wholesale assaults on the possibility of human sciences. We can reject the peculiar amalgam of transcendental ambitions and deductive arguments that preoccupied the central figures of the early Enlightenment, as well as the interpretivist and free-will based assaults on the viability of the social sciences. This leaves us free to affirm an empirical and fallibilist view of the social sciences that does not differentiate them in kind from the natural sciences. To be sure, there are many disagreements among mature Enlightenment thinkers, such as empiricists, positivists, pragmatists, and realists that should not be glossed over or otherwise minimized.[22] But the adherents of these different schools share in common the view that science is substantially an empirical enterprise, that it advances by rejecting unsuccessful theories, that all knowledge claims are corrigible and for that reason provisional, and that reliable knowledge of the human world is not in principle any less available to science than is reliable knowledge of the nonhuman world.

On the other hand, the record of achievement in the human sciences in general and political science in particular over the past two centuries is scarcely dazzling, whether they are taken on their own terms or evaluated in light of the stunning advances of the natural sciences. Certainly Bentham, Marx, and Dewey were from their different perspectives all much too optimistic about the possibility of scientific advances rendering political controversy obsolete. By the same token, from his point of view Mill worried unnecessarily that the advance of knowledge would yield so much agreement that people would cease to sharpen their wits through disputation, evolving into sheep-like mediocrities—ripe for indoctrination. Religions and ideologies have proved to be vastly more powerful and enduring features of contemporary politics than any of these theorists imagined, not to mention subsequent commentators who predicted that the world's ideologies would converge on a single set of liberal-democratic values as modernization advanced, or that we had finally reached, just before the radical student movements of the 1960s and the conservative revival of the 1980s and 1990s, "the end of ideology."[23] Ideologies and religions persist in politics, sometimes in tension with science, sometimes in tandem with it, partly because of the ways in which they facilitate competition for power in democracies. This process is far from well understood, but few social scientists today would bet much on the hope—or fear, depending on one's point of view—that these forces are likely to become obsolete in politics any time soon.

Moreover, it is often noted that political scientists often get the study of politics embarrassingly wrong. The most dramatic recent example of failure was the collapse of communism that took the political science discipline by at least as much surprise as the rest of the world, and has not been explained in a way that vindicates any particular theory after the fact. Failures of this kind, no matter how dramatic or consequential, say little about the quality of any science, however, since there are pertinent occurrences that every science fails to predict as well as phenomena that they all fail to explain. With sciences, as with people, if you focus on what they cannot do rather than what they can do, you are bound to be disappointed. The fairer approach is not to ask what political scientists have gotten wrong, but what they have gotten right.

Granting this, it is difficult to find a prepossessing stack of accomplishments to which political scientists can point to their credit. For instance, following communism's collapse and the wave of democratic transitions in Africa and Latin America, many countries were involved in writing new constitutions. Yet it soon became painfully obvious that there was no established stock of knowledge in the discipline on the best democratic constitutional arrangements, or even on the likely consequences of embracing different institutional setups.[24] Even in the most technically sophisticated precincts of political science, there has not been much bang for the buck in terms of intellectual investments made. For instance, the huge disciplinary commitment to adapting rational actor models from economics to the study of politics has yet to deliver significant advances in substantive knowledge about politics.[25] Likewise with the multi-decade investment in election-forecasting in the study of American national politics, the ratio of success to post hoc curve-fitting and explaining away failure is not good.[26] Similar failures attach to the attempts in the study of international relations to account for the incidence of international conflict by reference to strategic choice models and vast empirical datasets on the correlates of war.[27] Even if we are not looking only for the failures where do we locate the successes?

But the implied critique here is too harsh. Political science has not produced stunning predictive theories, but there are numerous ways in which it has added systematically to our knowledge of politics, partly by improving our descriptive understanding of the political world, partly by debunking stereotypes and bad theories, and partly by revealing which types of political phenomena do, and do not, call for general explanations. It has often been said, for instance, that the absence of a socialist tradition in the United States derives from the lack of entrenched hierarchies against which to react as there were in Europe, so that the formal and social egalitarianism in America forestalled more radical egalitarian demands. This orthodoxy began with Tocqueville but became conventional wisdom when restated by Louis Hartz in 1955.[28] But as Rogers Smith showed decisively in *Civic Ideals*, it rests on a descriptive falsehood. Throughout American history there have been explicit hierarchies based on race, ethnicity, and gender, whose effects are still very much with us.[29] Correcting misperceptions of this sort is itself an advance in the study of politics.

Getting a better-informed grip on political reality has displaced other entrenched orthodoxies in the study of politics. To take another example, it is often said that there is an economic cost to democracy resulting from inefficient inroads into the economy articulated through the political system. This is attributed to various causes ranging from voters' demands for government programs unfriendly to economic growth, to inefficiencies resulting from the pork-barrel politics in democratic legislatures, to rent-seeking behavior by strategically placed public officials, to claims that the spending pressures on democratic governments are inherently inflationary. It is now clear from the work of Adam Przeworski and others, however, that democracies do not grow more slowly than nondemocracies, so that there is no economic cost of democracy to be explained.[30] Comparable findings attend long-accepted beliefs about the importance of bills of rights and constitutional courts to interpret them. Despite the beliefs of many constitutional lawyers and advisers to the architects of new democracies to the contrary, we will see in §7.2.2 that the best evidence currently suggests that these institutional devices have no effect, over and above the effects of democracy generally, in ensuring institutional protections for human rights.

Findings of this kind might never cumulate to an arresting grand theory of politics, but they do add appreciably to our stock of knowledge about politics. Indeed, even failures of political science can contribute in this way. For instance, generations of scholars have theorized about the conditions that give rise to democracy. Tocqueville alleged it to be the product of egalitarian mores.[31] For Seymour Martin Lipset it was a byproduct of modernization.[32] Barrington Moore identified the emergence of a bourgeoisie as critical, while Evelyne Huber, Dietrich Rueschemeyer, and John Stephens held the presence of an organized working class to be decisive.[33] It now seems clear that there is no single path to democracy and, therefore, no generalization to be had about which conditions give rise to democratic transitions. Democracy can result from decades of gradual evolution (Britain and the United States), imitation (India), cascades (much of Eastern Europe in 1989), collapses (Russia after 1991), imposition from above (Chile), revolutions (Portugal), negotiated settlements (Poland, Nicaragua, and South Africa), or external imposition (Japan and West Germany).[34] In retrospect this may not be surprising. Once someone invents a toaster, there is no particular reason to think others must go through the same invention processes. Perhaps some will, but some may copy it, some may buy it, some may receive it as a gift, and so on.

Discovering the limits of general explanatory theory can help refocus the explanatory enterprise more appropriately. Thus although we now know that there is unlikely to be a general theory of what gives rise to democracy, it continues to seem reasonable to try to generalize about the conditions under which democracy, once established, will survive. For instance, political scientists have long debated whether some democratic institutional arrangements are more stable than others. A generation ago Juan Linz made the case that parliamentary systems are more stable than presidential ones.[35] Presidential systems, he argued, tend toward polarization both in the political culture and between presidents and legislatures, which presidentialism lacks the institutional mechanisms to alleviate. By contrast, he said that parliamentary systems are more stable and better able to deal with leadership crises. Linz's view has since been challenged by Matthew Shugart and others, who differentiate among more and less stable presidentialisms, showing that weak or "reactive" presidential systems, such as that in the United States, can be as stable as parliamentary ones.[36] Subsequent scholarship suggests that other institutional features, such as a substantial presence of the presidential party in the assembly, favorable conditions for coalition politics, and centralized executive authority in the government, may matter more than whether the regime is presidential or parliamentary. In Latin America, for instance, these factors seem to account for the differences between the institutionally more stable countries like Chile and Uruguay and less stable ones such as Ecuador, Peru, and contemporary Venezuela.[37]

Comparable advances have been made in understanding the relationship between economic development and democratic stability. For instance, Przeworski and others have shown that although the level of economic development does not predict the installation of democracy, there is a strong relationship between level of per capita income and the survival of democratic regimes. Democracies appear never to die in wealthy countries, whereas poor democracies are fragile, exceedingly so when annual per capita incomes fall below $2,000 (1975 dollars). When annual per capita incomes fall below this threshold, democracies have a one in ten chance of collapsing within a year. Between annual per capita incomes of $2,001 and $5,000 this ratio falls to one in sixteen. Above $6,055 annual per capita income, democracies, once established, appear to last indefinitely. Moreover, poor democracies are more likely to survive when governments succeed in generating development and avoiding economic crises.[38]

These illustrations should suffice to establish the point that the failures and limitations of political science do not support the view that cumulative advance in knowledge about politics is impossible. The findings of political scientists, like those in any empirical science, are always provisional, corrigible, and likely to be modified by future research, and we remain a vast distance from the kinds of terminus that Bentham, Marx, and Dewey sought and Mill and Tocqueville feared. Indeed, it is doubtful that we will ever reach such a point. For one thing, new questions continually arise in politics as a result of changing circumstances. In our own time globalization, worldwide population growth, nuclear proliferation, and global warming are obvious examples, but life has more imagination than most of us, and the twenty-first century will likely present human beings with political problems that cannot now be anticipated.

For another, there will always be those in politics who stand to gain from obscuring the truth and sustaining ideologies that are incompatible with the commitment to science—if not openly hostile to it. Weber was thus right to insist that a primary task for scholars of politics is to teach students "to recognize 'inconvenient' facts—I mean facts that are inconvenient for their party opinions." And for every party opinion, he noted, "there are facts that are extremely inconvenient."[39] The commitment to science involves resistance to arguments from authority or expediency, and a concomitant willingness to submit all claims to critical evaluation in light of the best available evidence. It often involves conceding that we do not know the right answer, even as we expose spurious claims by those who claim that they do. Giving up on the scientific attitude means giving up on this.

Commentators like Rorty, Lyotard, and William Connolly seem to think that adopting a post-Enlightenment stance leads naturally to a commitment to the left-leaning social-democratic politics they find congenial. But no reason has ever been supplied why this should be the case. Thus, although Lyotard reassures us that abandoning the Enlightenment "narrative" need not mean that we are "reduced to barbarity," he never explains why we should be confident that it will not.[40] Perhaps adopting the post-Enlightenment stance will lead people to a benign toleration of difference, but it might just as easily lead them to embrace fascism.[41] "If nothing is true, then everything is permitted" was Nietzsche's secular rendition of Ivan Karamazov's worry.[42] If we abandon the idea that anything can be said to be true, it is difficult to see how criteria can be developed for judging one type of political practice or regime superior to another. To say this is not to establish which political arrangements are most compatible with the mature Enlightenment outlook. Nor is it to say anything about how advances in knowledge are most likely to be pressed into the service of human improvement. Those subjects are taken up in chapter 7. It is to say, however, that without a commitment to some version of the possibility of genuine knowledge about politics, there is no chance of developing satisfying criteria for assessing political legitimacy.

6.5 Subordinating Rights to Communities

Resistance to the Enlightenment commitment to science often goes hand-in-hand with antipathy for its foundational political focus on individual rights. This, too, is rooted in a neo-Burkean outlook. Burke was appalled by the notion that rights might be seen as the normative building blocks of politics. It is sometimes said that he saw obligations as prior to rights.[43] He did, and in this he embraced a version of the timeless universal view of natural law that Locke rejected in favor of his voluntarist theology. But, more pertinent for our purposes here, he saw both rights and obligations as rooted in the inherited traditions that give life to political communities. This view of the primacy of collective traditions over individual rights and obligations is characteristic of the world view often called "communitarian," though the label sits uncomfortably with some to whom it is regularly applied.

These include theorists as different from one another as MacIntyre, Michael Sandel, Charles Taylor, Michael Walzer, and Will Kymlicka. In one way or another, they all recognize that inherited systems of affiliation are important, if not exclusive, sources of what people experience as morally legitimate.[44] These theorists differ over whether they regard systems of national membership, religious or ethnic identification, or other forms of inherited affiliation as most significant. They also differ over whether the imperatives embedded in systems of group affiliation should always trump other political considerations or whether they should sometimes be required to defer to other imperatives, and, if so, by whom and in accordance with what principles. Despite these differences, they share a common commitment to the idea that the communities into which people are born are wellsprings of the political claims that they recognize, and, in some formulations, even of their identities as individuals. Collective norms and practices constitute individuals as the beings that they are; they are, in Taylor's phrase, the "sources of the self." By this he means to convey not merely that collective norms and practices are historically prior to any given individual; they also supply her life with meaning and value.

The communitarian outlook differs from the various Enlightenment views considered thus far in two ways. The first, implicit
in what has just been said, is that it involves a proclivity for what
might be called collectivist teleology. Teleological views, it will be
recalled from §5.3, are those in which the good is defined independently of the right, which is then defined so as to maximize
the good. Not all teleological views are communitarian, however,
or necessarily at odds with the goals of the Enlightenment. From
Plato (c. 427 B.C.–c. 347 B.C.), to Bentham, to Leo Strauss (1899–
1973), there have always been teleological thinkers who believed
that the good for individuals can be discerned in natural law,
human nature, or rational reflection. The communitarian outlook is distinctive, and distinctively at odds with the Enlightenment, in that its proponents see the good as collectively given,
embedded in the evolving traditions and practices of political
communities. Locke had regarded legitimate human groups as
voluntary associations, reflecting his will-centered view of the
human condition. For writers with communitarian inclinations,
by contrast, the implication of choice implied by the idea of a
voluntary association belies reality. For them, one can no more
choose one's sense of obligation to a group, or the lack of it, than
one can choose one's personality. Even a "liberal culturalist" like
Kymlicka, who agrees that freedom involves choices among options, thinks it important to stress that "our societal culture not
only provides these options, but makes them meaningful to us."[45]

This leads to the other characteristic anti-Enlightenment feature of the communitarian outlook: its emphasis on the psychological, not to say emotional, dimensions of identification and
commitment, as distinct from what their bases in reason may or
may not be alleged to be. The intuition here is that it is pointless
to theorize about rights and obligations without taking account of
how people actually experience them. Perhaps the most explicit

articulation of this view is in Michael Walzer's discussion of political criticism by different "left" intellectuals during the Algerian war (1954–1962). Walzer is unsympathetic to Jean-Paul Sartre's conception of the intellectual as a "permanent critic" who cuts all parochial ties and affiliations. Sartre, Simone de Beauvoir, and Albert Camus all agreed that members of the *pied noir* community in Algeria were "historically in the wrong" and criticized them for it, but Walzer is far more impressed by Camus than by the other two. Camus refused to detach himself from the French and dehumanize them in the way that they did. "I believe in justice, but I will defend my mother before justice," Camus wrote, a proposition Walzer adapts and incorporates by rejecting as unacceptable any conception of justice that has no room for love. He notes with approval that "Camus had no use for philosophers who loved humanity and disdained the men and women among whom they lived." Along with him, Walzer rejects the idea, characteristic of cosmopolitan thinkers, of philosophical detachment. "Even 'true intellectuals' have parents, friends, familiar places, warm memories," he says. "Perfect solitude, like existential heroism, is a romantic idea."[46]

Part of Walzer's point is that criticism is more likely to move hearts and minds if it affirms the value of those at whom it is directed. But, more than this, his comments reveal a Hegelian view of human psychology characteristic of communitarian writers. This view appeals to the idea that recognition by valued others is essential to human well-being and motivation. Thus Hegel argued that slavery is an unstable system of social organization not merely because the slave will resist it, but also because the master seeks recognition from someone he can regard as an equal, whereas the recognition that arises between master and slave is "one-sided and unequal."[47]

This view differs from both the utilitarian view, according to which people maximize their preferences with a contingent, if any, interest, in the preferences of others, and the other-referential view characteristic of Marxists and others discussed in §4.2.2. On that account there is necessary reference to what others have—but only for the purposes of determining one's relative distributive position. On what I am calling the Hegelian account, by contrast, people are seen as wanting to be valued by others who matter to them. This makes their commitments to shared ideals intrinsic to their senses of themselves, and to the political arguments that will move them.

When we say that, on the communitarian view, rights and obligations are subordinate to collectively given conceptions of the good, we are thus saying that they are subordinate to quite a lot. People are seen as born into ongoing systems of collective norms and practices from which they derive meaning and value. Part of this meaning and value emanates from the knowledge that these norms and practices are also accepted by others who they care about and who they want and expect to care about them. The ties that bind are the individual's identification with the collective, buttressed by her need for recognition from pertinent others within it. Whereas the various liberal and Marxian views we have examined are all individualist in that the freedom or, in the case of utilitarianism, the happiness of each individual forms the moral foundation of the system, communitarian views are holist in that our goals and standards are artifacts of the collectively given conceptions of the good that define us as individuals and set our expectations about what we can do to and expect from others. This is why writers like Walzer treat membership as the primary or most basic political good.[48] We might say that "I belong, therefore I am" is the communitarian alternative to the Cartesian *cogito*.

The communitarian outlook is as hostile to the clean slate metaphor embedded in contractarian arguments as Burke was to the French Revolution. Even the hypothetical social contract arguments discussed in chapter 5 are seen as misleading from this perspective because of their deontological character. The suggestion that one can usefully speculate about what rights people should enjoy while kept in ignorance of their (collectively given) conceptions of the good seems to its adherents to be unthinkable. This is why critics of Rawls, like Sandel, complain that he operates with a deracinated conception of the individual, a self absurdly stripped of its affiliations:

> The vaunted independence of the deontological subject is a liberal illusion. It misunderstands the fundamentally "social" nature of man, the fact that we are conditioned beings "all the way down." There is no point of exemption, no transcendental subject capable of standing outside society or outside experience. We are at every moment what we have become, a concatenation of desires and inclinations with nothing left over to inhabit a noumenal realm.[49]

For Sandel, deontological liberalism's commitment to the priority of right makes it tone-deaf to the human condition, submerging us "in a circumstance that ceases to be ours."[50] As he elaborates in *Democracy's Discontent*, the flawed idea of an unencumbered self "cannot make sense of our moral experience, because it cannot account for certain moral and political obligations that we commonly recognize, even prize." Instead, we should "think of ourselves as encumbered selves, already claimed by certain projects and commitments."[51] The unencumbered self is objectionable, then, primarily because it factors out of consideration about political right the features of social life that give rights their meaning and purpose.[52] In a like spirit to Walzer's appeal to a politics that takes account of emotional attachments, Sandel assumes that it should be thought of on something much more like a familial model. It should involve extending the intimacies of our cultural attachments into an explicit theory of the political good, from which political rights should then be derived. This would be far superior to politics among "strangers," presupposed in the deontological vision.[53]

6.6 Difficulties With What Is Collectively Given

Plausible as many of the communitarian assertions about the human condition might be, there are serious difficulties that attend to embracing a politics in which claims of political right are subordinated to the demands and expectations of membership. I have already mentioned the issue of disagreement in connection with Rorty, but it applies more generally to writers in this camp.[54] In most, if not all, communities, there is considerable disagreement about how the collectively given norms and practices that have been inherited should be interpreted and what they require in practice. One only has to think of the political variation within MacIntyre's own Catholic tradition to recognize that there is scarcely a political issue that has not at some time been controversial within it. Certainly the question of which types of political arrangements are best, and why, admits no definitive Catholic answer. Individual Catholics, as well as members of the church hierarchy up to and including popes, locate themselves at various points on the ideological spectrum, notwithstanding their faith in the traditions of the church.[55]

Or consider Sandel's quasi-familial model. His claim is that by basing politics on particularistic attachments we can get away from the focus on rights and justice that is appropriate to the deontological world of strangers. Yet it is simply untrue that the idea of justice does not operate in such entities. The child who knows herself to be loved or valued less than her siblings, or the abused wife, will certainly believe that injustice has been done and that pertinent rights have been violated. Surely the same can be said of every particularistic community on which a communitarian might wish to model politics. They all have their conflicts, intrigues, and simmering disputes, their abusers and their abused, their well-adjusted and disaffected members, their winners and losers.

Moreover, different people stand to benefit, or to be harmed, by competing interpretations of inherited traditions and accepted practices. This makes manifest the need for procedures to determine which competing claims should prevail and how disagreements should be settled, issues about which communitarian writers are disconcertingly quiet. In the Catholic Church, these issues are dealt with in an authoritarian way that few communitarians would likely propose as a model for politics in the modern world. In the family, they are often dealt with in authoritarian ways too, or informally. It would be naïve to suppose that, when they are dealt with informally, disagreements are always satisfactorily resolved and some are not harmed by the ways in which they are managed. This is not to deny that there may well be good reasons to require pretty high thresholds of abuse to be crossed before we are willing to pay the costs of third-party interference in institutions such as families and churches.[56] But it must raise serious questions about the extent to which they can provide a model for governance in the larger polity.

In short, appealing to affective communities such as churches or families as a means of wishing away disagreement and conflict of interest seems a less than a promising strategy for developing models of legitimate political arrangements. Indeed, to the degree that we are persuaded, as we should be, that most forms of human interaction are not like Lockean voluntary associations—formed at will and dissolved when they no longer suit—we should be *more* concerned about appropriate mechanisms for the management of disagreement and conflict of interest. As the economist Albert Hirschman argued, when the costs of exit from a form of collective association go up for people, so does the importance of ensuring that there are mechanisms for them to influence it through participation or "voice."[57] In short, communitarians do not respond convincingly to the fact of pluralism that supplied much of the impetus for Rawls's deontological approach. Antipathy for his proffered solution scarcely obviates the need to deal with the reality he identified—that people who must live together in political associations have profound conflicts of interest and disagreements of value.[58]

Notice that even if there were widespread acceptance of a collectively given conception of the good, it might reasonably be judged wanting on the grounds that one person's consensus is another's hegemony. We can see this by noting that if, *per impossible,* politics could be based on family-life writ large, it is far from clear that this would lead us closer to a world that many of us would see as legitimate. Consider the changing position of women in most Western countries over the past century and a half. Until the passage of the Married Women's Property Acts in the second half of the nineteenth century, women lost title to their assets to their husbands—part of the suspension of their legal identities during marriage that was rooted in the common law presumption that made the wife the husband's chattel. Women could not vote in most universal franchise democracies until well into the twentieth century, and they suffered various related indignities of status and well-being. As recently as the 1950s it remained widely accepted in the United States that a wife could not deny her husband consortium. This was reflected in a conclusive legal presumption against the possibility of marital rape, as well as various shields from such criminal offenses as assault and battery when committed by husbands on wives—not to mention intra-spousal tort immunity that prevented even civil action in response to domestic violence.[59]

Today much of the subordination of women has been mitigated by concerted political and legal action on the part of feminist movements. Assets are no longer given up upon marriage. Women have the same voting rights as men, and politicians must pay lip-service, at least, to women's equality. Barriers to female participation in economic, social, and political life face tough scrutiny in the courts. The presumption against marital rape has largely been abandoned. It is now a felony in most U.S. jurisdictions, and other forms of domestic violence are prosecutable and, increasingly, prosecuted. Intra-spousal tort immunity has all but disappeared, and women have made significant economic advances. They continue to face numerous social and economic disadvantages, not to mention domestic violence, but in relative terms things have improved dramatically.[60]

None of these changes would have occurred had "traditional family life" been accepted as a kind of post-political political ideal. Indeed, if the case for drawing on the family as a model for political life had been seriously acted on in the nineteenth century, this would presumably have meant a return to the kind of patriarchalism in public life that Locke had attacked in the *First Treatise* two centuries earlier. It was the opposite move, of bringing principles of non-domination and rights to equal treatment that had by then become entrenched in the public realm to bear in areas that had previously been shielded from them, that was necessary to achieve the advances. In short, the suggestion that it would be desirable to transcend the realm or rights by modeling politics on traditional family life would be unattractive even if it was feasible.

The example underscores the reality that power relations are ubiquitous to human interaction. Just as we saw in §4.2.3 that Marx's impulse to get beyond politics by transcending scarcity in an ideal future was chimerical, so we see here that there is no good reason to suppose that there is an ideal private realm beyond conflict any more than there is one in the traditions of some distant past. To be sure, this raises serious questions about the limits of political involvement in every walk of social life. There are more and less plausible ways of tackling those questions, but it is surely one of the least plausible approaches to argue that politics should be modeled on an idealized conception of private association on the grounds that it gets us beyond the realm of right appropriate to "strangers."[61]

What of another characteristic feature of the communitarian outlook: elevating the psychological and emotional dimensions of belonging either above or into the idea of political right? Certainly one can understand Walzer's empathy for Camus's unwillingness to sacrifice his mother to the demands of justice. But what really follows from this? One can read in the newspaper every day of situations where a parent, spouse, or sibling feels she must stand by a family member who has committed an unspeakable crime. It is not difficult to understand why they feel this way, yet it scarcely means that there is something wrong with the criminal justice system. Wrenching though these situations often are, there is no contradiction in recognizing that affection for one's family members might exert a more powerful pull on someone than supporting what justice requires—or even in thinking there must be something wrong with someone for whom this was not so. Indeed, the legal system concedes as much through such devices as the bar on compelling testimony against a spouse. We love people who do wrong without disputing that they have done wrong. We may stand by them when they fail to measure up, yet not deny that people generally should be expected to measure up and that they should pay the price when they do not. We are unwilling to turn the justice system over to the anger and outrage of the victim's family members, sacrificing justice to vengeance, but we do not blame them for wanting revenge and might even think something was wrong with them if they did not. By the same token, we should be unwilling to see the demands of justice melt before the love of kith and kin—though we understand and value that love.

There is a less personalized version of the psychological-cum-emotional claim than Walzer's, to wit the suggestion often associated with the arguments of Taylor, Kymlicka, and others that

political arrangements should incorporate the affective commitments people feel to their communities. People want to feel that it
is legitimate for them to belong, and they want the entities to
which they belong to exemplify and reproduce the sources of their
attachments. This is why writers in this tradition are strongly
sympathetic to the claims of multiculturalism. From their perspective there is nothing sacrosanct about the nation-state. If some
sub-national ethnic group, religious or linguistic community, or
other collective source of meaning and value exerts a powerful pull
on some collection of people, then there is at least a *prima facie*
claim that the political system should accommodate their collective aspirations, perhaps even to the point of permitting secession.
The same would be true of a transnational ethnic group, such as
the Kurds who live partly in Iraq, partly in Turkey, and partly in
Iran. Many among them identify more strongly with one another
than with the nations of which they are citizens. Why suppress
aspirations to refashion political communities that reflect and
embody the communities of meaning that are most important to
people?

Put this way, the rhetorical question sounds reasonable enough,
but the formulation obscures the darker side of community. The
corollary of inclusion is exclusion, and often the desire to associate
with those one cares about is part and parcel of the desire to
disassociate from others. This can make eminent sense in personal life, but in politics it often goes hand-in-glove with depriving
people of resources, creating second-class citizens, or worse. Political sociologist Benedict Anderson suggests that this need not be
so. He distinguishes patriotism from nationalism on the grounds
that patriotism does not feed on the xenophobic hatred of others
that so often sustains nationalism. We can be patriots in identifying with our country and thinking it best without being troubled
by the thought that others can feel the same way with respect to
their countries.[62]

Attending to this difference between patriotism and national-ism underscores the difficulties associated with thinking of politi-cal communities on familial or other affective models. One can value one's children more highly than anyone else's children, finding it perfectly natural that other parents will feel the same way about their children. The groups that make up political en-tities differ from families, however, in that their members must be mobilized to identify with the group, and then kept together in the face of competing forms of potential mobilization. French Canadians, Zulu South Africans, and Spanish Basques are invari-ably pulled by secessionist leaders in the direction of their ethnic affiliations, while national leaders try to get them to identify with the larger political entity. In struggles of this kind, political entre-preneurs know that dehumanizing outsiders is one of the best ways to mobilize and sustain group solidarity. V. O. Key's *Southern Politics* is a classic discussion of how anti-black racism was ef-fectively deployed in political coalition-building in the American south.[63] More recent scholarship has illuminated the deployment of out-group dehumanization in building South African apart-heid and maintaining the conflict-ridden status quo over genera-tions in Northern Ireland.[64] This phenomenon may not be as old as the hills, but it is at least as old as the Ancient Greeks who famously described non-Greeks as barbarians.

Philosophers who argue that political arrangements should mirror group aspirations too often ignore or underplay the reality that groups do not just "have" political aspirations. These aspira-tions are at least partly mobilized from above by political entre-preneurs who stand to benefit from either maintaining existing systems of group solidarities, or from dismantling them and re-placing them with different ones. The temptation to pursue this by fomenting out-group hatred will often be irresistible to lead-ers and would-be leaders, just because political associations are not families. They consist of multiple overlapping coalitions and

potential coalitions whose members' interests are partly comple-
mentary and partly competing.

It is, indeed, ironic that defenders of the idea that political
institutions should embody strongly felt cultural attachments are
generally sympathetic to the social construction of reality thesis
discussed in §6.4, yet they pay so little attention to the ways in
which systems of cultural attachment are created, maintained,
and destroyed in actual politics.[65] Attending to this more would
lead them to be a good deal warier than they are of the idea that
ethnic, cultural, and religious attachments should be politicized.
The reasoning behind disestablishing the church after the religious wars of the seventeenth and eighteenth centuries was,
after all, not that religious affiliations are unimportant to people
but rather that they are intensely important to them, yet potentially conflicting in zero-sum ways. Those who find themselves
well disposed to the idea that politics should incorporate powerfully felt group aspirations should reflect on how destructive this
idea is in the contemporary Middle East, where almost everyone
feels compelled to recognize the political aspirations of both Jews
and Palestinians for their own national states. The conflict there
would be a lot more tractable if there were the possibility of a
single secular state throughout the region in which no government could support or interfere with any religious practice. But
when, as here, political aspirations for religious and ethnic conceptions of nationhood are not seriously questioned, it would
mean political suicide for any political leader to advocate this
possibility. The politicized religious ethnicities in the Middle East
may be beyond being depoliticized, at least for the moment. But
the example should give pause to those who think that intense
forms of group identity should be afforded political recognition
elsewhere on the grounds that they are important to people.

This is to say nothing of the possibility of internal domination.
As my earlier discussion of the history of patriarchy suggests, the

ties that bind can be more or less benign. Claims of the form "the American people believe" or "the Jewish people must stand together" may be attempts to mobilize group support vis-à-vis an out group, but they can also operate to suppress internal dissent and opposition. Less directly threatening, perhaps, than hauling someone before an un-American Activities Committee or calling them a self-hating Jew, they may be just as insidious. When political entrepreneurs claim to be articulating the values and aspirations of a group, we should always ask who within the group stands to be harmed by their demands. In debates about the distribution of authority in the post-1994 South African constitution, for example, traditional tribal leaders argued for strong regional autonomy, including the retention of marital law within their jurisdictional ambit. Among other things this means the retention of polygamy and related matrimonial and economic practices that subordinate women in the tribal order at least as much as pre-twentieth-century patriarchalism subordinated European and American women.[66] In practice, "respecting traditional communal practice" may amount to validating a system of internal oppression that would be difficult to justify on any grounds other than blunt appeal to existing practice.[67]

Given the evident possibilities of internal and external oppression, writers sympathetic to the communitarian outlook cannot push their deference to conventional practices to the limit without losing plausibility. For instance, in *Spheres of Justice*, Michael Walzer appeals to what he says are the accepted meanings within our culture to come up with appropriate principles for the distribution of different social goods in different spheres of social life. He then invokes to a meta-principle of nondomination to make the case that it is not legitimate for a good that is appropriate to one sphere to be deployed in another. When we describe the act of accepting money for political favors as bribery, we reveal that we have come to value the "art of separation" that renders behavior of this kind illegitimate.[68] Walzer claims that this idea of non-domination as maintaining the distinctions between spheres is widely accepted within our culture, a claim that becomes a substitute for his arguing for the principle's desirability. But the more seriously we take that claim, the less attractive his theory of justice becomes. If this idea was an historically contingent artifact of liberalism in the modern West as he claims, does that mean one cannot argue that the domination that occurred under feudalism was illegitimate—to say nothing of the domination that occurs in illiberal societies today?

Walzer responds to such objections by claiming that every culture contains ideological resources for criticism of prevailing practices within it.[69] This may be so, but the available ideological resources can be drawn on by the Adolf Hitlers and Timothy McVeighs of this world as well as by the likes of Albert Camus. By itself, the appeal to the possibility of social criticism does not get us very far. To be persuasive, it needs to be supplemented by an argument that it should be deployed to diminish domination rather than achieve some other goal for which there are also ideological resources in the culture—be it creating an Aryan master race or overthrowing the corrupt usurpers in Washington.

Moreover, even in the contemporary United States some forms of domination involve violating the integrity of Walzer's spheres, but some do not. My earlier discussion of the exploitation and physical abuse of women in patriarchal marriage revealed that the problem may be the widely accepted norm, not its contravention. If Walzer is unwilling to make the case that such practices are objectionable, his theory becomes available to buttress an unjust status quo rather than to undermine it. When women demand compensation for domestic work, or that the criminal law should outlaw marital rape, the conservative Walzerian will respond that they are seeking to violate the integrity of the sphere of family life by applying principles that belong in the workplace and the criminal law. In short, unless an independent argument is supplied for why domination is a bad thing, Walzer's appeals to culture as a source for standards of political legitimacy will quickly wear thin.

Kymlicka's liberal culturalism also illustrates the difficulty of developing a view that plausibly devolves critical standards of political legitimacy to locally accepted values. He insists, in what could be a cosmopolitan spirit, that multicultural accommodation should be conditioned on a principle of respecting autonomy. This requires "*freedom within* the minority group, and *equality between* the minority and majority groups."[70] As Kymlicka is aware, depending on how these requirements for respecting autonomy are unpacked, winning a policy of multicultural accommodation based on his ground rules may well be judged a Pyrrhic victory by the leaders of most groups that seek multicultural accommodation in the actual world. Applying Kymlicka's criteria for autonomy within and among groups would surely raise at least as many difficulties as we confronted with the interpretation of Mill's harm principle in §3.3. Who is to determine, by what criteria, whether autonomy is under sufficient threat to warrant interference, or what form that interference should take? Kymlicka thinks our willingness to defer to the demands for recognition emanating from minority cultures should be substantial, but he supplies no criteria for determining whether the limits of acceptable toleration have been breached.

Kymlicka does propose that consistency requires liberals to afford illiberal subnational groups the same hands-off policy they conventionally apply to illiberal foreign countries on the grounds that both "form distinct political communities, with their own claims to self-government." So he argues that we should take a hands-off approach to cultural minorities unless their violations of human rights are "gross and systematic," of the sort, that is, that would legitimate foreign intervention.[71] This, however, is doubly problematic. Reluctance to interfere abroad may spring from principled or pragmatic considerations. If the latter, the claim is usually some form of the assertion that international policing would fail, or that at any rate it is too costly. Judgments of this kind must be made case-by-case, but, even if they are often valid, there is no reason to expect that the logic of transnational policing applies to subnational policing. Except in cases of civil war or exceedingly weak states like contemporary Russia and Colombia, governments generally do enjoy effective domestic monopolies of coercive force. In any case, Kymlicka's formulation suggests that the reason for his view is principled, based on the obligation to recognize claims of self-government, not merely pragmatic.

Now liberals do indeed typically apply less demanding principles to practices in foreign nations than they do to their own, but they are not famous for articulating good reasons for this. Certainly Kymlicka does not purport to supply any. One could imagine defending the attitude on the grounds Rawls takes over from Kant, that a single worldwide standard would require a world government to enforce it, and that this, in turn, would lead to worse forms of tyranny than those that would be eradicated.[72] Whether this is true is difficult to know. Granting, for the sake of argument, that world government would bring with it serious attendant evils, there are many measures that can be imposed on recalcitrant governments within the existing international regime, from tariffs, to sanctions, to trade embargoes. In any event, there is nothing in this argument to support the notion that national governments should abdicate their domestic political responsibilities. As Sarah Song points out, Kymlicka's analogy "between appropriate liberal attitudes toward illiberal nation-states and appropriate attitudes toward national minorities fails for a very obvious reason, namely that a liberal state does not have the same responsibility to protect the rights of non-nationals that it has to protect its own citizens."[73]

Song's critique takes the legitimacy of the nation-state for granted, yet it is an open secret that political theorists have yet to come up with a compelling justification for it. Certainly none of the theorists considered thus far in this book supplies a convincing justification for the current division of the world into nation-states sharing in common the right to have their sovereignty recognized by others and to exclude whomever they wish, but containing huge variations in population, resources, freedoms, opportunities, and income and wealth. Classical utilitarians would tell us that the world should be divided up, if at all, so as to maximize happiness, neoclassical utilitarians to maximize Pareto-efficiency. Marxism is thoroughly cosmopolitan in spirit and generates no justification for nation-states, even if Marx— among many others—was wrong in supposing that the increasingly global character of capitalism would lead to the disappearance of the nation-state.[74] Indeed, the very idea that there could be socialism in one country is antithetical to Marx's analysis of capitalism. It was dreamed up by Lenin and his successors as a rationalization for the Russian revolution.

The social contract tradition scarcely does better. As noted in §5.1, Locke's theory of tacit consent is unpersuasive given the immense costs of entry into and exit from countries for most people. National boundaries are of no moral significance on Nozick's neo-Lockean account. Nation-states exist because they acquire monopoly control of coercive force in a given area, which is another way of saying that they are byproducts of prevailing technologies of violence. With respect to Rawls, if ever a feature of social life met his criterion for being morally arbitrary it is surely the distribution of citizenship and the benefits and burdens associated with one's geographical location on the world's surface. Unsurprisingly, therefore, Rawls has drawn heavy critical fire for his undefended assumption in A Theory of Justice that his principles apply only to closed national states. Numerous commentators have argued that, taken seriously, his argument entails that principles of justice should be applied worldwide.[75]

What of the Burkean and neo-Burkean outlooks that inform communitarian thinking? Here, too, we find ourselves bereft of convincing arguments. A strict Burkean would hold that we should oppose existing nation-states only if they threaten inherited liberties and obligations (as Burke thought the British did in the American colonies), or if such opposition is needed to prevent the inherited system from deteriorating. The idea of replacing it with something better would have been anathema to him. But the difficulty here is that the division of the world into nation-states reinforces the inherited system of liberties and obligations that amounts to little more than apartheid on a world scale. The privileged minorities in the rich countries shield themselves behind the accepted principles of citizenship, national sovereignty, and the self-determination of peoples just as surely as South Africa's National Party government used the idea of "separate development" to rationalize its stance during the heyday of apartheid.

The international manifestation of the phenomenon is more resilient, however, partly because there is no significant outside force to create pressure for change but also because the ideas of sovereignty and the self-determination of peoples have so much legitimacy as inherited norms in the international order. Critics of multiculturalism and group rights within countries point out that appeals to them can divert attention from distributive injustice.[76] The same is true in the international arena, where successful demands for national recognition that work to the advantage of local elites divert attention from distributive injustice and limit the available means for addressing it. By recognizing the sovereignty of poor countries and their rights to self-determination, governments of wealthy countries also divest themselves of responsibility for distributive injustice within those sovereign poor countries. Redistribution from wealthy to poor countries then falls within the charitable category of "aid" rather than what justice requires, limiting what people are obliged to recognize as legitimate demands. In short, appealing to historically accepted norms is not going to get us very far in coming up with a satisfying argument for the legitimacy of the nation-state system.

Nor is it going to supply us with norms for political legitimacy within countries that obviate the imperative to concern ourselves with people's rights. Adherents to the Burkean outlook who reject individual rights must either embrace palpably implausible accounts of the moral claims of collectivities or find proxies for individual rights, such as Walzer's non-domination or Kymlicka's autonomy, to render their accounts plausible. Doing this involves recognizing, albeit implicitly, that it is no easier to jettison the characteristic Enlightenment commitment to individual rights than it is to jettison the commitment to science.

CHAPTER 7 | Democracy

Some will be surprised that our discussion has proceeded to this point without engaging democracy as a normative ideal. Given the prevalence of democracy in the contemporary world, any inquiry into the moral foundations of politics must surely attend to democracy's role in legitimating political regimes. That governments of all ideological stripes in every region of the world try to shroud themselves in the mantle of democracy is further evidence, were it needed, that a commitment to democracy is a necessary component of political legitimacy. Aspiring political leaders can be liberals or conservatives, meritocrats or egalitarians, nationalists or cosmopolitans, multiculturalists or uniculturalists. It is considerably more difficult, and rare, for them openly to oppose democracy than to adopt any of these outlooks. They can attack democracy's corruption or perversion, or argue that a particular system of democratic representation is unfair. They can argue about what democracy means and what institutions it requires. They may even try to argue that their country is not ready for democracy "yet"—conceding democracy's legitimacy even as they evade it.

Endorsement of the democratic idea, then, is close to nonnegotiable in the contemporary world. International institutions often try to condition aid to developing countries on their embrace of regular elections and other democratic reform. Liberation movements insist that they are more democratic than the regimes they seek to replace. Constitutional systems sometimes limit democracy's range, to be sure, particularly in separation-of-powers systems such as the United States. But constitutions generally contain entrenched guarantees of democratic government as well. Moreover, they are themselves revisable at constitutional conventions or via amendment procedures whose legitimacy is popularly authorized. Even liberal constitutionalists such as Bruce Ackerman agree that critical moments of constitutional founding and change require popular democratic validation if they are to be seen as legitimate over time.[1]

That the utilitarian, Marxian, and contractarian traditions attend so little to democratic considerations is testimony, I think, to the captivating allure of the Enlightenment enterprise in politics. There are many variants of democratic theory, but we will see that there are important respects in which they all involve giving up on the more ambitious versions of the Enlightenment enterprise—both with respect to replacing political choices with technical ones, and to treating individual rights as prior to, and in need of protection from, politics. Anti-Enlightenment outlooks also pay surprisingly little heed to democracy, though for the different reason that it can threaten the inherited norms and constitutive practices that are integral to the Burkean outlook. These various reasons for academic skepticism of democracy have been buttressed by scholarship purporting to show that democracy fails on its own terms as a device for measuring and representing the will of the citizenry.

There is thus a tension between democracy's non-negotiable political status and a widespread skepticism of it among political theorists. John Dunn captured this well in 1979 by observing that although most people think of themselves as democrats, democratic theory oscillates between two variants, "one dismally ideological and the other fairly blatantly utopian."[2] The oscillation he had in mind was between cold war rhetoric and arguments for participatory democracy that lacked convincing attention to how they might be deployed in the actual world. In the years since Dunn wrote there has been a revival of interest in democratic theory, as we will see, but democracy continues to be widely regarded as a limited procedural device that does not guarantee correct answers, protect individual rights, or respect cultures and traditions. My own view is that these fears are misguided. Appropriately construed and institutionalized, democracy offers the best hope that the truth will prevail in the political arena over time, that human rights will be respected, and that those elements of traditions and constitutive cultures meriting preservation will be preserved. That is, democracy is more likely than the going alternatives to deliver on a suitably chastened Enlightenment project while speaking to the fears of those who identify with the undertow of the anti-Enlightenment. Instead of resisting the popular view that political legitimacy inheres in democracy, it therefore makes better sense to adapt our thinking to incorporate it. Or so I will argue. Before getting to this we need to attend to the democratic tradition itself.

7.1 Democracy and the Truth

The democratic tradition is older than the others I have discussed here in that its roots go back to the ancient Greek city-states, most famously Athens. By contemporary standards Athenian democracy was at best radically incomplete. Women were not recognized as citizens and the economy was based on slavery. Any impulse to romanticize ancient democracy should therefore be resisted. Moreover, the small size of the Ancient polis suggests obvious limitations on its viability as a model for thinking about democracy in the modern world. Given these caveats, Athenian democracy was recognizably democratic by comparison with the prevalent alternatives in the ancient world, which were either monarchies or oligarchies of various sorts.[3] It also contained enduring elements of subsequent democratic ideologies. Most importantly, from the beginning, commitment to democracy involved rejecting the idea that political power should be the hereditary preserve of kings, a select few, or committed to the trust of experts. Its cardinal principle has always been that, in matters affecting their collective life and interests, the people appropriately rule themselves.

7.1.1 Plato's Critique

This commitment to the sovereignty of the people has obvious potential for collision with any idea that good regimes should be based on true principles, or even committed to the search for the truth. The people might want to know the truth, but there is no guarantee of this. They might just as easily be superstitious, bigoted, shortsighted, and perhaps even openly hostile to the truth. Even Mill, who was progressively egalitarian for his day, feared these possibilities; this was one of the reasons he favored a second vote for university graduates.[4] Yet just as democratic theory is much older than the Enlightenment, so, too is the worry that it is hostile to the truth. Indeed the theory of democracy and this critique were both developed in ancient Greece. One of the earliest discussions of both that we have is to be found in Plato's *Republic*. Plato wrote out of the bitter knowledge that the truth can be fatally dangerous to its proponent. His friend and teacher, Socrates, had been executed in 399 B.C. This reinforced Plato's contempt for the corrupt Athenian polity, and his conviction that the kind of knowledge needed to cure the world's evils could never be realized in a democracy. It could be realized only in a world governed by reluctant philosopher kings who would prefer the pursuit of truth to the exercise of power. Even if such a society could be created Plato believed that it would be unstable—decaying eventually into a corrupt regime.[5]

Plato's most dramatic discussion of the tensions between

democracy and the truth appears in book six of *The Republic.* He pursues it by analogy to a somewhat deaf, shortsighted, and inept ship's captain who we might think of as representing bureaucratic wielders of the instruments of public power: people of limited horizon, heavily subject to inertia, with a limited capacity to respond well to changing conditions. The crew, representing the common people, quarrel over how to navigate the ship, each thinking he ought to be in charge even though none has learned anything about navigation. Indeed, and this is the core of Plato's concern about democracy given the death of Socrates, they threaten to kill anyone who even suggests that there is any such thing as an art of navigation, let alone that it can be taught. Because they have no idea that a true navigator "must study the seasons of the year, the sky, the stars, the winds, and all the other subjects appropriate to his profession if he is to be really fit to control a ship," they would regard someone who does have these skills as "a word-spinner and a star-gazer" who is of no use to them.[6]

The purpose of the ship's captain analogy is to drive home Plato's view that under democratic conditions the truth about politics will generally not be sought after, and not spoken when it is known. The common people will more likely be impressed by the Sophists, who "in fact teach nothing but the conventional views held and expressed by the mass of the people." Although they call this science, Plato thinks of it as the ancient equivalent of opinion research and spin-doctoring:

> Suppose a man was in charge of a large and powerful animal, and made a study of its moods and wants; he would learn when to approach and handle it, when and why it was especially savage or gentle, what the different noises it made meant, and what tone of voice to use to soothe or annoy it. All this he might learn by long experience and familiarity, and then call it a science, and reduce it to a system and set up to teach it. But he would not really know

which of the creature's tastes and desires was admirable or shameful, good or bad, right or wrong; he would simply use the terms on the basis of its reactions, calling what pleased it good, what annoyed it bad.[7]

In the short run the masses find democracy pleasant just because rulers cater to their whims by learning the "science" of the Sophists. Over time, however, democracy breeds undisciplined and self-indulgent people whose excessive desire for liberty makes them manipulable by pandering politicians or "drones." The drones impose confiscatory taxes on the rich, keep as much as they can for themselves, and redistribute the rest to the masses. The squabbling among politicians and competing factions of the rich leads to a downward spiral of corruption and mutual accusation, opening the way for a popular leader to take power. But he soon becomes a tyrant. Taking advantage of the peoples' weakness to consolidate his power, he transforms them into slaves.[8]

Plato's account of democracy's collapse into tyranny is part of a more general discussion of the inevitable decay of all political regimes that will concern us more fully anon; here I attend to his discussion of the tensions between democracy and the truth. Like the authors discussed previously, Plato's argument suggests that, in principle at least, the legitimacy of a political order is dependent on its being friendly to the pursuit of truth. Knowledge is the greatest good, for Plato, and if a regime could be based on the truth, it would be the best regime. Democracy is not dependent on the pursuit of truth, however. As we have seen, Plato takes its constitutive principle to be pandering to the masses who are generally incapable of recognizing the truth and indeed are hostile to it when it conflicts with their prejudices.

Whether it is reasonable to assume democratic publics must invariably be hostile to truth-telling is a question to which I return below. Casual observation of the massive reliance on polling, focus groups, and spin-doctors in modern electoral politics suggests, at least, that Plato's concern was not groundless. And if his account of democratic politicians as extracting what they can from the rich and redistributing with an eye to what is necessary to ensure reelection is a little crude, it is surely recognizable to the contemporary eye even without the benefit of the political science literatures on rent-seeking and the electoral strategies of politicians.[9] Democratic politicians face incentives to tell people what they want to hear and to gratify popular desires; there is no prima facie reason to suppose that this will engender fidelity to the truth.

Perhaps this is often the case, but the obvious question to ask of Plato's view is: Compared to what? Posing it inevitably gets us to the much-debated issue of whether *The Republic* should be read as providing a blueprint for a perfectly just society or a demonstration of its impossibility. Plato insisted that such a society would have to be run autocratically by philosopher kings who were committed to knowing and acting on the truth. Only philosophers have knowledge of, and love for, the good, which is "the end of all endeavors."[10] Much of *The Republic* is a description of the disciplined hierarchical order that would be needed to create a just society. Partly shaped by Plato's admiration for Sparta, it included centralized control of all aspects of social life from reproduction, to childrearing, to economic organization, and, most important, to an exacting educational system designed to uncover and train those with the capacity to rule as philosopher kings. This included general education to the age of eighteen followed by two years of rigorous physical and military training, and then a decade of training, for those sufficiently capable, in the mathematical disciplines. At the age of thirty those deemed trustworthy enough to learn the potentially dangerous art of rhetoric were to be taught it for five years, whereupon they would be appointed to subordinate leadership offices until the age of fifty. Those who survived would become fully qualified philosopher kings, dividing their time between their preferred activity of philosophy and governing— which they would recognize as their obligation.[11]

Some commentators, most notably Karl Popper in *The Open Society and Its Enemies,* have attacked this as a recipe for totalitarianism. Writing in the midst of World War II, Popper was thoroughly appalled that Plato's views could be taken seriously by humane intellectuals. Giving the sorts of power to the state that Plato proposes seemed to Popper to be a recipe for the type of regime Britain was then fighting in Hitler's Germany, not to mention the communist totalitarianism further east.[12] Others, by contrast, have argued that, far from advocating the perfect society, Plato's purpose was to demonstrate its impossibility. For instance, Leo Strauss read Plato in this way partly on the grounds, among others, that philosophers would have to be compelled to rule, and partly because Plato's account of a perfectly just society requires equality of the sexes and absolute communism, both of which are "against nature."[13] In a brilliant polemic Miles Burnyeat contests this reading as implausible, arguably leaving Popper's literal interpretation as the more plausible.[14]

Yet there is a different reason, not grappled with by Popper and independent of the interpretive disagreements between Burnyeat and Strauss just mentioned, for thinking that Plato intends the message of *The Republic* to be that the just society is unattainable. One need not indulge in extravagant claims about esoteric meanings to notice that Plato's Socrates is unequivocal in *The Republic* that the just society, were it created, would not be exempt from what he takes to be the general rule that all regimes decay. A properly constituted just society will be unusually stable, "but since all created things must decay, even a social order of this kind cannot last for all time, but will decline."[15] The rulers will make errors in breeding the next cohort, resulting in debasement of future rulers who will become consumed with internal strife. As a result, the communal principles of ownership on which the ideal republic is based will be abandoned, and the rot will then set in. Initially it will be replaced by a timarchy or military aristocracy. This will in turn degenerate into an oligarchy, then be replaced by democracy, and eventually collapse into tyranny.[16] Tyranny will presumably be unstable as well, but Plato does not pursue the question what would replace it in *The Republic*.[17] Instead he moves into a discussion of why the life of the philosopher, who desires not to rule, is happier than any other.[18]

Plato's account reflects the fact that he worked with a contemplative ideal of truth, best realized outside the political realm. For him, discovering the truth is like basking in sunlight. This is expressed both in his comparison of the good, which is the source of reality and truth, with the sun,[19] and in his famous comparison of the search for truth with struggling to understand reality in an underground cave that is dimly lit by indirect light from above.[20] If, *per impossible,* a just society could be created, those with access to the truth would be reluctant rulers, accepting the necessity that they must rule because the alternative would be regimes in which there would be no space for them to engage in the pursuit of knowledge. As far as the world of imperfect regimes is concerned, those who value the pursuit of truth do best to withdraw from politics, particularly democratic politics, lest they share the fate of Socrates. It is not entirely clear what they will discover; on many readings of Plato it is a politically unpalatable fact that we know nothing. Philosophers are those with the courage to face up to, and grasp the full implications of, this awful reality about the human condition. But they had better keep it to themselves.

In some respects the view of truth that informs Plato's account of its incompatibility with democracy is unlike any we have encountered thus far. It is an elitist conception in that Plato thought only the elect few capable of the disciplined reflection that discovering the truth requires. "Philosophy," we are told, "is impossible among the common people."[21] Only philosophers have what it takes to venture outside of the cave into the sunlight. The Enlightenment, by contrast, is about reason for everyman. Plato's view is also distinctive in that truth for him is defined by reference to "forms" or timeless universals that are exogenous to human beings and their intentions.[22] This stands in stark contrast to the early Enlightenment conception in which will-dependence is the gold standard for authoritative knowledge, an irreducibly endogenous conception.

Putting the elitism, or what Popper describes as Plato's "intellectualism"[23] to one side, his view shares with that of the early Enlightenment thinkers a concern with what can be known beyond all doubt—even if adopting this absolutist criterion involves conceding that ultimately nothing can be known. Also like that of the early Enlightenment thinkers, Plato's method of inquiry involved rigorous introspection. Like the thinkers of the mature Enlightenment, however, Plato believed the truth to be a good deal more slippery and elusive than the early Enlightenment thinkers thought was the case, and that it is a frequent casualty of corruption and competing interests that vie with one another in politics. Indeed, he was a good deal less sanguine, and perhaps more realistic, than even Mill and Dewey on this front. Their faith in the alluring attraction of an unbiased science geared to the pursuit of truth is often belied by events as we have seen; Plato's account seems closer to the mark.

Yet Plato's account of the tension between democracy and the truth seems less than fully adequate for establishing criteria for the legitimacy of political institutions. Because his view of the pursuit of truth is essentially contemplative, it has little to offer for evaluating the different imperfect regimes in which we actually live, and no sound basis, therefore, for arguing for the relative merits of one rather than another. On some interpretations Plato is said to prefer the regime that is most likely to leave the philosopher alone to engage in the pursuit of knowledge; hence the Straussian story that the philosopher should humor the gentleman so as to be supported in his craft.[24] Granting this, for the sake of argument, as a correct account of Plato's stance, it is far from

clear that it should lead us to reject democracy that, as I note in
§7.2, has a better record than nondemocracy in protecting negative rights such as freedom of speech and association that are
needed for unfettered philosophical reflection.

But this is scarcely a compelling test for political legitimacy. By
its terms it is meaningless to the great majority who, on Plato's
account, are incapable of philosophical reflection. They would
therefore have no interest in, and would be unimpressed by, the
proposition that effectiveness in making the world safe for philosophy should be the criterion to judge the legitimacy of regimes.
This might be said to call for various forms of subterfuge and
indoctrination of the masses to get them to support the regime
most friendly to the pursuit of philosophy. Leaving the unattrac-
tiveness of such a manipulative view to one side, it seems doubtful that it could work in an era of mass literacy and contested
politics, where there will always be people with an interest in, and
a capacity for, exposing hypocrisy and dishonesty. Plato's system
of indoctrination was part of his account of what would be needed
to maintain a perfectly just order, not for the world of imperfect
societies in which we actually live.[25]

7.1.2 Democratic Competition as Truth's Ally

Democracy as we know it might well involve much of the pandering and capture by special interests conjured up in Plato's analogies to the ship's captain and the animal, but democratic leaders
can never be entirely free from a commitment to truth-telling. For
instance, even though political parties and the governments they
form may often work in the interests of some subset of the population, they invariably claim to be acting in the interests of all.[26] This
opens the way for opposition parties to point to the ways in which
they fail to live up to their promises and misrepresent reality.
Indeed, one of the principal reasons why opposition and political
competition are essential to democratic politics is that they pro-

vide the mechanisms through which democratic leaders are held to account.[27] Appalling as President Bill Clinton's ability to manipulate the truth was, he suffered impeachment and contributed to Vice-President Albert Gore's loss in the 2000 Presidential election when his dishonesty was incontrovertibly exposed.

To be sure, the truth does not always win out in democratic politics, but fidelity to it is a significant regulative ideal in democratic political debate. Senator Joseph Biden's exposure as a fraud for plagiarizing a "personal" speech about his childhood from Neil Kinnock in the 1988 elections finished him as a viable presidential candidate. Gary Hart suffered a similar fate for dishonest taunting of the press over extramarital affairs. The FBI's Abscam sting operation in the late 1970s ended careers of numerous public officials who were exposed as dishonest. Even as powerful a figure as long time Congressman and House Ways and Means Committee Chairman Dan Rostenkowski found himself convicted and sent to prison in disgrace in 1996 for fraudulent use of taxpayer funds. These types of dishonesty and corruption would be less likely to be exposed in nondemocratic regimes, where there is no competition for power and opposition politics, and hence no institutionalized incentive to expose dishonesty.

Commitment to truth-telling in politics is integral to legitimacy, I think, because most people recognize that they have an interest in knowing and acting on the truth. As I noted in discussing Nozick's experience machine in §2.3, one reason people become uncomfortable with classical utilitarianism's identification of the good life with pleasure is that they need to believe that their experiences are authentic—rooted, that is, in reality. To be sure, people are generally aware that those who have, or are seeking, power will always discover incentives to distort or manipulate the truth. Lord Acton's epithet to the effect that "all power tends to corrupt and absolute power corrupts absolutely" may be an overstatement, but it is widely recognized to capture enough reality, for reasons given in Plato's *Republic* among others, so that mechanisms to expose corruption and dishonesty must be integral to any legitimate political regime. Democracy does better than the going alternatives just because it institutionalizes such mechanisms, giving political aspirants incentives to shine light in dark corners and expose one another's failures and dissembling. Democracy is thus an important antidote to power monopolies that are all too easily held hostage to the imperatives for their own maintenance. Just as the Pareto system embodies Mill's notion of consent, so democracy institutionalizes the competition over ideas that both Mill and Dewey thought essential to the maintenance of freedom.

Joseph Schumpeter forcefully articulated a competitive democratic ideal in *Capitalism, Socialism, and Democracy* in 1942 by pressing the analogy between political and economic competition. He suggested that we think of voters as analogues of consumers, parties and politicians as corresponding to firms, the votes politicians seek as proxies for profits, and the policies governments enact as political goods and services.[28] To be sure, democracy is not reducible to competition. Often it involves other things as well, notably rights to participate in agenda setting and a deree of public deliberation.[29] But competition for power is indispensable.[30] This is why contemporary Schumpeterians such as Samuel Huntington insist that to call a country democratic a government must twice have given up power upon losing an election—a tough test that arguably rules out the United States until 1840, Japan and India for much of the twentieth century, and most of the so-called third wave democracies that have emerged in the ex-communist countries and sub-Saharan Africa since the 1980s.[31] The imperatives of competition also render opposition rights indispensable in democracies: meaningful political competition requires that there be opposition parties waiting in the wings, criticizing the government and offering voters potential alternatives.

Just as the Pareto system embodies Mill's idea of consent only imperfectly, so Schumpeterian democracy leads to less than fully adequate political competition. In theory at least, the standard left criticism of markets—that they reward those with greater resources—does not apply. One-person-one-vote is a resource equalizer that is widely seen as a non-negotiable requirement of democracy, despite occasional defenses of markets in votes on efficiency or intensity grounds.[32] The difficulty in practice is that, particularly in the United States but increasingly in other democracies, politicians compete first for campaign contributions and second for votes. Perhaps there would be decisive voter support for confiscatory taxes on estates worth more than ten million dollars, but no party proposes this. Indeed, in 2000 and 2001 the U.S. Congress gave strong bipartisan support to a bill that would abolish the existing estate tax—paid by only the wealthiest two percent of Americans.[33] It seems likely that politicians avoid taxing the wealthy for fear of the funds that would be channeled to their electoral opponents if they sought to do so. Empirical study of such claims is inherently difficult, but it seems reasonable to suppose that the proposals politicians offer are heavily shaped by the agendas of campaign contributors; why else would they contribute? Add to this the fact that the small number of major parties means that what we actually get is oligopolistic competition, and it becomes clear that the sense in which parties are as attentive to voters as firms in competitive markets are to consumers is quite attenuated.

Notice that these powerful objections are not aimed at the idea of political competition itself, but rather to the ways in which the system is imperfectly competitive. Disproportionate power of campaign contributors could be reduced (proposals for reform abound),[34] and reforms could be instituted to increase the number of parties, facilitating more competition. Indeed, it is remarkable that public interest litigants, activists, and political commentators (not to mention political theorists) do not argue for attempts to use antitrust laws to attack the existing duopoly. If competition for power is the life blood of democracy, then the search for bipartisan consensus (and the ideal of deliberative agreement that lies behind it) is really anti-competitive collusion in restraint of democracy. Why is it that people do not challenge legislation that has bipartisan backing, or other forms of bipartisan agreement, on *these* grounds? It seems that there are at least as many meritorious reasons to break up the Democratic and Republican parties as there are to break up AT&T and Microsoft.[35]

As the comparison between bipartisan agreement and collusion in restraint of democracy suggests, the ideal of institutionalized political competition should not be confused with the notion of deliberation that is taken by some to be the essence of democracy.[36] Deliberation has its place in democratic politics, particularly in ensuring that peoples' views are well informed, but in most theories the goal of deliberation is to produce agreement.[37] Competition for power is focused, by contrast, on contests that are carried out in structured settings in which people know they have to abide by certain rules, but in which they intend to win the argument in the eyes of their constituents—not reach an agreement with their adversaries. Institutionalizing mechanisms that require people to agree does nothing to promote their convergence on the truth. They might agree that the earth is flat, that foreigners are barbarians, or that blacks are inferior to whites. One of the reasons Mill thought argument so important in public life was that it creates openings for dissenters to expose misguided conventions and orthodox prejudices. When it operates well, competitive democracy facilitates vigorous ongoing debate in which power-seekers are forced to justify their claims to the public while being interrogated by opponents who have incentives to persuade the public of the shortcomings of their views and the advantages of different ones.[38]

For political competition to be meaningful, in addition to a supply of alternatives by those seeking power, there must also be demand for alternatives from a voting public whose members can think critically about these alternatives and evaluate the adequacy of political arguments. Creating and sustaining the requisite critical skills in the population at large was one of the reasons for Dewey's support of democracy against Plato's "aristocratic" principle of social organization. Dewey contested the idea that what is good for people can, even in principle, be imposed upon them. Conceding that Plato might be right that an individual obtains "his completest development" when he has found "that place in society for which he is best fitted and is exercising the function proper to that place," Dewey insisted that "he must find this place and assume this work in the main for himself."[39] Buttressing this universal defense of individuality was a strongly anti-vanguardist outlook that led Dewey always to be suspicious of apparently benign authoritarian rulers. Plato's aristocratic ideal fails in his view because "the practical consequence of giving the few wise and good power is that they cease to remain wise and good. They become ignorant of the needs and requirements of the many; they leave the many outside the pale with no real share in the commonwealth." Moreover, they are all too easily corrupted by their position so that they use "their wisdom and strength for themselves, for the assertion of privilege and status and to the detriment of the common good."[40] In maintaining power monopolies, political elites should thus be expected to try to dumb down the population, undermining the critical demands that are needed to keep leaders honest and on their toes.

These political arguments for democracy's superiority to the going alternatives are reinforced, in Dewey's view, by epistemological considerations. Once we abandon the absolutist features that Plato's theory of truth shares with the arguments of the early Enlightenment in favor of the mature Enlightenment's fallibilism, then, democracy's connection to the truth is cast in a different light.[41] In the cumulative and experimental venture of pushing back the frontiers of ignorance, democracy is the truth's most reliable ally. The democratic attitude and the scientific attitude are mutually reinforcing just because both require public contestation. Every new idea and theory, Dewey argued in *Individuality in Our Day*, must be submitted to the scientific community for critical evaluation.

> Experimental method is something other than the use of blow pipes, retorts and reagents. It is the foe of every belief that permit habit and wont to dominate invention and discovery, and ready-made system to override verifiable fact. Constant revision is the work of experimental inquiry. By revision of knowledge and ideas, power to effect transformation is given us. This attitude, once incarnated in the individual mind, would find an operative outlet. If dogmas and institutions tremble when a new idea appears, this shiver is nothing to what would happen if the idea were armed with the means for the continuous discovery of new truth and the criticism of old belief. To "acquiesce" in science is dangerous only for those who would maintain affairs in the existing social order unchanged because of lazy habit or self-interest. For the scientific attitude demands faithfulness to whatever is discovered and steadfastness in adhering to new truth.[42]

Dewey envisaged mass education as diffusion of this outlook throughout society, promoting a "general adoption of the scientific attitude in human affairs."[43] Conceding that "it would be absurd to believe it desirable or possible for every one to become a scientist when science is defined from the side of the subject matter," he nonetheless insisted in *Freedom and Culture* that "the future of democracy is allied with the spread of the scientific attitude. It is the sole guarantee against wholesale misleading by propaganda. More important still, it is the only assurance of the possibility of a public opinion intelligent enough to meet present social problems."[44]

Dewey wrote these words on the eve of World War II. We saw in

§6.3 that he was more sanguine than he should have been, both
about how rapidly the scientific attitude would spread and about
its cumulative capacity to displace prejudice, bigotry, and superstition. From the vantage point of the twenty-first century it is
clear that the reality is more of a continuous battle without any
guarantee that the critical scientific attitude will always prevail.
The perpetual existence of contending interests in democratic
politics means that Plato was right to suggest, via the ship's captain and animal analogies, that there will always be those who
succumb to the impulse to distort the truth and play to passion
and prejudice in the quest to attain or retain political power. But
he was wrong, for epistemological reasons as well as political
ones, to suggest that the answer to this was to vest power in a
political elite. His absolutist view of knowledge shares many unpersuasive features in common with the early Enlightenment
views we have seen fit to reject in favor of the experimental fallibilism of modern science. Democracy offers no guarantee of the
pursuit of truth through science and its application to politics, but
Dewey was right that the democratic and scientific attitudes share
elective affinities, and that democracy offers a better chance than
any alternative political system for the truth to prevail in politics
over time. No doubt this is part of what Winston Churchill had in
mind when he insisted that democracy is "the worst form of
government except all those other forms that have been tried
from time to time."[45]

7.2 Democracy and Rights

No less venerable than Plato's contention that democracy is hostile to the truth is the claim, usually associated with the "tyranny
of the majority" discussed by Tocqueville and Mill, that democracy is hostile to individual rights.[46] In its modern form it is
traceable at least to Rousseau's concern, echoed by Madison in

Federalist #10 with "majority factions," that a majority might satisfy its members' interests at the expense of a minority.[47]

7.2.1 Democracy's Alleged Irrationality

Modern social choice theorists have held that the problem is worse than these classical authors realized in that majority rule can lead to arbitrary outcomes and even minority tyranny. Extending an old insight of the Marquis de Condorcet (1743–1794), Kenneth Arrow showed that under some exceedingly weak assumptions, majority rule can lead to outcomes that are opposed by a majority of the population. For instance, if voter I's ranked preferences are ABC, voter II's are CAB and voter III's are BCA, then there is a potential majority for A over B (voters I and II), a potential majority for B over C (voters I and III), and a potential majority for C over A (voters II and III).[48] This outcome, known as a voting cycle, violates the principle of transitivity—generally taken to be an indispensable feature of rationality. Whoever controls the order of voting can determine the outcome when there is the potential for such a cycle, provided that she knows the preferences of the voters. Even if outcomes are not manipulated by an agenda setter, they might nonetheless be arbitrary in the sense that had the alternatives been voted on in some order other than they actually were, the result would have been different. In short, democracy might lead to tyranny of the majority, but it might also lead to tyranny of a strategically well-placed minority or to tyranny of irrational arbitrariness.

None of these possibilities would seem to augur well for democracy as a protector of individual rights. Fear of tyranny by majority factions led Madison and the Federalists to devise a political system comprised of multiple vetoes in order to make majority political action difficult. These included a separation of powers system in which "ambition will be made to counteract ambition,"[49] including an independent court with the power to declare legislation unconstitutional and a President whose election and hence legitimacy are independent of the legislature; strong bicameralism in which legislation must pass both houses and in which two-thirds majorities in both houses can override the President's veto power; and a federal system in which there is constant jurisdictional tension between federal and state governments. The findings in the post-Arrovian social choice literature have led commentators such as William Riker and Barry Weingast to endorse this multiplication of institutional veto points on the possibility of governmental action and argue that courts should hem in legislatures as much as possible, lest they compromise individual rights, particularly property rights.[50]

We should distinguish the claim that majority rule produces results threatening to individual rights from the claim that it produces irrational results. True, if majority rule were a perfect aggregator of individual preferences, we might be tempted to say that it embodied the choices of the governed—thereby protecting the rights of individuals as expressed through the system. This is presumably what Rousseau had in mind when he said that decision procedures should converge on a general will that he famously, if vaguely, characterized by saying that we start with "the sum of individual desires," subtract "the plusses and minuses which cancel each other out," then "the sum of the difference is the general will."[51] But this idea of a general will, described in the modern literature as a social welfare function, is just what Arrow showed to be unavailable.

Yet we can grant Arrow his victory over Rousseau without being persuaded that democracy poses any particular threat to individual rights as a result. The decisive question, after all, is: compared to what? Arrow's finding deals not merely with majority rule. His theorem shows that, given the diversity of preferences he postulates, his modest institutional conditions, and his unexceptionable constraints on rationality, *no* mechanism is guaranteed to produce a rational collective decision. But what is the alternative? Libertarians like Riker and Weingast claim that it is to minimize governmental action as much as possible, but that is inadequate for two reasons. First, as noted in §3.4, making governmental action difficult is in effect to privilege the status quo, but it is mistaken to suppose this does not involve collective action. Perhaps due to their proclivity for thinking in a social contract idiom, libertarian commentators often write as if "not having" collective action is a coherent option in societies that nonetheless have private property, enforcement of contracts, and the standard panoply of negative freedoms. The recent experience of post-communist countries such as Russia should remind us that these are all costly institutions requiring continual collective enforcement.[52] The libertarian constitutional scheme is a collective action regime maintained by the state, one that is disproportionately financed by implicit taxes on those who would prefer an alternative regime. The more appropriate question, then, is not "whether-or-not collective action?" but rather "what sort of collective action?"

Second, libertarians like Riker and Weingast tend to focus on potential institutional pathologies of legislatures while ignoring those of the institutions, such as courts, that they would have curbed legislative action. At least in the United States, appellate courts are themselves majoritarian institutions (including the U.S. Supreme Court, which has nine members). There is every reason to believe they would be at least as vulnerable to cycles as are legislatures, and possibly even more susceptible to manipulation. Chief justices, who have considerable control over court agendas and the order in which issues are taken up, know a good deal about their colleagues' preferences because they decide many closely related cases and personnel turnover is incremental and slow. It seems reasonable to suppose that less of the information pertinent to manipulation is available in a Senate of a hundred, a third of whom are up for election every two years, or a House of Representatives of four hundred and thirty-five, all of whom are up for reelection every two years—not to mention the population at large. True, high incumbent reelection rates slow down turnover of legislators, and much of their work is done in smaller committees. Granting this, there is still no compelling reason to believe legislatures more susceptible than courts to the potential for arbitrary or manipulated outcomes identified by Arrow.[53]

More important, perhaps, than these weaknesses in the libertarian critique of democracy are the expectations it rests on concerning what would be a nonarbitrary decision-making outcome. Arrow might have established that often there may be no such thing as a Rousseauian general will, but to say that we should be troubled by this is to buy into a kind of epistemological absolutism that is a cousin of Plato's. Transitivity might well be a reasonable property of individual rationality, but it is far from clear that it makes sense to require it of many collective decisions. If the New York Giants beat the Dallas Cowboys who in turn beat the Washington Redskins, no one suggests that the Redskins should not play the Giants lest the principle of transitivity be violated. Deadlocked committees sometimes make decisions by the toss of a coin—arbitrary perhaps, but necessary for collective life to go on. In such circumstances it matters more that each contest or decision-mechanism was perceived to be fair than that a different outcome might have occurred on a different day.[54]

If we abandon the expectation that there is a Rousseauian general will or social welfare function waiting out there to be discovered like a Platonic form in metaphysical space, we might nonetheless be persuaded of the merits of majority rule as a decision-making mechanism in many circumstances. That it promotes competition of ideas as discussed in §7.1 is one reason to favor it. Another is that majority rule can contribute to political stability just because there is the perpetual possibility of upsetting the status quo. Democratic theorists such as Guiseppe Di Palma and Adam Przeworski note that it is institutionalized uncertainty about the future that gives people who lose in any given round the incentive to remain committed to the process rather than reach for their guns or otherwise become alienated from the political system.[55] This will not happen when there is a single dominant cleavage in the society, as when a majority of the population has identical preference orderings. Such a preference structure will forestall an Arrovian cycle, but quite possibly at the price of turning loyal opposition (where the democratic system is endorsed though the government of the day is opposed), into disloyal opposition where those who lose try to overthrow the system itself. Generalizing this, Nicholas Miller has noted that there is a contradiction between the notion of stability in the public choice literature since Arrow, where various restrictions on preferences are intended to prevent cycling, and the pluralist idea of stability. The periodic turnover of government required by the latter notion is facilitated by just the kind of heterogeneous preferences that create the possibility of cycling.[56] Indeed, students of comparative politics often contend that competitive democracy does not work when heterogeneous preferences are lacking. If the preference-cleavages in the population are not sufficiently cross-cutting to produce this result, they propose alternative institutional arrangements, such as Arend Lijphart's "consociational democracy," which includes entrenched minority vetoes and forces elites representing different groups to govern by consensus as a cartel, avoiding political competition.[57]

Closer inspection thus reveals that the possibility of voting cycles is not especially troubling, and it may even be advantageous for the stability of democratic institutions. How likely it is that cycles actually occur is another matter. I have already noted that they are ruled out if an absolute majority has identical preferences. Various other constraints on preferences will also reduce their likelihood or eliminate them.[58] At least one theoretical result suggests that cycles are comparatively unlikely in large populations even when preferences are heterogeneous, and an exhaustive empirical study by Gerry Mackie has revealed every alleged cycle identified in the social choice literature to be based on spurious claims or faulty data.[59] It may be that democracies turn out to enjoy the best of both worlds. The possibility of cycles gives those who lose in any given election an incentive to remain committed to the system in hopes of prevailing in the future, but the fact that cycles are actually rare means that government policies are not perpetually being reversed.[60] In the area of tax policy, for instance, there is undoubtedly a potential coalition to upset every conceivable status quo, as can be seen by reflecting on a society of three voting to divide a dollar by majority rule: whatever the distribution, some majority coalition will have an interest in changing it. Yet tax policy remains remarkably stable over time.[61]

7.2.2 Tyranny of the Majority?

If the findings in the public choice literature are less threatening to democratic legitimacy than is often assumed, what of the more traditional worry about the tyranny of the majority associated with the arguments of Tocqueville and Mill and the counter majoritarian elements that the Framers built into the American Constitution? Tocqueville's forecasts were particularly apocalyptic on this point. "Formerly tyranny used the clumsy weapons of chains and hangmen," he noted in 1835, yet "nowadays even despotism, though it seemed to have nothing more to learn, has been perfected by civilization." The possibility of majority tyranny struck him as the greatest threat posed by democracy in America. Quoting Madison's worry in *Federalist* #51 that "in a society under the forms of which the stronger faction can readily unite and oppress the weaker, anarchy may truly be said to reign," Tocqueville opined that "if ever freedom is lost in America, that will be due to the omnipotence of the majority driving the minorities to desperation and forcing them to appeal to physical force." The result might be anarchy as Madison said, "but it will have come as a result of despotism."[62]

An influential theoretical response to this danger put forward by James Buchanan and Gordon Tullock in 1962 builds on the Framers' impulse to make some rights and liberties more difficult to change by majority rule than others. Deploying the style of reasoning that Rawls would later make famous, they asked the question: What decision rules would mutually disinterested citizens choose at a constitutional convention where everyone is uncertain "as to what his own precise role will be in any one of the whole chain of later collective choices that will actually have to be made." Whether selfish or altruistic, each agent is forced by circumstances "to act, from self-interest, *as if* he were choosing the best set of rules for the social group."[63] Thus considered, they argued, there is no reason to prefer majority rule to the possible alternatives. Collective decision-making invariably has costs and benefits for any individual, and an optimal decision rule would minimize the sum of "external costs" (the costs to an individual of the legal but harmful actions of third parties) and "decision-making costs" (those of negotiating agreement on collective action). The external costs of collective action diminish as increasingly large majorities are required; in the limiting case of unanimity rule every individual is absolutely protected because anyone can veto a proposed action. Conversely, decision-making costs typically increase with the proportion required, because the costs of negotiation increase. The choice problem at the constitutional stage is to determine the point at which the combined costs are smallest for different types of collective action, and to agree on a range of decision rules to be applied in different future circumstances.[64]

At least three kinds of collective action can be distinguished requiring different decision rules. First is the initial decision rule that must prevail for other decision rules to be decided on. Buchanan and Tullock "assume, without elaboration, that at this ultimate stage . . . the rule of unanimity holds." Next come "those possible collective or public decisions which modify or restrict the structure of individual human or property rights after these have once been defined and generally accepted by the community." Foreseeing that collective action may "impose very severe costs on him," the individual will tend "to place a high value on the attainment of his consent, and he may be quite willing to undergo substantial decision-making costs in order to insure that he will, in fact, be reasonably protected against confiscation." He will thus require a decision rule approaching unanimity. Last is the class of collective actions characteristically undertaken by governments. For these "the individual will recognize that private organization will impose some interdependence costs on him, perhaps in significant amount, and he will, by hypothesis, have supported a shift of such activities to the public sector." Examples include provision of public education, enforcement of building and fire codes, and maintenance of adequate police forces. For such "general legislation" an individual at the constitutional stage will support less inclusive decision rules, though not necessarily simple majority rule, and indeed within this class different majorities might be agreed on as optimal for different purposes. "The number of categories, and the number of decision-making rules chosen, will depend on the situation which the individual expects to prevail and the 'returns to scale' expected to result from using the same rule over many activities."[65]

This argument is defective in various ways that need not concern us now.[66] The point to be emphasized here is that their inertial bias in favor of unanimity rule turns on two dubious assumptions that make democracy look less attractive than it should. First is the social contract fiction, the implausibility of which has already been noted, that there could be an initial stage in which only private action prevails in society—without being underwritten by collective institutions. This is not to mention that Buchanan and Tullock's assumption—that pre-political people "own" their resources and endowments—runs afoul of Rawls's powerful moral arbitrariness argument discussed in §5.2.2. The second defect arises even if we engage in the thought experiment Buchanan and Tullock propose. Unanimity as a decision rule has the unique property, they argue, that if decision-making costs are zero, it is the only rational decision rule for all proposed collective action.[67] But this argument confuses unanimity *qua* decision rule with unanimity *qua* social state, that is, a condition in the world where everyone actually wants the same outcome. Building on earlier work by Brian Barry, Douglas Rae has pointed out that from the standpoint of their constitutional convention, we would have to assume that we are as likely to be ill-disposed toward any future status quo as we would be well-disposed toward it; and that in cases where we are ill-disposed, a decision rule requiring unanimity will frustrate our preferences. Buchanan and Tullock assume throughout that it is departures from the status quo that need to be justified, but this is not warranted. Externalities over time, or "utility drift" (Rae's term), might change our evaluations of the status quo. We might feel in certain circumstances that those who favor failures to act collectively, rather than collective action itself, should shoulder the burden of proof.[68] People might change their minds for other reasons, foreseen or unforeseen, or someone might be opposed to, and not wish to be bound by, a status quo that was the product of the unanimous agreement of a previous generation. Indeed Rae has shown formally that if we assume we are as likely to be against any proposal as for it, which the condition of uncertainty at the constitutional convention would seem to require, then majority rule, or something very

close to it, is the unique solution to Buchanan and Tullock's
choice problem.[69]

Ultimately, it is an empirical question whether majoritarian
democracy undermines individual rights in the ways that concerned Tocqueville, Mill, and the American Framers, necessitating the implementation counter-majoritarian devices designed to
limit its range. In the United States the institutional device that
has attracted the most debate and attention is the judiciary, given
the Supreme Court's extensive powers of judicial review. The
Rawlsian enterprise is one of constitutional constraint that has
had some impact on the behavior of the American judiciary.[70]
Theorists such as Bruce Ackerman, Ronald Dworkin, and G. A.
Cohen have put forward alternative theories that may have been
less influential to date, but all are premised on the notion that
some independent enforcer of their proffered principles, presumably a constitutional court, should set the limits on what democracies may do.[71]

Yet it is difficult to find convincing evidence to support the
worry that democracy is threatening to individual rights and liberties. Robert Dahl has recently reminded us that in the century and
a half since Tocqueville articulated his apocalyptic fears, political
freedoms have turned out to be substantially better respected in
democracies than in nondemocracies. The countries in which
there is meaningful freedom of speech, association, respect
for personal and property rights, prohibitions on torture, and
guarantees of equality before the law are overwhelmingly the
countries that have democratic political systems.[72] Even if we ex-
pand the definition of individual rights to include social and economic guarantees, one could not make a credible case that nondemocracies supply these better than do democracies.[73] This issue
is, concededly, difficult to study empirically. Most of the world's
wealthy countries, with the resources for meaningful socio-
economic guarantees, are also democracies, and the failures of

the communist systems arguably had more to do with their economies than their political systems. Yet one would scarcely want the Tocquevillian case to rest on the communist example, where civil and political freedoms were substantially less well-respected than in democracies, and the level of social provision was generally low. At a minimum, one is bound to conclude that the Tocquevillian case has not been established and that the converse of it seems more likely to be true, to wit, that the best way to guarantee individual rights and civil liberties is to work to create and entrench democracy.

Do constitutional courts make a difference among democracies? In the United States there have certainly been eras when the federal judiciary has successfully championed individual rights and civil liberties against the legislative branch of government, that of the Warren Court being the best known.[74] But there have also been eras when it has legitimated racial oppression and the denial of civil liberties.[75] Until recently there has been surprisingly little systematic study of this question beyond the trading of anecdotes. As early as 1956 Dahl had registered skepticism that democracies with constitutional courts could be shown to have a positive effect on the degree to which individual freedoms are respected when compared to democracies without them, a view he developed more fully two years later in his seminal article titled "Decisionmaking in a democracy: The Supreme Court as national policymaker."[76] Subsequent scholarship has shown Dahl's skepticism to have been well-founded.[77] Indeed, there are reasons for thinking that the popularity of independent courts in new democracies may have more in common with the popularity of independent banks than with the protection of individual freedoms. They can operate as devices to signal foreign investors and those who control international economic institutions that the capacity of elected officials to engage in redistributive policies or interfere with property rights will be limited. That is, they may be devices for limiting domestic political opposition to unpopular policies by taking them off the table.[78]

7.2.3 Whose Rights?

We saw in earlier chapters that an important question about rights that has not been convincingly dealt with in much political theory concerns *whose* rights? On the face of it, the democratic tradition would seem to be equally handicapped in this regard. If democracy requires the use of a decision rule such as majority rule, this presupposes that the question "majority of whom?" has been settled—that the demos has already been established. Yet this suggests that some of the most fundamental and contentious questions of politics must be presumed to have been settled before democracy can come into play. Certainly going back to the roots of the democratic tradition is less than helpful here. The Ancient Greeks famously denied citizenship to women and slaves as we saw, and they recognized no political obligations to foreign barbarians. The universal franchise is a comparatively recent development in democratic countries, yet citizenship continues in most instances to be an absolute bar on democratic participation. Down through the contemporary literature, it has frequently been noted that the failure to come up with an adequate theory of membership is an enduring embarrassment of democratic theory.[79]

In fact the democratic tradition contains distinctive resources for tackling this issue, because the basis for its legitimacy rests on the causal notion of having an affected interest. That is, the reason why democracy is argued to be justified is that people should have a say in the decisions that affect them. Hence the appeal of Nelson Mandela's statement to the Apartheid South African court before his sentencing for treason in 1963: he should not be bound by "a law which neither I nor any of my people had any say in preparing."[80] The causal principle of affected interest suggests that ideally the structure of decision rules should follow the contours of power relationships, not that of memberships or citizenships: if you are affected by the results, you are presumptively entitled to a say. This view provides grounds for a potential response to the morally arbitrary distribution of citizenships in the world: either the distribution of citizenship should be reformed to bring it into closer conformity to the realities of power, or rights to participate in decision-making should be detached from citizenship better to follow the contours of power relations.

One comment on this line of reasoning is that, just as there may be versions of democratic theory that do not stumble headlong into the membership problem, so there are versions of the other traditions we have discussed that also eschew national membership as a legitimating basis for politics. There are utilitarian writers who insist on a global metric of account.[81] The Marxist tradition, too, was cosmopolitan from the beginning—if unrealistically so. Some critics of Rawls argue that his contractarian theory of justice should be applied on a global basis, as we saw in §6.6. Other liberal writers defend self-consciously cosmopolitan theories, criticizing the unthinking fetishism of nation-states in much of the liberal tradition.[82] Even writers in the communitarian tradition are willing to question the trumping supremacy of the nation-state. If strands, at least, in all these traditions problematize the primacy of national citizenship, why single out that strand of democratic theory as superior on this ground?

The answer is that the democratic tradition offers more plausible and realistic resources for dealing with the issue in practice. Some communitarian writers reject the primacy of national political membership, but we saw in §6.6, this tends to be replaced with characteristic blind spots concerning their own assumptions about membership. The principal difficulty with the different variants of liberal and utilitarian cosmopolitanism, not to mention cosmopolitan Marxism, is that they lack plausible mechanisms of application. Nozick may overstate things when, following Weber, he defines a state by reference to a monopoly of coercive force in a given territory.[83] States can often be viable while enjoying something considerably short of that, but the capacity for international enforcement is so limited that the idea of world government presupposed by cosmopolitan philosophies seems inherently chimerical.

True, international courts have been created, and have had some limited success in prosecuting war crimes and other criminal acts. But they can be ignored with impunity by the most powerful players in the international system, and in any case it is difficult to imagine them as engines of ongoing international government. Some, such as David Held, suggest that it is possible to create an international legal order or *rechtstaat* that mimics how power was centralized in national states between the seventeenth and nineteenth centuries. But Held's critics point out that this is not a plausible analogy. The decisive difference is that in today's international arena there are huge obstacles to forming global political institutions that have no analogues from the era of national state-formation, namely powerful national governments whose leaders command both widespread political legitimacy and coercive resources.[84] Moreover, to the extent the power of national states is being eroded (which can be overstated),[85] this erosion is caused by transnational economic forces. The idea that national governments are going to roll over and play dead for global political institutions any time soon is difficult to take seriously. Global political institutions would, in any case, confront major difficulties of efficiency and legitimacy, raising serious questions as to their desirability.[86] Because cosmopolitan theories so often ignore the subject of global enforcement institutions, they can easily seem curiously disengaged from obvious questions concerning how their theories could actually work or even begin to garner public legitimacy.[87]

By contrast, the principle of affected interest that legitimates the democratic tradition lends itself to the disaggregation of decision-making: defining the demos decision by decision rather than people by people. As such, it is compatible with a number of arguments that have recently been developed whose purpose is to decenter membership-based sovereignty as the decisive determinant of participation, replacing it with systems of overlapping jurisdiction in which different groups of persons are sovereign over different classes of decisions. The emerging structure of the European Union is a prototypical model.[88] At the same time as it might make sense for the United Kingdom to centralize some decision-making in Brussels, it might make sense to devolve other decision-making to regional parliaments in Scotland and Wales and even to local governments.

I have discussed this view in detail elsewhere.[89] Suffice to note here that, from a democratic perspective, the goal should be to refashion decision-making so as better to embody participation of those whose interests are affected by the decisions that are actually made, with the strongest presumption of inclusion going to those whose basic interests are vitally at stake. In addition to disaggregating decisions among different groups of citizens for different types of decisions, this approach also suggests that noncitizens should often vote on particular issues—militating against the practice in many countries to disenfranchise guest-workers and other long-term noncitizen residents. It might be reasonable to withhold citizenship from them, but not to deny them a vote concerning taxes they pay or the governance of the schools that their children attend. To be sure, there will be many arenas in which those whose basic interests are vitally at stake will continue to be ignored. Yet the principle of affected interest is helpful even in these cases. It suggests that decisions taken in such arenas will lack legitimacy, and it points the way to the types of reforms that would improve their legitimacy. Moreover, moving toward a world governed by the principle of affected interest can be approached in a piecemeal way. There may be insuperable obstacles to achieving it in some arenas, but it can still be pursued in others.

Major difficulties will arise in determining who is affected and how much by a particular decision, and about who is to determine which claims about being affected should be accepted. These are serious difficulties, to be sure, but two points should be noted in mitigation. First, although who is affected by a decision is bound to be controversial, this fact scarcely distinguishes causally based arguments from membership-based arguments about participation. Who is to decide, and by what authority, who is to be a member is as fraught with conceptual and ideological baggage as who is to decide, and by what authority, who is causally affected by a particular collective decision. These difficulties should not therefore count as decisive against the causally based view if the membership-based view is seen as the alternative. Second, there is considerable experience with causally based arguments in tort law. Tort actions are often concerned with the causal effects of individual rather than collective decisions, but in dealing with them courts have developed mechanisms for determining whose claims should be heard, for sorting genuine claims from frivolous ones, and for distinguishing weaker from stronger claims to have been adversely affected by an action. This is not an argument for turning politics into tort law; the point of the comparison is to illustrate that in other areas of social life, institutional mechanisms have been developed to assess and manage conflicting claims of being causally affected by actions. They may be imperfect mechanisms, but they should be evaluated by reference to the other imperfect mechanisms of collective decision-making that actually prevail in the world, not by comparison with an ideal that prevails nowhere.

CHAPTER 8

Democracy in the Mature Enlightenment

Arguments in the democratic tradition over the past several centuries, like the other traditions examined in this book, have been centrally shaped by the characteristic Enlightenment preoccupations with science and individual rights. To be sure, these concerns enjoy a lineage that predates the Enlightenment. Plato's discussion of democracy reminds us that political philosophers had been concerned both with potential tensions between democracy and the truth for over two millennia and with the possibility that, in a democracy, respect for individual freedom might be threatened by mob tyranny. This underscores the reality that there is nothing entirely new under the modern sun. Indeed, we saw that Plato's conceptualization of both issues bears a striking resemblance to many Enlightenment preoccupations.

Despite important differences between what I described as Plato's exogenous theory of truth and the endogenous character of the early Enlightenment conception, both exhibit an absolutist character that leads naturally to a vanguardist approach to politics. If there are indisputable right answers to questions concerning how the state should be organized and what policies it should pursue, then it makes sense to give political power to those who know the answers—be they philosopher kings, utilitarian calculators, or ideological leaders of a revolutionary working class party. By contrast, although the mature Enlightenment view of science does not go all the way with the postmodern critique, it differs from early Enlightenment views in recognizing that knowledge claims are invariably corrigible and subject to revision. Moreover, from the perspective of the mature Enlightenment we are bound to recognize that enduring differences of value and interest mean that in politics there will always be people with incentives to misrepresent and obscure the truth. As a result, partisans of the mature Enlightenment have good reasons for skepticism of all forms of political vanguardism.

We saw in §5.5 that the Rawlsian appeal to overlapping consensus has its attractions, given the assumption of enduring disagreement about fundamental beliefs and world views. The advantage is that it takes a "political, not metaphysical" approach to questions of ultimate truth and the justification of political beliefs, focusing instead on who is advantaged and who disadvantaged in the event that particular views rather than others are underwritten by the state. But the overlapping consensus approach does not deliver the results that Rawls claims for it. Overlapping consensus could be self-consciously defined so as to include the views that yield his principles and exclude those that do not, but this would render the enterprise trivially circular. If overlapping consensus is identified, instead, from the ground up it becomes potentially more interesting, but then there is no reason to think that in any country, let alone the contemporary United States, it will yield his principles. Despite these difficulties, we saw in Chapter 6 that abandoning the Enlightenment project *tout court* is not a viable option. The propensity of anti-Enlightenment writers like Rorty to identify the search for truth with the flawed foundationalist project can convincingly be stated only as a critique of the early Enlightenment. It offers no criteria for adjudicating among conflicting fallible truth-claims, or, indeed, claims that are not even said to be true.

Rather than deal with conflicting claims by trying to identify the elusive and shifting intersecting sets of people's beliefs (which may in any case converge on falsehoods), the democratic approach involves recognizing the importance of truth as a regulative ideal in public debate, and institutionalizing means of bringing the truth to bear on contending political positions. Mill was right to insist on the importance of argument in public life, even if he overestimated the likelihood that the advances in science would lead to diminished contestation, and he underestimated the possibilities offered by democratic institutions to foster the vigorous debate that he prized. The dynamics of democratic competition with robust opposition institutions, when combined with the permissive freedoms of thought and discussion Mill championed in the second chapter of *On Liberty*, offer the best hope of achieving this debate. To be sure, the actual political argument we see in contemporary democracies is far from adequate, largely because of the extent to which the process has become sullied by money. An important creative challenge for the present generation of democratic innovators is to find ways to diminish money's influence, so as to bring actual democratic argument closer to the disciplined debate, envisaged by Mill and Dewey, in which the truth operates as a regulative ideal.[1]

Just as the fear that democracy is truth's foe in politics turns out to be chimerical, once absolutist conceptions of truth are abandoned in favor of the mature Enlightenment's fallibilism and the merits of competitive democracy are assessed against the going alternatives, so too democracy's supposed threat to individual rights turns out on inspection to be overblown. Despite Mill's and Tocqueville's fears, the historical record reveals that democracies are better respecters of individual rights and civil liberties than nondemocracies. In the end this is surely the appropriate basis for comparison. People who live in countries lacking democratic political institutions must endure authoritarian ones, as must most of those living in democracies when their institutions are abandoned or fall apart.

The democratic tradition also does comparatively well when considered alongside the other intellectual traditions discussed in this book. Classical utilitarianism, we saw, was indifferent to individual rights, rendering it vulnerable to Rawls's critique that it fails to take seriously the differences among persons. Neoclassical utilitarianism avoids this charge, but at the price of taking on new difficulties with respect to individual rights. In some formulations it operates with so robust a libertarian conception of individual autonomy that it violates the rights of others once unintended harms and the broader context of resources is taken into account. In others, as with the consequentialist reading of Mill's harm principle, this problem is avoided. However, because there is no uncontroversial tortometer or consequentialist calculus for applying his principle, Mill is unconvincing as to how this should be done, and he is disconcertingly silent about to whom those doing the calculating should be answerable.

The Marxist tradition oscillates between an implausible utopian ideal, according to which the need for rights would be rendered obsolete with the abolition of injustice, and a strong version of Locke's workmanship ideal. This is incoherently cashed out as the theory of exploitation and it is in any case vulnerable to Rawls's argument about moral arbitrariness. As with Mill's definition of harm, some versions of exploitation that are independent of the labor theory of value are plausible, but in the neo-Marxist tradition there is no convincing account of who will wield the exploitometer. Nor is there an account of who will decide how, and to what extent, minimizing exploitation should be traded off against other goods such as efficiency, or of who will hold decision-makers accountable for their decisions about these matters. The vanguardist impulse within Marxism is strong, even if its main historical impetus came from Lenin rather than Marx himself. As a result, Marxists have never devoted serious attention to democratic procedures, except for how they might operate in their utopian world, which, if it could exist, would render them unnecessary. Certainly the record of nondemocratic socialist and communist states that have existed in the world is scarcely encouraging.

The Rawlsian critiques of the ways in which other traditions handle individual rights is powerful, but this is not matched by a compelling positive account of his own. We saw in §§5.4 and 5.5 that there are internal contradictions in Rawls's inconstant adherence to his "grave risks" assumption in ordering his principles and in his refusal to extend his discussion of moral arbitrariness to differences in people's capacities to use resources. Exceedingly different accounts of rights would result if one resolved these issues differently than he does. In any case, the early Rawls does not make a convincing case that they would be dealt with as he does in the original position, and the later Rawls does not show that his principles, internally contradictory or not, would command an overlapping consensus as we have seen. We also saw in Chapter 5 that others who write in the contractarian idiom, such as Buchanan and Tullock, Nozick, and Dworkin are no more successful at dealing with these issues.

The anti-Enlightenment move is profoundly unsatisfactory with respect to individual rights. Burke's argument is a caution against making things worse by trying to make them better, and he reasonably reminds us that changing our political institutions has an inescapable dimension of rebuilding a ship at sea. Well taken as his admonitions against vanguardism undoubtedly are, ships sometimes rot and decay, and they can sometimes be improved upon. That a system of institutions has endured may create a presumption in favor of its legitimacy, but it is a rebuttable one. Standards immanent in inherited languages and practices can provide tools for criticizing them, but our engagement with the various postmodern and communitarian schools of thought in §6.6 revealed that they may often leave objectionable practices unscathed, and that in any case immanent criticism need not press inherited practices to evolve in better directions. In contrast, the democratic approach creates an impetus to reform inherited practices as they are reproduced into the future: Minimizing the domination they can foster by pressing for decision-making in accordance with the principle of affected interest and opening up avenues for meaningful opposition. When it operates well, democratization leads to a world in which collective practices achieve, and deserve, increasing legitimacy.

Last, but by no means least important, the democratic tradition offers fruitful resources to manage the potential tensions between the Enlightenment commitments to the pursuit of truth through science and the centrality of individual rights. Certainly there are interpretations of these values that would not lead us to this conclusion. In particular, claims deriving from the post-Arrovian literature on cycles might be thought to suggest that democracy leads to results that not only tyrannize the individual, but are, in scientific terms, irrational. Leaving the empirical likelihood of cycles to one side, we have seen that this conception of irrationality appeals to an absolutist conception of right answers in politics that is a cousin of the early Enlightenment's absolutist idea of truth. The idea of political stability presupposed by this view would foster neither individual freedom nor the pursuit of truth in collective life. Both values are better served by the structured instability of power relations that proponents of democracy seek to institutionalize. Democracy is a system in which those who are disadvantaged by present arrangements have both the incentive and the resources to point to the defects of those arrangements, show how the truth about them is being obscured, and try to get those arrangements changed. In a world in which those contending for power must appeal to the human interest in knowing and acting on the truth, there will always be those who try to twist the truth to their purposes, thereby taking advantage of others. Democratic competition for power as I have described it here is the best available response to this state of affairs. It is, however, better thought of as essential medicine for a chronic malady than as a cure that will ever render the treatment redundant.

Introduction

1. For discussion of Eichmann's claim that his actions were legitimate, see Hannah Arendt, *Eichmann in Jerusalem* (New York: Penguin Books, 1963).

2. Charles Taylor, *Sources of the Self: The Making of Modern Identity* (Cambridge, Mass.: Harvard University Press, 1992).

Chapter 1: Enlightenment Politics

1. Perhaps the best general study of the Enlightenment is Jonathan Israel's *Radical Enlightenment: Philosophy and the Making of Modernity, 1650–1750* (Oxford: Oxford University Press, 2001).

2. René Descartes, *Discourse on the Method* (Notre Dame: University of Notre Dame Press, 1994 [1637]), p. 53.

3. Immanuel Kant, *The Critique of Pure Reason* (London: Macmillan, 1976 [1781]), p. 17.

4. Francis Bacon, *Selected Philosophical Works* (Indianapolis: Hackett Publishing, 1999), p. xv.

5. Kant, *The Critique of Pure Reason*, p. 48.

6. See W. V. Quine, "Two dogmas of empiricism," in W. V. Quine, *From a Logical Point of View: Logico-Philosophical Essays* (New York: Harper Torchbooks, 1953), pp. 20–46.

7. Thomas Hobbes, *De Homine* (New York: Anchor, 1972 [1658]), p. 42.

8. Thomas Hobbes, *The English Works of Thomas Hobbes* (London: John Bohn, 1966) VII pp. 183–84.

9. Thomas Hobbes, *Leviathan* (London: Pelican Books, 1968 [1651]), p. 83.

10. John Locke, *Two Treatises of Government*, ed. Peter Laslett (Cambridge: Cambridge University Press, 1988), pp. 306, 358. For discussion see Patrick Riley, *Will and Political Legitimacy* (Cambridge, Mass.: Harvard University Press), pp. 61–97. See also Ian Shapiro, *The Evolution of Rights in Liberal Theory* (New York: Cambridge University Press, 1986), pp. 100–18.

11. See T. J. Hochstrasser, *Natural Law Theories in the Early Enlightenment* (Cambridge: Cambridge University Press, 2001); Ian Hunter, *Rival*

Enlightenments: Civil and Metaphysical Philosophy in Early Modern Germany (Cambridge: Cambridge University Press, 2001); and James Tully, *A Discourse on Property: John Locke and His Adversaries* (Cambridge: Cambridge University Press, 1980).

12. See John Locke, *An Essay Concerning Human Understanding*, ed. Peter Nidditch (Oxford: Clarendon Press, 1975 [1690]) Book II, Chapters 31–32, Book III, Chapter 3, 6. For further discussion, see Tully, *A Discourse on Property*, pp. 9–27; and Ian Shapiro, *The Evolution of Rights in Liberal Theory*, pp. 109–10.

13. See Carl G. Hempel, *Aspects of Scientific Explanation and Other Essays in the Philosophy of Science* (New York: Free Press, 1965), pp. 298–303, for discussion of Hempel's deductive-nomological model, and see Karl R. Popper, *Conjectures and Refutations: The Growth of Scientific Knowledge* (London: Routledge & Kegan Paul, 1963), pp. 228, 238 for discussion of Popper's falsificationism.

14. J. K. Webb, M. T. Murphy, V. V. Flambaum, V. A. Dzuba, J. D. Barrow, C. W. Churchill, J. X. Prochaska, and A. M. Wolfe, "Further evidence for cosmological evolution of the fine structure constant," *Physical Review Letters* 87 (August 2001): 091301–091601.

15. Alfred J. Ayer, *Language, Truth, and Logic* (Harmondsworth: Penguin Books, 1971 [1936]), p. 29.

16. *Ibid.*, pp. 149–50.

17. Hobbes, *Leviathan*, p. 189.

18. John Locke, *Essays on the Law of Nature*, ed. W. Von Leiden (Oxford: Clarendon Press, 1958 [1660]), p. 111.

19. By following Hobbes and Pufendorf in this formulation of the distinction, Locke was embracing an important departure from the Thomist tradition, rooted in Grotius's revival of the Roman law conception of a right as one's *suum*, a kind of moral power or *facultas* that every man has, and that has its conceptual roots, as Quentin Skinner has established, in the writings of Francisco Suarez and ultimately Jean Gerson and the conciliarist tradition. Quentin Skinner, *The Foundations of Modern Political Thought* (Cambridge: Cambridge University Press, 1978), vol. 2, pp. 117, 176–78. See also Richard Tuck, *Natural Rights Theories* (Cambridge: Cambridge University Press, 1979); and John Finnis, *Natural Law and Natural Right* (Oxford: Clarendon Press, 1980), pp. 207–208.

20. Locke, *Essays on the Law of Nature*, pp. 111, 187.

21. John Locke, *Two Treatises of Government*, p. 271. For further discussion see Tully, *A Discourse on Property*, pp. 35–38; and John Dunn, *The Political Thought of John Locke* (Cambridge: Cambridge University Press, 1969), p. 95.

22. See John Locke, *An Essay Concerning Human Understanding*, Book II, Chapter 27 and Book I, Chapter 30. See also Tully, *A Discourse on Property*, pp. 108–10, 121.

23. Hobbes, *Leviathan*, pp. 268–70.

24. John Locke, *Two Treatises of Government*, p. 173. For further analysis, see Richard Ashcraft, *Locke's Two Treatises of Government* (London: Allen & Unwin, 1986), Chapter 3.

Chapter 2: Classical Utilitarianism

1. Jeremy Bentham, *An Introduction to the Principles of Morals and Legislation* (New York: Hafner Publishing Co., 1948 [1789]), p. 1. All italics in quotations follow the original.

2. *Ibid.*, pp. 126–27.

3. Hence Engels's famous comment to the effect that under genuine socialism "the government of persons is replaced by the administration of things." See Frederick Engels, *Anti-Dühring* (Moscow: Foreign Language Publishing House, 1959 [1878]), p. 387.

4. Jeremy Bentham, *Anarchical Fallacies*, reprinted in *The Works of Jeremy Bentham*, published under the superintendence of his executor, John Bowring (Edinburgh: William Tait, 1843), vol. 2, p. 501.

5. *Ibid.*, p. 500.

6. Bentham, *Introduction to Principles of Morals and Legislation*, pp. 4–5.

7. *Ibid.*, p. 9. Bentham might have pointed, in this regard, to the early Christian Circumcelliones who were noted for practicing suicide to eliminate the risk that they would sin and suffer eternal damnation as a result. It was thought particularly good to provoke an infidel to martyr you or to adopt austerities that would lead to your death, but in the last resort other means were acceptable. See G. Steven Neeley, *The Constitutional Right to Suicide: A Legal and Philosophical Examination* (New York: Peter Lang, 1994), p. 40.

8. Darwin's *Origin of the Species* was first published in 1859.

9. Bentham, *Introduction to the Principles of Morals and Legislation*, p. 27.

10. *Ibid.*, p. 4.

11. Bentham, *The Psychology of Economic Man*, reprinted in W. Stark, ed., *Jeremy Bentham's Economic Writings*, vol. 3 (London: George Allen & Unwin, 1954), p. 422. This title is supplied by Stark to a collection of Bentham's writings that had an influence on subsequent economic psychology.

12. *Ibid.*, p. 421.

13. Jeremy Bentham, *Principles of the Civil Code*, reprinted in *The Works of Jeremy Bentham*, vol. 1, p. 301.

14. *Ibid.*, p. 308.

15. For further discussion of Bentham's emphasis on law's fundamental purpose as providing security, see Nancy Rosenblum, *Bentham's Theory of the Modern State* (Cambridge, Mass.: Harvard University Press, 1978), p. 53.

16. Bentham, *Psychology of Economic Man*, p. 429.

17. Public goods are goods, such as clean air or national defense, that by

their nature require joint supply and from which it is impossible to exclude some members of the group. As a result, they are vulnerable to free riders. For a general discussion of free riding, see Mancur Olson, *The Logic of Collective Action* (Cambridge, Mass.: Harvard University Press, 1971), pp. 1-3, 64-65, 125-26.

18. Bentham, *Psychology of Economic Man*, p. 431.

19. Charles L. Stevenson, *Ethics and Language* (New Haven: Yale University Press, 1944), p. 275. Hume is, of course, more famous for his insistence that it is impossible to derive an "ought" from an "is." See David Hume, *A Treatise on Human Nature* (New York: Everyman, 1974 [1739]), vol. 2, pp. 177-78. However, it is precisely because Hume assumed psychology is substantially alike for everyone that his view of the fact/value gap did not seem threatening to his ability to reach conclusions about what justice requires and what is in the general interest of society. See Alasdair MacIntyre, "Hume on 'is' and 'ought,'" in Vere C. Chappell, ed., *Hume* (London: Macmillan, 1966), pp. 240-64; Geoffrey Hunter, "Hume on *is* and *ought*," *Philosophy* vol. 37 (1962), pp. 148-52; the exchange between Hunter and Anthony Flew in Chappell, *Hume*, pp. 278-94; and W. D. Hudson, "Hume on *is* and *ought*," *ibid.*, pp. 295-307.

20. Bentham, *Psychology of Economic Man*, p. 425.

21. Bentham, *Introduction to the Principles of Morals and Legislation*, pp. 29-32. He also believed "fecundity," or the likelihood that the pleasure or pain resulting from an act would be followed by similar pleasure or pain in the future, could be calculated, as could its "purity," the chance of its "*not* being followed by sensations of the *opposite* kind: that is, pains, if it be pleasure: pleasures, if it be a pain." These last two features "are, in strictness scarcely to be deemed properties of the pleasure or the pain itself; they are not, therefore, in strictness to be taken into account of the value of that pleasure or that pain." *Ibid.*, p. 30.

22. Bentham, *Psychology of Economic Man*, p. 443.

23. *Ibid.*, pp. 152-54.

24. Bentham, *The Philosophy of Economic Science*, reprinted in Stark, *Jeremy Bentham's Economic Writings*, vol. 1, p. 118. This title is supplied by Stark to a collection of Bentham's writings that had an influence on subsequent political economy.

25. *Ibid.*, p. 117.

26. Bentham, *Psychology of Economic Man*, p. 438.

27. Bentham, *Philosophy of Economic Science*, p. 117.

28. Thus Richard Posner notes that if a minority group was "so hated that their extermination would increase the total happiness of the society, the consistent utilitarian would find it hard to denounce their extermination." *The Economics of Justice* (Cambridge, Mass.: Harvard University Press, 1981),

p. 58. Posner's own theory involves the maximization of wealth rather than utility and rules out interpersonal comparisons, so it avoids this difficulty. It does not, however, avoid the difficulty that disabled people who contribute nothing to the production of wealth should on his account be permitted to starve to death. *Ibid.*, pp. 60–87. Generally, see Alan Donagan, "Is there a credible form of utilitarianism?" in *Contemporary Utilitarianism*, ed. by Michael Bayes (Garden City, N.Y.: Anchor Books, 1968), pp. 187–202.

29. Robert Nozick, *Anarchy, State and Utopia* (New York: Basic Books, 1974), pp. 42–45.

30. Aldous Huxley, *Brave New World* (New York: Harper, 1946 [1932]).

31. Bentham, *Philosophy of Economic Science*, p. 113.

32. *Ibid.*, p. 115.

33. *Ibid.*, p. 114.

34. Elie Halévy, *The Growth of Philosophic Radicalism* (Bath, England: Faber & Faber, 1972 [1928]), p. 254.

35. Jeremy Bentham, *Resolutions on Parliamentary Reform*, printed in *The Works of Jeremy Bentham*, vol. 10, pp. 495–97.

36. For the story of Bentham's gradual political radicalization, as well as his eventual break with demagogic revolutionaries such as William Cobbett and Henry Hunt, see Halévy, *Growth of Philosophic Radicalism*, pp. 251–64.

37. Bentham, *Philosophy of Economic Science*, pp. 115–16.

38. Bentham, *Psychology of Economic Man*, p. 442n.

39. *Ibid.*, p. 442.

40. *Ibid.*, p. 443n.

41. See Ian Shapiro, *Democracy's Place* (Ithaca, N.Y.: Cornell University Press, 1996), pp. 197–204.

42. See Joseph A. Pechman, *Federal Tax Policy* (Washington: Brookings Institute, 1971), p. 255. The peak tax years in the United States occurred from 1944–1945, in which the highest tax bracket paid a maximum of 94 percent of their adjusted gross income. Also see Alan Peacock and Jack Wiseman, *The Growth of Public Expenditures in the United Kingdom* (Princeton: Princeton University Press, 1961), Chapter 1. Peacock and Wiseman note that the public is more receptive to the idea of higher taxation during wars or other social disturbances. Approximately 32 percent of World War II expenditures in the United Kingdom were financed by taxation, resulting in a tax level that was 3.4 times higher in 1946 than it was in 1939.

43. Notice that this logic does not apply to every specific good. As is obviously the case with consuming aspirin or alcohol, beyond some threshold the good becomes an evil. It is because money can always be exchanged for other goods that saturation and negative effects can be staved off through exchange, perhaps indefinitely.

44. Halévy, *Growth of Philosophic Radicalism*, p. 264.

45. See Jean-Jacques Rousseau, *The Social Contract and Discourses* (New York: Hafner Publishing, 1947 [1762]), pp. 26–27. For Madison's description of factions, which is found in *Federalist #10*, see James Madison, Alexander Hamilton, and John Jay, *The Federalist Papers* (London: Penguin Books, 1987), pp. 122–28.

46. This follows from the logic of the divide-a-dollar game. If three people vote self-interestedly on how to divide up a dollar under conditions of majority rule, no matter what the status quo there is always a potential majority to overturn it in favor of some new distribution. This result is perfectly general. See Dennis Mueller, *Public Choice* (Cambridge: Cambridge University Press, 1979), pp. 19–31, for elaboration. Given this potential for perpetual instability, it is remarkable how stable tax regimes are in democracies over time. See Joseph Pechman, *Who Paid the Taxes, 1966–85?* (Washington: Brookings Institute, 1985), pp. 3–10; and Sven Steinmo, *Taxation and Democracy* (New Haven: Yale University Press, 1993).

47. Rosenblum, *Bentham's Theory of the Modern State*, pp. 152, 120.

48. Halévy, *Growth of Philosophic Radicalism*, p. 264.

Chapter 3: Synthesizing Rights and Utility

1. This weakness of classical utilitarianism is most forcefully articulated by John Rawls in relation to Henry Sidgwick's version of the doctrine. See John Rawls, *A Theory of Justice* (Cambridge: Belknap Press, 1971), pp. 183–92.

2. Vilfredo Pareto, *Manual of Political Economy* (New York: Augustus Kelley, 1971 [1909]), pp. 1–2.

3. *Ibid.*, pp. 104–105.

4. *Ibid.*, p. 48.

5. *Ibid.*, p. 49.

6. Mark Blaug, *Economic Theory in Retrospect*, third ed. (Cambridge: Cambridge University Press, 1978), p. 618.

7. Pareto, *Manual of Political Economy*, p. 39.

8. *Ibid.*, p. 111.

9. See, for example, G. E. Moore's argument that the utilitarian identification of happiness with pleasure involved a version of the genetic fallacy in George Edward Moore, *Principia Ethica* (Cambridge: Cambridge University Press, 1960 [1903]), pp. 59–109.

10. Pareto, *Manual of Political Economy*, p. 13.

11. *Ibid.*, p. 38.

12. *Ibid.*, p. 10.

13. *Ibid.*, p. 8.

14. *Ibid.*, p. 9.

15. *Ibid.*, p. 11.

16. Pareto did admit the existence of exceptions, such as building a collection or the behavior of a "miser." See *ibid.*, p. 193. In general, however, like all the classical and neoclassical theorists, he assumed that diminishing marginal utility holds enough of the time that it does better as an assumption than alternative view of the matter.

17. See Dennis C. Mueller, *Public Choice* (Cambridge: Cambridge University Press, 1979), pp. 189–94 for explication of the concept of transitivity.

18. Pareto, *Manual of Political Economy*, p. 105.

19. *Ibid.*, pp. 113, 10.

20. For more elaborate explication of these basic Paretian concepts, see Charles E. Ferguson and John P. Gould, *Microeconomic Theory* (Homewood, Ill.: R. D. Irwin, 1975), chapters 1 and 15.

21. Note that the axes in figure 3.2 represent the utilities of A and B, not their holdings of bread and wine.

22. Sometimes a strong version of Pareto-superiority, requiring that everyone be made better off, is distinguished from the weaker version discussed in the text, which requires only that no one be made worse off. Assuming point x in figure 3.2 to be the status quo, on the strong interpretation we would say that the entire class of Pareto-superior changes lies to the north-east of x, whereas the weak interpretation would also include points to the northeast of x that fall on the lines mn and st.

23. For his general disclaimer, see the *Manual of Political Economy*, pp. 1–2. It is clear, however, from his chapter on population that Pareto was skeptical, from a social Darwinist perspective, of the long-term benefits of humanitarian-inspired redistribution from the strong to the weak, which would tend to preserve society's "inferior elements." Thus, alcoholism "is a powerful agent of selection and causes the disappearance of individuals and races who do not know how to resist it. . . . Tuberculosis is also a powerful means of selection, since only a small number of the strong are affected, while it destroys a very large number of the weak." *Ibid.*, pp. 288–89.

24. Peter Singer, *Practical Ethics*, second ed. (New York: Cambridge University Press, 1993), pp. 182–88. This is not to mention the issue of nonhuman utility, and the demands it might legitimately make on us on an objective utilitarian account. See *ibid.*, pp. 63–68, 134.

25. See the scathing essay in which Mill argues that despite Bentham's impressive philosophical acumen, he was hampered by a hopelessly superficial grasp of human motivation. "How much of human nature slumbered in him he knew not, nor can we know. . . . Knowing so little of human feelings, he knew still less of the influences by which those feelings are formed: all the more subtle workings both of the mind upon itself, and of external things upon the mind, escaped him; and no one, probably, who in a highly instructed age, ever attempted to give a rule to all human conduct, set

out with a more limited conception either of the agencies by which human conduct *is*, or those by which it *should* be, influenced." John Stuart Mill, *Mill on Bentham and Coleridge*, ed. by F. R. Leavis (Cambridge: Cambridge University Press, 1980 [1950]), p. 63.

26. John Stuart Mill, *On Liberty* (Indianapolis: Hackett, 1978 [1859]), p. 9.

27. *Ibid.*, p. 54.

28. *Ibid.*, pp. 55–56.

29. *Ibid.*, p. 55.

30. *Ibid.*, p. 62.

31. John Stuart Mill, *Representative Government*, reprinted in Mill, *Three Essays* (Oxford: Oxford University Press, 1975), pp. 284–85.

32. Mill, *On Liberty*, p. 10.

33. *Ibid.*, p. 50.

34. *Ibid.*, p. 70.

35. *Ibid.*, pp. 38–39.

36. *Ibid.*, pp. 93–94.

37. *Ibid.*, p. 94.

38. *Ibid.*, p. 94.

39. *Ibid.*, p. 4. See Alexis de Tocqueville, *Democracy in America* (New York: Anchor Doubleday, 1966 [1832]), pp. 250–76.

40. Mill, *On Liberty*, p. 4.

41. *Ibid.*, p. 73.

42. On the distinction between act- and rule-utilitarianism see D. H. Hodgson, *Consequences of Utilitarianism* (Oxford: Clarendon Press, 1967), pp. 1–8.

43. A lucid account of the harm principle's logic can be found in Joel Feinberg, *Social Philosophy* (Englewood Cliffs, N.J.: Prentice Hall, 1973), pp. 25–54.

44. In Anglo-American legal systems a tort is generally understood to be a civil harm or injury, other than a breach of contract, for which courts provide remedies—usually in the form of damages. The term derives from the Latin *torquere*, to twist, or *tortus*, twisted or wrested aside. See *Black's Law Dictionary*, fifth edition (St. Paul, Minn.: West Publishing Co., 1983), p. 774.

45. Joseph Hamburger points out in *John Stuart Mill on Liberty and Control* (Princeton: Princeton University Press, 1999) that, considering his oeuvre as a whole, Mill in fact favored significant quantities of social control.

46. Mill, *On Liberty*, p. 53.

47. *Ibid.*, p. 9.

48. *Ibid.*, pp. 79–80.

49. We are concerned here with harmful or "negative" externalities, though Pigou was well aware that there could also be beneficial or "positive" externalities to actions in many circumstances. See A. C. Pigou, *The Economics of Welfare*, fourth edition (London: Macmillan, 1948), pp. 167–203.

50. Mill, *On Liberty*, 89–90, 87–89. Mill insists that fornication or gambling must be tolerated for similar reasons, though he equivocates about whether one is "free to be a pimp" or to "keep a gambling house," acknowledging that there are good arguments on both sides of the issue. *Ibid.*, p. 98.

51. *Ibid.*, pp. 79–88.

52. *Ibid.*, p. 87.

53. *Ibid.*, p. 80.

54. It might be said that there are exceptions to this, such as drunk driving, where the capacity to form the relevant malevolent intent is impaired. But this type of exception proves the rule in the sense that common knowledge of the fact that drunk driving can be harmful permits constructive intent. Even if you were so drunk that you cannot remember getting into your car before you ran someone over, if you put yourself into a situation where you are going to drive after drinking we impute the relevant intention to you.

55. See Guido Calabresi, *The Costs of Accidents: A Legal and Economic Analysis* (New Haven: Yale University Press, 1970), pp. 24–31.

56. We have seen a move of this kind away from negligence and toward strict liability in the United States since the 1970s. See *ibid.*, pp. 13–14, and, for a synoptic overview, Guido Calabresi and A. Douglas Melamed, "Property rules, liability rules and inalienability: One view of the cathedral," *Harvard Law Review*, vol. 85 (April 1972), pp. 1089–1128.

57. See Calabresi, "Optimal deterrence and accidents," *Yale Law Journal*, vol. 84, pp. 656–71.

58. Earl Warren was Chief Justice from 1953 to 1969; Warren E. Burger from 1969 to 1986, when William Rehnquist was elevated to that rank by Ronald Reagan.

59. *Green v. County School Board*, 391 U.S. 430 (1968); *Swann v. Charlotte Mecklenburg Board of Education*, 402 U.S. 1 (1971).

60. *Freeman v. Pitts*, 503 U.S. 467 (1992); *Missouri v. Jenkins*, 495 U.S. 33 (1990).

61. *Griggs v. Duke Power Co.*, 401 U.S. 424 (1971); *Washington v. Davis*, 426 U.S. 229 (1976) at 240; also see *Alexander v. Sandoval*, 121 S. Ct. 1511 (2001), in which the Court ruled that there is no private right of action to enforce disparate-impact regulations promulgated under Title VI of the 1964 Civil Rights Act. Henceforth a cause of action can only be initiated to enforce the ban on intentional discrimination as specified by Section 601 of Title VI. Disparate impact claims remain viable under Title VII, however.

62. See *Mobile v. Bolden*, 446 U.S. 55 (1980), *City of Rome v. United States*, 446 U.S. 156 (1980), *Rogers v. Lodge*, 458 U.S. 613 (1982). The revised statute, Section 2 of the Voting Rights Act of 1965 as amended June 29, 1982, was upheld by the Court in *Thornburg v. Gingles*, 478 U.S. 30 (1986).

63. See Brian Barry, *Political Argument* (London: Routledge and Kegan

Paul, 1965), pp. 237–59. Douglas W. Rae, "Decision-rules and individual values in Constitutional choice," *American Political Science Review*, vol. 63, no. 1 (1969), pp. 40–46, 51; and "The limits of consensual decision," *American Political Science Review*, vol. 69, no. 4 (1975), pp. 1270–94.

64. As Hamburger notes, Mill felt compelled to obscure his anti-religious and anti-Christian opinions throughout his life for fear not only of compromising his social standing, but his chances of being read and taken seriously. *Mill on Liberty and Control*, pp. 55–85.

65. For a more extensive discussion of Mill's failure to marry individual autonomy with a determinist view of science, see Alan Ryan, *The Philosophy of John Stuart Mill* (London: Macmillan, 1970), pp. 103–31.

Chapter 4: Marxism

1. See Graeme Duncan, *Marx and Mill: Two Views of Social Conflict and Social Harmony* (Cambridge: Cambridge University Press, 1973).

2. Karl Marx and Frederick Engels, *The Communist Manifesto* (New York: Monthly Review Press, 1964 [1848]), pp. 39, 25–26.

3. V. I. Lenin, *State and Revolution* (New York: International Publishers, 1943 [1918]), pp. 23–24.

4. Karl Marx, *Theses on Feuerbach*, reprinted in Karl Marx and Frederick Engels, *Selected Works* (Moscow: Progress Publishers, 1969), vol. I, p. 13.

5. See Ernest Mandel, *Late Capitalism* (London: New Left Books, 1975).

6. This term refers to a group of European intellectuals led by Theodor Adorno (1903–1969), Herbert Marcuse (1898–1979), and Max Horkheimer (1895–1973), who left Europe to escape Hitler, and founded the New School for Social Research in New York in 1933. Jürgen Habermas, born in 1929, is generally seen as their contemporary heir.

7. For a vivid description of Marxist ideas on the architects of the British Labour Party in the early twentieth century, see Michael Foot, *Aneurin Bevan, A Biography, 1897–1960* (New York: Athenum, 1963).

8. Hence the statement at the start of *Capital* that the capitalist system "appears as" an immense collection of commodities, setting up his claim that these appearances conceal a different reality. See Karl Marx, *Capital: A Critique of Political Economy*, Vol. 1, Ernest Mandel, ed. (Harmondsworth, England: Penguin Books, 1976), p. 125.

9. Karl Marx and Frederick Engels, *The German Ideology*, Part I, C. J. Arthur, ed. (New York: International Publishers, 1970 [1845–46]), p. 42.

10. This labeling was not Hegel's. First deployed by Johann Gottlieb Fichte (1762–1814) to explain the structure of Hegel's dialectical reasoning in the *Phenomenology* and elsewhere, it was Marx's attribution of the thesis-antithesis-synthesis formula to Hegel in *The Poverty of Philosophy* that seems to have caused it to stick. See Walter Kaufmann, *Hegel: Reinterpretation, Texts,*

and Commentary (Garden City, N.Y.: Doubleday, 1965), pp. 165–75; and G. E. Muller, "The Hegel legend of thesis-antithesis-synthesis," *Journal of the History of Ideas*, vol. 19, no. 3 (1958), pp. 411–14.

11. Marx and Engels, *Communist Manifesto* (New York: Monthly Review Press, 1964 [1848]), p. 2.

12. Marx and Engels, *German Ideology*, Part I, p. 57.

13. Karl Marx, *Address of the Central Committee to the Communist League* (1850), reprinted in Robert C. Tucker, ed., *The Marx-Engels Reader* (New York: Norton, 1978), p. 506; Marx and Engels, *Communist Manifesto*, p. 24.

14. As Engels points out in *The Origin of the Family, Private Property, and the State* (New York: International Publishers, 1972 [1884]), the division of labor begins in a rudimentary form within the family. Marx took occasional note of this fact, e.g., in *The German Ideology*, part I, pp. 44, 51–53, but the division of labor among the sexes never entered seriously into his analysis of exploitation under capitalism, rendering the theory vulnerable to the feminist critique discussed in §4.2.3.

15. Adam Smith, *An Inquiry into the Nature and Causes of the Wealth of Nations*, Edwin Cannan, ed. (Chicago: University of Chicago Press, 1976 [1776]), pp. 7–9.

16. Marx and Engels, *German Ideology*, part I, pp. 82, 85, 94.

17. *Ibid.*, p. 54. "The social power i.e. the multiplied productive force . . . appears to these individuals . . . not as their own united power, but as an alien force existing outside of them, of origin and goal of which they are ignorant, which they thus cannot control, which on the contrary passes through a particular series of phases and stages independent of the will and action of man, nay even being the prime governor of these."

18. Marx and Engels, *Communist Manifesto*, p. 22.

19. Karl Marx, *Critique of the Gotha Programme* (Peking: Foreign Languages Publishers, 1972 [1875]), pp. 12–16.

20. *Ibid.*, p. 17.

21. *Ibid.*, pp. 8, 10.

22. *Ibid.*, p. 10.

23. Marx, *A Contribution to the Critique of Political Economy*, pp. 20–21.

24. Karl Marx, *The Eighteenth Brumaire of Louis Bonaparte* (New York: International Publishers, 1963 [1852]), p. 15.

25. These formulations come from Louis Althusser, *For Marx* (London: Verso, 1979). See also Nicos Poulantzas, *Classes in Contemporary Capitalism* (London: Verso, 1979). For an analytical reconstruction of the materialist conception of history, see G. A. Cohen, *Karl Marx's Theory of History: A Defense* (Princeton: Princeton University Press, 1978).

26. See, for example, Alasdair MacIntyre, *After Virtue* (Notre Dame, Indiana: University of Notre Dame Press, 1984), pp. 88–108.

27. Generally, see the discussions of partial and segmented universalism in

Donald Green and Ian Shapiro, *Pathologies of Rational Choice Theory* (New Haven, Conn.: Yale University Press, 1994), pp. 26–28, 192–93.

28. See *ibid.*, especially chapter 8, as well as Green and Shapiro, "Pathologies revisited: Reflections on our critics," in Jeffrey Friedman, ed., *The Rational Choice Controversy: Economic Models of Politics Reconsidered* (New Haven, Conn.: Yale University Press), pp. 235–76.

29. Rousseau, *The Social Contract*, p. 64.

30. On Marx's methodological individualism, see Jon Elster, *Making Sense of Marx* (New York: Cambridge University Press, 1985).

31. Marx and Engels, *The German Ideology*, Part 1, p. 53.

32. Marx and Engels, *The Communist Manifesto*, p. 41.

33. Isaiah Berlin, "Two concepts of liberty," in his *Four Essays on Liberty* (London: Oxford University Press, 1969), pp. 118–72.

34. Arguments between negative and positive libertarians can thus sometimes reduce to semantic disputes over whether a prisoner is unfree because of the presence of chains or the absence of a key. See Gerald C. MacCallum, "Negative and positive freedom," in Peter Laslett, W. G. Runciman, and Quentin Skinner, eds., *Philosophy, Politics, and Society*, fourth series (Oxford: Blackwell, 1972), pp. 174–93.

35. Anatole France, *Le Lys Rouge* (Paris: Calmann-Lévy, 1923 ed. [c. 1895]), p. 113.

36. Niccolò Machiavelli, *The Discourses* (London: Routledge & Kegan Paul, 1950 [1517]) § I.5, p. 220–22.

37. For further discussion of the labor theories of value embraced by Petty and Hobbes, see Shapiro, *Evolution of Rights in Liberal Theory*, pp. 35–38.

38. The best general treatment of this subject is Maurice Dobb, *Theories of Value and Distribution Since Adam Smith* (Cambridge: Cambridge University Press, 1973).

39. Thus Marx often writes of prices varying in response to fluctuations in supply and demand, as in chapter three of *Wage, Labor, and Capital* (New York: International Publishers, 1978 [1849]).

40. Marx, *Capital*, vol. 1, pp. 129, 131.

41. Marx, *Capital*, vol. 1, pp. 781–793.

42. Marx, *Capital*, vol. 1, p. 275. See also pp. 701–706.

43. See Marx, *Capital*, vol. 1, pp. 389–410. The Ten Hours Bill was part of the 1847 Factory Act in England. See R. W. Cooke-Taylor, *The Factory System and the Factory Acts* (London: Methuen & Co., 1894).

44. See Lenin, *Imperialism: The Highest Stage of Capitalism* (New York: International Publishers, 1939 [1916]); and Samir Amin, *Accumulation on a World Scale: A Critique of the Theory of Underdevelopment* (New York: Monthly Review, 1974).

45. Marx, *Capital*, vol. 1, pp. 227–31.

46. Marx and Engels, *Communist Manifesto*, pp. 11–13. See also Marx's

discussion of capitalist overproduction in the course of his critique of Ricardo in Karl Marx, *Theories of Surplus Value*, vol. 2 (London: Lawrence & Wishart, 1969 [1861-63]), pp. 499-535.

47. Marx, *Capital*, vol. II, p. 250.

48. Marx and Engels, *Communist Manifesto*, p. 5. For his more general discussion of the limitations of bourgeois rights, see Marx, *On the Jewish Question* (1844) reprinted in Karl Marx and Frederick Engels, *Collected Works*, vol. 3 (London: Lawrence and Wisehart, 1975), pp. 146-74.

49. See David Gordon, Richard Edwards, and Michael Reich, "Long swings and stages of capitalism," in David Kotz, Terrence McDonough, and Michael Reich, eds., *Social Structures of Accumulation: The Political Economy of Growth and Crisis* (Cambridge: Cambridge University Press, 1994), pp. 11-28; David Kotz, "Interpreting the social structure of accumulation theory," *ibid.*, pp. 50-69; and Terrence McDonough, "Social structures of accumulation, contingent history, and stages of capitalism," *ibid.*, pp. 72-84.

50. See Ralph Miliband, *The State in Capitalist Society* (New York: Basic Books, 1974).

51. Marx and Engels, *Communist Manifesto*, p. 62.

52. See Robert Frank, *Choosing the Right Pond: Human Behavior and the Quest for Status* (New York: Oxford University Press, 1985), pp. 39-107.

53. Generally, see Jonathan Kelley and M. D. R. Evans, "Class and class conflict in six Western nations," *American Sociological Review*, vol. 60 (April, 1995), pp. 157-78. On availability heuristics, see Amos Tversky and Daniel Kahneman, "The framing of decisions and the rationality of choice," *Science* No. 211 (1981), pp. 543-58; Daniel Kahneman, Paul Stovic, and Amos Tversky, *Judgment Under Uncertainty* (Cambridge: Cambridge University Press, 1982).

54. For the classic statement see W. G. Runciman, *Relative Deprivation and Social Justice* (London: Routledge & Kegan Paul, 1996), pp. 3-52. For a recent discussion of the evidence, arguing that physical proximity is an important variable in mobilizing, see Damarys Canache, "Looking out of my back door: The neighborhood context and the perceptions of relative deprivation," *Political Research Quarterly*, vol. 49, no. 3 (September 1996), pp. 547-71.

55. Kelley and Evans, "Class and class conflict in six Western nations," pp. 174-75.

56. M. D. R. Evans, Jonathan Kelley, and Tamas Kolosi, "Images of class: Public perceptions in Hungary and Australia," *American Sociological Review*, vol. 57 (1992), pp. 461-82; Robert Hodge and Donald Trieman, "Class identification in the United States," *American Journal of Sociology*, vol. 73 (1968), pp. 535-47. See also Canache's argument that poor people are more prone to violence if they find themselves in comparatively homogeneous rich neighborhoods where "the contextual evidence of deprivation is most explicit" than in more diverse neighborhoods, even if they are equally wealthy

overall. "Looking out of my back door: The neighborhood context and the perceptions of relative deprivation," pp. 556–57.

57. Pierro Sraffa, *The Production of Commodities by Means of Commodities* (Cambridge: Cambridge University Press, 1960), pp. 3–4, 7–8, 10, 74, 78.

58. See John Roemer, "Should Marxists be interested in exploitation?" *Philosophy and Public Affairs*, vol. 14, no. 1 (Winter 1985), pp. 36–37.

59. See Engels, *Anti-Dühring*, p. 387.

60. See John Roemer, *A Future for Socialism* (Cambridge, Mass.: Harvard University Press, 1994).

61. Locke, *Two Treatises*, I, sec. 53, p. 179, and I, sec. 54, pp. 179–80.

62. *Ibid.*, II, sec. 6, p. 271.

63. Marx, *Capital*, vol. 1, pp. 716, 990, 1003.

64. For discussion of this and related analytical difficulties in Marx's formulation of the labor theory of value, see Roemer, "Should Marxists be interested in exploitation?" pp. 30–65 and G. A. Cohen, "The labor theory of value and the concept of exploitation," *Philosophy and Public Affairs*, vol. 8, no. 4 (Summer 1979), pp. 338–60; and "Freedom, Justice and Capitalism," *New Left Review*, no. 125 (1981), pp. 3–16.

65. See *O'Brien v. O'Brien* 66 NY 2d 576 (1985), in which the Appellate Division of the Supreme Court in the Second Judicial Department of New York upheld a decision that a husband's license to practice medicine was marital property on the grounds that "[t]he contributions of one spouse to the other's profession or career . . . represent investments in the economic partnership of the marriage and the product of the parties' joint efforts. . . ." Thus although New York is not a community property state, the divorcing wife was awarded 40 percent of the estimated value of the license to be paid over eleven years, and the divorcing husband was ordered to maintain a life insurance policy for the unpaid balance of the award, with the divorcing wife as the beneficiary.

66. See Nancy Folbre, "Exploitation comes home: A critique of the Marxian theory of family labor," *Cambridge Journal of Economics*, vol. 6, no. 4, pp. 317–29.

67. For Cohen's account, see "The structure of proletarian unfreedom," in G. A. Cohen, *History, Labour, and Freedom* (Oxford: Clarendon Press, 1988), pp. 255–85. See also Cohen, "The labor theory of value and the concept of exploitation," *Philosophy and Public Affairs*, vol. 8, no. 4 (1979), pp. 338–60.

68. See Douglas Rae, "Knowing power," in Ian Shapiro and Grant Reeher, eds., *Power, Inequality, and Democratic Politics* (Boulder: Westview Press, 1988), pp. 17–49; and "Democratic liberty and tyrannies of place," in Ian Shapiro and Casiano Hacker-Cordón, ed., *Democracy's Edges* (Cambridge: Cambridge University Press, 1999), pp. 165–92; and Clarissa Hayward, *Defacing Power* (Cambridge: Cambridge University Press, 2000), pp. 161–78.

69. See §4.1.2.

Chapter 5: The Social Contract

1. Robert Nozick, *Anarchy, State, and Utopia* (New York: Basic Books, 1974), pp. 150–53.

2. John Rawls, *A Theory of Justice*, second edition (Cambridge, Mass.: Harvard University Press, 1999), pp. 6–7.

3. See Richard Tuck, *Natural Rights Theories: Their Origin and Development* (Cambridge: Cambridge University Press, 1982).

4. See Rawls, *A Theory of Justice*, pp. 19–24, 284–85.

5. Hobbes, *Leviathan*, p. 187. For elaboration, see Shapiro, *Evolution of Rights*, pp. 26–27.

6. Locke, *Two Treatises*, II, sec. 225, p. 415.

7. Aristotle, *The Politics*, Books I and II, trans. Trevor Saunders (Oxford: Clarendon Press, 1995 [c. 350 BC]), 1253a1–39, pp. 3–4.

8. Rousseau, *The First and Second Discourses*, ed. R. D. Masters, trans. J. R. Masters (New York: St. Martin's Press, 1964), p. 129.

9. Nozick, *Anarchy, State, and Utopia*, p. 54.

10. See Locke, *Two Treatises*, II, sec. 95–99, pp. 330–33, sec. 121, p. 349.

11. James Buchanan and Gordon Tullock, *The Calculus of Consent: Logical Foundations of Constitutional Democracy* (Ann Arbor: University of Michigan Press, 1962).

12. See Nozick, *Anarchy, State, and Utopia*, pp. 10–35.

13. See Rawls, *A Theory of Justice*, pp. 18–19, 42–45, 507–508.

14. See Ian Shapiro, "Optimal deliberation?" *The Journal of Political Philosophy* (vol. 10, no. 2, June 2002), p. 197.

15. See Jürgen Habermas, *Communication and the Evolution of Society*, trans. Thomas McCarthy (Boston: Beacon Press, 1979); Jürgen Habermas, *Theory of Communicative Action*, 2 vols., trans. Thomas McCarthy (Boston: Beacon Press, 1984, 1987); and Bruce Ackerman, *Social Justice in the Liberal State* (New Haven, Conn.: Yale University Press, 1980).

16. See Hobbes's discussion of the causes of the English civil war in *Behemoth* [1679], reprinted in *The English Works of Thomas Hobbes* (London: John Bohn, 1966), vol. VI, p. 166.

17. Locke, *Two Treatises*, II, sec. 168, p. 379.

18. Nozick, *Anarchy, State, and Utopia*, pp. 54–87.

19. Hobbes, *Leviathan*, p. 186.

20. See Locke, *Two Treatises*, II, sec. 89, p. 325.

21. See Hobbes, *Leviathan*, pp. 239–51; Locke, *Two Treatises*, II, sec. 132–33, pp. 354–55; and Rousseau, *The Social Contract*, pp. 110–23.

22. Rawls, *A Theory of Justice*, p. 113.

23. Hobbes, *Leviathan*, pp. 129–30, 160–61.

24. See Fyodor Dostoevsky, *The Brothers Karamazov* (Hammondsworth: Penguin, 1958), pp. 35–95.

25. James Tully, *A Discourse Concerning Property: John Locke and His Adversaries* (Cambridge: Cambridge University Press, 1980).

26. Richard Tuck, *Natural Law Theories: Their Origin and Development* (Cambridge: Cambridge University Press, 1979); Quentin Skinner, *The Foundations of Modern Political Thought*, vol. I: *The Renaissance* (Cambridge: Cambridge University Press, 1978); J. G. A. Pocock, *The Ancient Constitution and The Feudal Law* (Cambridge: Cambridge University Press, 1957) and *The Machiavellian Moment* (Princeton: Princeton University Press, 1975); and Otto von Gierke, *Natural Law and the Theory of Society*, 2 vols. (Cambridge: Cambridge University Press, 1934).

27. Hobbes, *Leviathan*, p. 186.

28. See Locke, *Two Treatises*, II, sec. 123–131, pp. 350–53.

29. Nozick, *Anarchy, State, and Utopia*, pp. 9–12, 26–28.

30. See Shapiro, *Evolution of Rights*, pp. 240, 249–51.

31. Rawls, *Political Liberalism* (New York: Columbia University Press, 1993), p. 15.

32. *Ibid.*, pp. 9–11, 133–72. See also Cass Sunstein, "On legal theory and legal practice," in *NOMOS XXXVII: Theory and Practice*, ed. Ian Shapiro and Judith Wagner DeCew (New York: New York University Press, 1995), pp. 267–87.

33. Rawls, *Political Liberalism* pp. 150–58.

34. Rawls, *A Theory of Justice*, pp. 222–23.

35. Richard J. Herrnstein and Charles Murray, *The Bell Curve: Intelligence and Class Structure in American Life* (New York: Free Press, 1994). For a sampling of the subsequent controversy, see Joe Kincheloe, Shirley Steinberg, and Aaron Gresson, eds., *Measured Lies: The Bell Curve Examined* (New York: St. Martin's Press, 1997); Bernie Devlin, Stephen Fienburg, Daniel Resnick, and Kathryn Roeder, eds., *Intelligence, Genes, and Success: Scientists Respond to The Bell Curve* (New York: Copernicus Books, 1997); and Steven Fraser, ed., *The Bell Curve Wars: Race, Intelligence, and the Future of America* (New York: Basic Books, 1995).

36. Rawls, *A Theory of Justice*, p. 63.

37. According to Learned Hand's famous efficiency−based rule in torts, a person should be held liable for an injury done to another only if the cost of taking precautions to prevent the harm is less than the cost of the harm times the probability of the event. Unless this criterion is met, losses should lie where they fall. See *U.S. v. Carroll Towing Co.* (1947).

38. John Harsanyi, "Democracy, equality, and popular consent," in *Power, Inequality, and Democratic Politics*, ed. Ian Shapiro and Grant Reeher (Boulder: Westview, 1988), p. 297.

39. Rawls, *A Theory of Justice*, pp. 21–22, 26–27, 35–36.

40. *Ibid.*, pp. 350–58.

41. For his initial formulation of the general conception see *Ibid.*, p. 53-54. For the final formulation see p. 266.

42. See Douglas Rae, "Maximin justice and an alternative principle of general advantage," *American Political Science Review*, vol. 69, no. 2 (1975), pp. 630-47; and John Harsanyi, "Can the maximin principle serve as a basis for morality? A critique of John Rawls's Theory," *American Political Science Review*, vol. 69, no. 2 (1975), pp. 594-606; as well as my discussion in *Evolution of Rights*, pp. 226-34.

43. Rawls, *A Theory of Justice*, pp. 132-35. Rawls gives additional, and in my view less plausible, reasons for treating the standpoint of the least advantaged as an implicit proxy for the standpoint of all, such as his discussion of "chain connection," a kind of Keynesian assumption according to which improving the condition of those at the bottom will have positive ripple effects for everyone else. See my discussion in Shapiro, *Evolution of Rights*, pp. 225-34.

44. Nozick, *Anarchy, State, and Utopia*, pp. 160-64.

45. See Bruce Kogut, Gerald McDermott, and Andrew Spicer, "Entrepreneurship and privatization in Central Europe: The tenuous balance between destruction and creation," *Academy of Management Review*, vol. 25, no. 3 (July 2000), pp. 630-49; Gerald McDermott, *Embedded Politics: Industrial Networks and Institution Building in Post-Communism* (Ann Arbor: Michigan University Press, 2001).

46. Nozick, *Anarchy, State, and Utopia*, pp. 169-72, 152-55. Nozick further argues that a minimal state, the "nightwatchman state" of classical liberal theory can be justified on the grounds that, although some "independents" would object to it, their forced participation is inevitable because coercive force is a natural monopoly. Those who are forced to become members could in principle be compensated for the unavoidable harm done them; as a result their forced incorporation is legitimate. Ibid., pp. 23-24, 108-118. For discussion of why this argument fails, see my *Evolution of Rights*, pp. 174-78.

47. Nozick, *Anarchy, State, and Utopia*, p. 29.

48. Nozick never actually defends his embrace of self-ownership, except with his opening insistence that "individuals have rights, and there are things no person or group may do to them (without violating their rights)." *Ibid.*, p. ix. His discussion of the presumptive illegitimacy of taxation makes it clear that he means these rights to include ownership of what one produces.

49. For a useful review of this debate, see Ronald Dworkin, "What is equality? Part I: Equality of welfare," *Philosophy and Public Affairs*, vol. 10, no. 3 (Summer 1981), pp. 185-246.

50. Rawls, *A Theory of Justice*, pp. 54-55, 78-81.

51. See, for example, Dworkin, "What is equality? Part II: Equality of resources," *Philosophy and Public Affairs*, vol. 10, no. 4 (Fall 1981), pp. 283-345. For defense of "middle ground" metrics, intermediate between resourcism

and welfarism, see Amartya Sen, "Well-being, agency and freedom," *The Journal of Philosophy*, vol. 82, no. 4 (April 1985), pp. 169–221; Richard Arneson, "Equality and equal opportunity for welfare," *Philosophical Studies*, vol. 56 (1989), pp. 77–93; and G. A. Cohen, "On the currency of egalitarian justice," *Ethics*, vol. 99, no. 4 (July 1989), pp. 906–44.

52. Roemer has shown that this is generally true of resourcist arguments. See Roemer, "Equality of resources implies equality of welfare," *Quarterly Journal of Economics*, vol. 101, no. 4 (1986), pp. 751–84. See also Thomas Scanlon, "Equality of resources and equality of welfare: A forced marriage?" *Ethics*, vol. 97, no. 1 (1986), pp. 111–18.

53. Rawls, *A Theory of Justice*, p. 266.

54. *Ibid.*

55. On gender differences in labor participation and wages, see Claudia Goldin, "The gender gap in historical perspective," in Peter Kilby, ed., *Quantity and Quiddity* (Middletown, Conn.: Wesleyan University Press, 1987), pp. 135–68: and Claudia Goldin, *Understanding the Gender Gap* (New York: Oxford University Press, 1990), pp. 58–118. See also Susan Okin, *Justice, Gender, and the Family*, pp. 144–45.

56. See Shapiro, *Evolution of Rights*, pp. 231–32, 266–70.

57. Locke, *Two Treatises*, II, sec. 27, p. 288.

58. *Ibid.*, sec. 37, p. 298.

59. When a "fundamental" liberty is potentially at risk (usually a freedom protected by the Bill of Rights), American courts subject proposed governmental action to "strict scrutiny." This requires showing that the governmental objective is unusually important, that a "compelling state interest" is at stake. Government is usually also required to show that this objective cannot be accomplished in a less intrusive way. This is contrasted with "intermediate" scrutiny, which requires only the showing of a "substantial relationship" between the proposed policy and an "important government objective," and "minimal scrutiny" which merely requires demonstration of a "rational relationship" to legitimate governmental objectives. These calibrations are meant to be linked not only to the importance of the right in question but also to the magnitude of the injustice to which ameliorative policies are addressed. American courts are not always consistent about this, however. In the affirmative action area, for instance, with a few exceptions that have not been followed, the Court has insisted on strict scrutiny of all race classifications, though since *Craig v. Boren* 429 U.S. 190 (1976) gender classifications have been subject to intermediate scrutiny only, producing the anomaly that affirmative action designed to benefit women is less suspect than that to benefit blacks. Generally, see Laurence H. Tribe, *American Constitutional Law*, 2d ed. (New York: Foundation Press, 1988), pp. 251–75.

60. For elaboration, see Shapiro, *Evolution of Rights*, pp. 218–23.

61. Rawls, *A Theory of Justice*, p. 18.

62. Harsanyi argues powerfully that risk-neutral people would choose utilitarianism rather than maximin in the original position. See J. Harsanyi, "Can the maximin principle serve as a basis for morality? A critique of John Rawls's theory," *American Political Science Review*, vol. 69, no. 2 (June, 1975), pp. 594–606.

63. Wolff's argument is developed in *In Defense of Anarchism* (New York: Harper and Row, 1970). For a critical appraisal of it, see my "Gross concepts in political argument," *Political Theory*, vol. 17, no. 1 (February 1989), pp. 51–76. For discussion of Buchanan and Tullock's hierarchy of principles see their *Calculus of Consent*, pp. 3–97, and, for critical discussion, my *Democracy's Place*, pp. 17–29. Dworkin's view is taken up in §5.5. below. For further evaluation of the empirical assumptions built into Nozick's and Rawls's arguments, see *Evolution of Rights*, pp. 155–95 and 205–51.

64. Dworkin "What Is equality? I," pp. 300–301.

65. Nozick, *Anarchy, State, and Utopia*, pp. 174–75.

66. See Amartya Sen, "Equality of what?" in *The Tanner Lectures on Human Values*, vol. 4, ed. Sterling McMurrin (Salt Lake City: University of Utah Press, 1980), pp. 212–20; and Sen, "Well-being, agency and freedom," *Journal of Philosophy*, vol. 82, no. 4 (April, 1985), pp. 185–221.

67. Rawls's most explicit statement of the view that people must be regarded as responsible for their preferences can be found in "Social unity and primary goods," Amartya Sen and Bernard Williams, eds., *Utilitarianism and Beyond* (Cambridge: Cambridge University Press, 1982), pp. 168–9. For discussion of the tensions between this claim and the argument that differences in capacity are arbitrary, which Rawls defends most fully in *A Theory of Justice* at pp. 101–104, see Thomas Scanlon, "Equality of resources and equality of welfare," pp. 116–17, "The significance of choice," *The Tanner Lectures on Human Values*, vol. 8 (Salt Lake City: University of Utah Press, 1988), pp. 192–201; Arneson, "Equality and equal opportunity for welfare"; and Cohen, "Equality of what?" pp. 7–10.

68. Ronald Dworkin, "What is equality?" part I, pp. 185–246, part II, pp. 283–385. Dworkin's hypothetical auction, described at "What is equality? Part II," pp. 283–90, fails on its own terms as a device for deciding on what could count as an equal initial allocation of resources. For example, in the hypothetical auction Dworkin describes it would be quite possible for some player or players to bid up the price of a good that he or they did not want, but that he or they knew someone else had to have at all costs (such as the available stock of insulin on the island in Dworkin's example, assuming there was one diabetic). In this way the diabetic could be forced either to spend all (or at least a disproportionate quantity) of his initial resources on insulin, thereby making other bundles of goods relatively cheaper for the other inhabitants, or he

might be forced to buy it at an artificially high price from whoever had bought it in the initial auction. As this example illustrates, Dworkin's hypothetical auction assumes that people do not have different strategic resources and powers to bargain, and that they will not have reasons to misrepresent their preferences. But there is no good reason to suppose that either of these assumptions is true, and so no reason to believe that his auction would equalize resources as he claims.

69. *Ibid.*, pp. 300–301.

70. *Ibid.*, pp. 292–304.

71. *Ibid.*, p. 301.

72. See *ibid.*, pp. 300, where he notes in opposition to the idea that there can be a view of "normal" human powers that no amount of initial compensation could make someone born blind or mentally incompetent equal in physical or mental resources with someone taken to be "normal" in these ways.

73. "Someone who is born with a serious handicap faces his life with what we concede to be fewer resources, just on that account, than others do. This justifies compensation, under a scheme devoted to equality of resources, and though the hypothetical insurance market does not right the balance—*nothing can*—it seeks to remedy one aspect of the resulting unfairness." *Ibid.*, p. 302, italics added.

74. *Ibid.*, pp. 311, 288, 302.

75. *Ibid.*, p. 311ff.

76. I am not saying here that people always have the capacities to achieve their ambitions, or even that we cannot develop ambitions which we know we cannot achieve, although I suspect that sustained analysis would reveal part of the difference between an ambition and a fantasy to reside in the fact that an ambition is generally a spur to action in a way that a fantasy need not be. Here I want only to establish that it is not credible to believe that our ambitions are developed independently of our capacities, which Dworkin's categorial distinction requires.

77. Dworkin, "What is equality? II," pp. 302–303ff.

78. Cohen has tried to minimize the extent of such difficulties by suggesting that we should not confuse the true claim that our capacities for effort are "influenced" by factors beyond our control with the false claim that people like Nozick mistakenly attribute to egalitarians like Rawls that those capacities are "determined" by factors beyond our control. Preserving this distinction enables him to say that although not all effort deserves reward, it is not the case that no effort deserves reward, that effort "is partly praiseworthy, partly not," although he concedes that in practice "we cannot separate the parts." Cohen, "Equality of what?" pp. 8–10. As I note below, however, once it is conceded that the very decision to choose to expend effort is influenced by factors that are conceded to be morally arbitrary, the difficulty becomes one of

principle rather than practicality; certainly Cohen offers no account of how that component of effort meriting reward might in principle be singled out.

79. Cohen, "On the currency of egalitarian justice," p. 922.

80. As noted in note 78 above, Cohen does not claim to have resolved these difficulties. I remain skeptical that they can be resolved.

Chapter 6: Anti-Enlightenment Politics

1. See Christopher Hill, *The World Turned Upside Down* (London: Temple Smith, 1972); Malcolm Thomis, *The Luddites: Machine-Breaking in Regency England* (Newton Abbot, England: David & Charles, 1970); George Woodcock, *Pierre-Joseph Proudhon: A Biography* (New York: Black Rose Books, 1987); Christopher Lasch, *The True and Only Heaven: Progress and Its Critics* (New York : Norton, 1991); Thomas Poguntke, *Alternative Politics: the German Green Party* (Edinburgh: Edinburgh University Press, 1993).

2. See the "Biographical Note" in Burke's *Reflections on the Revolution in France* (Harmondsworth: Penguin, 1969), p. 77.

3. *Ibid.*, p. 141.

4. *Ibid.*, p. 119.

5. *Ibid.*, pp. 194−95.

6. *Ibid.*, p. 140.

7. Burke himself had nothing but contempt for Rousseau, whom he saw as vain and unprincipled and whose refusal to acknowledge any unchosen obligations appalled him. Burke would have thought Rousseau merely pathetic had he not been appealed to by the French revolutionaries. See his furious denunciation of Rousseau in the 1791 "Letter to a member of the National Assembly," in *The Works of the Right Honourable Edmund Burke* (London: F. & C. Rivington, 1803), vol. 6, pp. 1−68. It is in the *First Discourse: On the Arts and Sciences*, in Jean-Jacques Rousseau, *The First and Second Discourses*, ed. Roger Masters (New York: St. Martin's Press, 1964 [1750]) that Rousseau's antimodernist sentiments are most fully articulated.

8. Richard Rorty, *Philosophy and the Mirror of Nature* (Princeton, N.J.: Princeton University Press, 1979), pp. 136−64.

9. See Ludwig Wittgenstein, *Philosophical Investigations* (Oxford: Blackwell, 1953).

10. Rorty, *Philosophy and the Mirror of Nature*, p. 136, and "Postmodernist bourgeois liberalism," *The Journal of Philosophy*, vol. 80, no. 10 (1983), pp. 583−89.

11. See my *Political Criticism* (Berkeley: University of California Press, 1990), pp. 36−53; and Richard Rorty, *Achieving Our Country* (Cambridge, Mass.: Harvard University Press, 1998), pp. 27−29, 34−35, 96−97.

12. Rorty, *Achieving Our Country*, p. 96−97.

13. Max Weber, "Science as a vocation," lecture delivered at Munich University in 1918, in H. H. Gerth and C. Wright Mills, *From Max Weber: Essays in Sociology* (New York: Oxford University Press, 1946), pp. 135–36.

14. John Dewey, *Characters and Events: Popular Essays in Social and Political Philosophy* (New York: Henry Holt, 1929), vol. 1, p. iii.

15. John Dewey, *Individualism Old and New* (New York: Capricorn Books, 1962 [1929]), p. 164.

16. On the rise of hostility to rehabilitative views of punishment in the last part of the twentieth century, see Francis A. Allen, *The Borderland of Criminal Justice* (Chicago: University of Chicago Press, 1964). On the role of interest-group lobbying for stiffer sentences, see Edwin Bender, "Private prisons, politics, and profits," National Institute on Money in State Politics (July 2000, *mimeo*), available at *www.followthemoney.org/issues/private_prison/private__prison.html*; and Eric Blumenson and Eva Nilsen, "Policing for profit," *University of Chicago Law Review*, vol. 65 (1998), pp. 35–114. On the relationship between the war on drugs and racial discrimination, see Michael Tonry, *Malign Neglect: Race, Crime, and Punishment in America* (New York: Oxford University Press, 1996); and Mark Mauer, *Race to Incarcerate* (New York: New Press, 1998). On the politicization of crime generally, see Stuart Scheingold, "The politics of street crime and criminal justice," in *Crime, Community, and Public Policy*, ed. Lawrence Joseph (Chicago: University of Illinois Press, 1995), pp. 265–94.

17. Don Herzog, *Without Foundations: Justification in Political Theory* (Ithaca: Cornell University Press, 1985), p. 27.

18. See Peter Winch, *The Idea of a Social Science* (London: Routledge and Kegan Paul, 1958).

19. See J. L. Austin, *Sense and Sensibilia* (New York: Oxford University Press, 1964); and *How to Do Things With Words* (Cambridge, Mass.: Harvard University Press, 1962).

20. See Roy Bhaskar, *A Realist Theory of Science* (Sussex: Harvester and Humanities, 1978); and *The Possibility of Naturalism* (Sussex: Harvester and Humanities, 1979); Richard Miller, *Fact and Method: Explanation, Confirmation and Realism in the Natural and Social Sciences* (Princeton, N.J.: Princeton University Press, 1987); Ian Shapiro and Alexander Wendt, "The difference that realism makes: Social science and the politics of consent," *Politics and Society*, vol. 20, no. 2 (June 1992), pp. 197–224; and Alexander Wendt and Ian Shapiro, "The false promise of realist social theory," in Kristen Monroe ed., *Empirical Political Theory* (Berkeley: University of California Press, 1997), pp. 166–87.

21. Alasdair MacIntyre, *After Virtue*, second edition (Notre Dame: University of Notre Dame Press, 1984), pp. 88–108.

22. See my *Political Criticism*, pp. 232–42, as well as the works cited in note 20 of this chapter for exploration of these differences.

23. Daniel Bell, *The End of Ideology: The Exhaustion of Political Ideas in the Fifties* (Glencoe, Ill.: Free Press, 1960). On the convergence predictions of modernization theory, see Seymour Martin Lipset, *Political Man: The Social Bases of Politics* (Baltimore: Johns Hopkins University Press, 1981 [1960]), pp. 82–83; and David Apter, *The Politics of Modernization* (Chicago: University of Chicago Press, 1965), pp. 313–56. For a recent version of the idea that ideological politics has reached its terminus following communism's collapse, see Francis Fukuyama, *The End of History and the Last Man* (New York: Avon Books, 1993).

24. For one heroic attempt to distill the accumulated wisdom in the literature at the time of the South African transition, see the three-volume study put together by the South African Law Commission, *Report on Constitutional Models* Project 77 (Pretoria: South African Government Printer, 1991).

25. See Donald Green and Ian Shapiro, *Pathologies of Rational Choice Theory: A Critique of Applications in Political Science* (New Haven, Conn.: Yale University Press, 1994); and Jeffrey Friedman, ed., *The Rational Choice Controversy: Economic Models of Politics Reconsidered* (New Haven, Conn.: Yale University Press, 1996).

26. For a series of postmortems on failed election-forecasting models in light of the 2000 U.S. Presidential election, see *P.S.: Political Science and Politics*, vol. 34, no. 1 (March 2001), pp. 9–44.

27. On the application of rational choice models to the study of international relations, see Stephen Walt, "Rigor or rigor mortis?: Rational choice and security studies," *International Security*, vol. 23, no. 4 (Spring 1999), pp. 5–48; and Alexander Wendt, *Social Theory of International Politics* (New York: Cambridge University Press, 1999), pp. 113–38, 313–43. On the difficulties with the correlates of war empirical studies, see Donald Green, Soo Yeon Kim, and David Yoon, "Dirty pool," *International Organization*, vol. 55 (2001), pp. 441–68.

28. Louis Hartz, *The Liberal Tradition in America* (New York: Harcourt Brace & World, 1955).

29. Rogers Smith: *Civic Ideals: Conflicting Visions of Citizenship in U.S. History* (New Haven, Conn.: Yale University Press, 1995).

30. Adam Przeworski, Michael E. Alvarez, Jose Antonio Cheibub, and Fernando Limongi, *Democracy and Development: Political Institutions and Well-being in the World 1950–1990* (New York: Cambridge University Press, 2000), pp. 142–75.

31. Alexis de Tocqueville, *Democracy in America*, ed. J. P. Mayer, trans. George Lawrence (New York: Harper Perennial, 1966 [1832]), pp. 31–47.

32. Seymour Martin Lipset, "Some social requisites of democracy: Economic development and political legitimacy," *American Political Science Review*, vol. 53, 1959, pp. 69–105.

33. Barrington Moore, *The Social Origins of Dictatorship and Democracy: Lord and Peasant in the Making of the Modern World* (Boston: Beacon Press, 1965), pp. 413–32; Evelyne Huber, Dietrich Rueschemeyer, and John D. Stephens, *Capitalist Development and Democracy* (Oxford: Polity, 1992).

34. See Adam Przeworski, *Democracy and the Market* (Cambridge University Press, 1991), chapter 1; Samuel Huntington, *The Third Wave: Democratization in the Late Twentieth Century* (Norman: University of Oklahoma Press, 1991), chapter 1; and Ian Shapiro, *Democracy's Place* (Ithaca: Cornell University Press, 1996), chapter 4.

35. See Juan J. Linz, *The Breakdown of Democratic Regimes: Crises, Breakdown, and Reequilibration* (Baltimore: Johns Hopkins University Press, 1978); and "Presidential or Parliamentary democracy: Does it make a difference?" in *The Failure of Presidential Democracy*, Linz and Arturo Valenzuela, eds. (Baltimore: Johns Hopkins University Press, 1994).

36. Matthew Shugart and John M. Carey, *Presidents and Assemblies: Constitutional Design and Electoral Dynamics* (New York: Cambridge University Press, 1992), chapter 3; and Matthew Shugart and Scott Mainwaring, eds., *Presidentialism and Democracy in Latin America* (Cambridge: Cambridge University Press, 1997), pp. 12–55.

37. See Joe Foweraker, "Institutional design, party systems, and governability—Differentiating the Presidential regimes of Latin America," in *British Journal of Political Science*, vol. 28, 1998, pp. 665–70; and Cheibub and Limongi, "Parliamentarism, Presidentialism, is there a difference," *mimeo*, Yale University, 2000.

38. Przeworski et al., *Democracy and the Market*, pp. 106–117.

39. Weber, "Science as a vocation," Gerth and Mills, *From Max Weber*, p. 147. Weber was less than sanguine about the ongoing capacity of scientists to speak the truth to power, because he expected—over-apocalyptically, as it has turned out—that the conduct of science would increasingly be dominated by a vast government bureaucracy. He underestimated the pluralism that would endure, particularly in the United States, due to research being funded by multiple corporations, independent foundations, and wealthy private universities in addition to the federal government, not to mention economies of smallness in branches of knowledge, such as information technology that renders them able to resist bureaucratization.

40. Jean-Francois Lyotard, *The Postmodern Condition: A Report on Knowledge* (Minneapolis: University of Minnesota Press, 1988), p. 41. See also Rorty, "Postmodernist bourgeois liberalism," *The Journal of Philosophy*, vol. 80, no. 10, pp. 583–89; and "Thugs and theorists," *Political Theory*, vol. 15, no. 4, pp.

564–80; and William Connolly, *Identity/Difference. Democratic Negotiations of Political Paradox* (Ithaca: Cornell University Press, 1991), pp. 158–97; and *The Ethos of Pluralization*, pp. 75–104 (Minneapolis: University of Minnesota Press, 1995).

41. For extended discussion of this point, see my *Political Criticism*, chapter 2.

42. Friedrich Nietzsche, *On the Genealogy of Morals and Ecce Homo*, trans. Walter Kaufmann (New York: Vintage Books, 1967), chapter 3, §24.

43. See Connor Cruise O'Brien's introduction to Edmund Burke, *Reflections on the Revolution in France* (London: Penguin Books, 1968), pp. 9–76.

44. See MacIntyre, *After Virtue*; Michael Sandel, *Liberalism and the Limits of Justice* (Cambridge: Cambridge University Press, 1982); and *Democracy's Discontent* (Cambridge, Mass.: Harvard University Press, 1996); Michael Walzer, *Spheres of Justice: A Defense of Pluralism and Equality* (New York: Basic Books, 1983); and *Interpretation and Social Criticism* (Cambridge, Mass.:Harvard University Press, 1987), Charles Taylor, *Sources of the Self* (Harvard University Press, 1989); and Will Kymlicka, *Multicultural Citizenship: A Liberal Theory of Minority Rights* (New York: Oxford University Press, 1995); and *Politics in the Vernacular: Nationalism, Multiculturalism, and Citizenship* (New York: Oxford University Press, 2001).

45. Kymlicka, *Multicultural Citizenship*, p. 83.

46. Walzer, "Commitment and social criticism: Camus's Algerian war," *Dissent* (Fall 1984), pp. 428–30.

47. Hegel, *Phenomenology of Spirit*, trans. A.V. Miller (Oxford: Clarendon Press, 1977 [1807]), pp. 115–17. See also Alexandre Kojève, *Introduction to the Reading of Hegel* (New York: Basic Books, 1969), pp. 3–30.

48. Walzer, *Spheres of Justice*, pp. 31–63.

49. Sandel, *Liberalism and the Limits of Justice*, p. 11.

50. *Ibid.*, p. 183.

51. Sandel, *Democracy's Discontent*, pp. 13–14.

52. It should be noted that Sandel's critique misses the mark in that asking yourself which policy on racial preferences you would prefer if you did not know whether you were going to be black or white does not require you to imagine people without color, as his reference to Kant's noumenal realm implies.

53. Sandel, *Liberalism and the Limits of Justice*, pp. 11–14, 183.

54. For extended critical discussion of Walzer and MacIntyre in this regard, see my *Political Criticism*, pp. 75–88, 141–65.

55. Interestingly, in this connection, until the "third wave" of democratic transitions that got underway in the world after 1984, it was widely believed among social scientists that Catholicism is incompatible with democracy. But many of the third wave transitions were in predominantly Catholic countries,

revealing this orthodoxy to have been misguided. As with Protestantism, Judaism, Islam, and other major religions, different variants of Catholicism seem compatible with different political regimes and ideologies. See Samuel Huntington, "Democracy's third wave," in *Journal of Democracy*, vol. 2, no. 2, Spring 1991, pp. 12–34.

56. See Shapiro, *Democratic Justice*, pp. 64–109, for discussion of these thresholds as they relate to children and pp. 110–42 as they relate to adult domestic relations.

57. Albert O. Hirschman, *Exit, Voice, and Loyalty* (Cambridge, Mass.: Harvard University Press, 1970).

58. Notice that when Walzer subtitles *Spheres of Justice* as "A Defense of Pluralism and Equality" he deploys the term *pluralism* idiosyncratically to convey his claim that different principles of justice are appropriate to different spheres of social life (healthcare to be distributed on the basis of need, education to prepare people for democratic citizenship, etc.) that are not reducible to a single index such as utility. However, Walzer assumes, implausibly, that there is agreement, i.e. lack of pluralism, in society as to what the appropriate metric within each sphere should be. See my *Political Criticism*, pp. 82–85, for discussion.

59. See Susan Moller Okin, *Justice, Gender, and the Family* (New York: Basic Books, 1989), pp. 134–69. On the changing law of marital rape in the United States, see Diana E. H. Russell, *Rape in Marriage*, second edition (Indiana University Press, 1990), and Rebecca M. Ryan, "The sex right: A legal history of the marital rape exception," *Law and Social Inquiry*, vol. 20, no. 4 (Fall 1995), pp. 941–1001.

60. On gender differences in labor-force participation and wages, see Claudia Goldin, *Understanding the Gender Gap* (New York: Oxford University Press, 1990), pp. 58–118. On economic disparities between men and women after divorce, see Susan Moller Okin, "Economic equality after divorce: 'Equal rights or special benefits?'" *Dissent* (Summer 1991), pp. 383–87; and Richard R. Peterson, "A re-evaluation of the economic consequences of divorce," *American Sociological Review*, vol. 61, no. 3 (June 1996), pp. 528–36. On domestic violence, see Daniel J. Sonkin, ed., *Domestic Violence on Trial: Psychological and Legal Dimensions of Family Violence* (New York: Springer, 1987).

61. For my answer to the question, see *Democratic Justice*, chapters 2–3.

62. Benedict Anderson, *Imagined Communities* (London: Verso, 1983), pp. 129–40.

63. V. O. Key, *Southern Politics in State and Nation* (New York: A. A. Knopf, 1949).

64. See Anthony Marx, *Making Race and Nation* (New York: Cambridge University Press, 1998); on South Africa, and, on Northern Ireland, John Cash, *Identity, Ideology and Conflict: The Structuration of Politics in Northern Ireland* (New York: Cambridge University Press, 1996).

65. For an illuminating discussion of the political mobilization of group identities among Zulus, Afrikaners, and Cape Colourds in South Africa before, during, and after the transition from apartheid to democracy, see Courtney Jung, *Then I Was Black: South African Political Identities in Transition* (New Haven, Conn.: Yale University Press, 2000).

66. For helpful discussions of the tensions between the egalitarian aspects of South Africa's post-Apartheid constitution and the ways in which Zulu customary law operates to the disadvantage of Zulu women, see Davis Chambers, "Civilizing the natives: Marriage in post-Apartheid South Africa," *Daedalus*, vol. 129, no. 4 (Fall 2000), pp. 101–24; and the Human Rights Watch report "South Africa: The state response to domestic violence and rape," available at www.hrw.org/reports/1995/Safricawm-02.htm. Generally see, T. W. Bennett, *Human Rights and African Customary Law* (Johannesburg: Jutas, 1995).

67. For discussion of many of the forms this can take, see Brian Barry, *Culture and Equality: An Egalitarian Critique of Multiculturalism* (Cambridge, Mass.: Harvard University Press, 2000), pp. 155–93.

68. See Walzer, *Spheres of Justice*, p. 100; and "Liberalism and the art of separation," *Political Theory*, vol. 12, no. 3 (1984), pp. 315–30.

69. Walzer, *Interpretation and Social Criticism*, pp. 33–66.

70. Kymlicka, *Multicultural Citizenship*, pp. 152–53, Kymlicka's italics. See also *Politics in the Vernacular*, pp. 17–48.

71. Kymlicka, *Multicultural Citizenship*, p. 167–69.

72. Rawls, *The Law of Peoples* (Cambridge, Mass.: Harvard University Press, 1999), pp. 36, 48. For discussion of other variants of this claim, see my *Democratic Justice*, pp. 234–37.

73. Sarah Song, "Liberalism, multiculturalism, and the problem of gender," Ph.D. dissertation prospectus, Department of Political Science, Yale University, *mimeo*, 2001.

74. This old saw has surfaced again in our own era of globalization. For reasons why it is overblown, see Geoffrey Garrett, *Partisan Politics in the Global Economy* (New York: Cambridge University Press, 1998).

75. See Thomas Pogge, *Realizing Rawls* (Ithaca, N.Y.: Cornell University Press, 1989); Charles Beitz, *Political Theory and International Relations*, second edition (Princeton, N.J.: Princeton University Press, 1999); and Ian Shapiro and Lea Brilmayer, eds., *NOMOS XLI: Global Justice* (New York: New York University Press, 1999).

76. See Brian Barry, *Culture and Equality*, pp. 252–328.

Chapter 7: Democracy

1. Bruce Ackerman, *We The People: Foundations* (Cambridge, Mass.: Harvard University Press, 1993).

2. John Dunn, *Western Political Theory in the Face of the Future* (Cambridge: Cambridge University Press, 1979), p. 26.

3. For useful discussions of the theory and practice of Athenian democracy, see H. D. F. Kitto, *The Greeks* (Middlesex, Penguin, 1956); and David Held, *Models of Democracy* (Cambridge: Polity Press, 1987), ch. 1. On the relations between Athenian democracy and the slave economy, see M. I. Finley, *The Ancient Economy*, second edition (London: Hogarth, 1985).

4. J. S. Mill, *Representative Government*, reprinted in Mill, *Three Essays* (Oxford: Oxford University Press, 1975 [1861]), pp. 284-85.

5. Plato, *The Republic*, trans. Desmond Lee, second edition (Harmondsworth: Penguin, 1974), pp. 359-64.

6. *Ibid.*, p. 282.

7. *Ibid.*, p. 288.

8. *Ibid.*, pp. 359-91.

9. On rent-seeking politicians, see Dennis C. Mueller, *Public Choice II* (Cambridge: Cambridge University Press, 1989), pp. 235-44. On the electoral behavior of politicians, see David Mayhew, *The Electoral Connection* (New Haven, Conn.: Yale University Press, 1974).

10. Plato, *The Republic*, p. 300.

11. *Ibid.*, pp. 347-55.

12. Karl Popper, *The Open Society and Its Enemies* (Princeton, N.J.: Princeton University Press, 1966 [1943]), pp. 86-7, 388.

13. See Leo Strauss, *The City and Man* (Chicago: University of Chicago Press, 1964), pp. 124-27.

14. Miles Burnyeat, "Sphinx without a secret," *The New York Review of Books* (May 30, 1985), pp. 35-36.

15. Plato, *The Republic*, p. 360.

16. *Ibid.*, pp. 360-98.

17. His discussion is, however, the first of many that explored the conditions for regime stability and ways in which political regimes evolve into one another. These subjects were taken up in greater detail in Aristotle's *Politics* and were developed into a six-fold classification of regime types and then historicized by the second century B.C. Stoic philosopher and Greek exile Polybius as a theory of *anakuklōsis politeiōn* or cycle of constitutions. They were thought to evolve from monarchy to tyranny, aristocracy, oligarchy, democracy and then ochlocracy (mob rule or anarchy) after which the cycle would begin again. In the civic humanist tradition that grew out of this study of the Polybian cycle, the science of politics became construed as that of determining where one was in the regime cycle and how to make government as virtuous as possible given that constraint. See J. G. A. Pocock, *The Machiavellian Moment: Florentine Political Thought and the Atlantic Republican Tradition* (Princeton, N.J.: Princeton University Press, 1975), pp. 76-80.

18. Plato, *The Republic*, pp. 398-420.

19. *Ibid.*, p. 306.

20. *Ibid.*, pp. 316-25.

21. *Ibid.*, p. 289.

22. *Ibid.*, pp. 260-80.

23. Popper, *Open Society*, p. 131.

24. See Leo Strauss, *Natural Right and History* (Chicago: University of Chicago Press, 1953), pp. 138-43; and "Liberal education and responsibility," in *Liberalism Ancient and Modern* (New York: Basic Books, 1968), pp. 9-25.

25. See, for example, his discussion of military discipline in *The Laws*, where the goal is to promote unthinking obedience to authority on the part of the common people. Plato, *The Laws* (Harmondsworth: Penguin, 1970), pp. 489-91. For additional discussion see Popper, *The Open Society and Its Enemies*, pp. 131-33.

26. See John Roemer, "Does democracy engender justice?" in Shapiro and Hacker-Cordón, *Democracy's Value*, p. 60; and Margaret Levi, "Death and taxes: Extractive equality and the development of democratic institutions," in *ibid.*, pp. 112-27.

27. See my *Democracy's Place*, pp. 180-84, 234-42.

28. Joseph Schumpeter, *Capitalism, Socialism, and Democracy* (New York: Harper, 1942). The analogy was in fact first explored by an economist, Harold Hotelling, in "Stability in competition," *Economic Journal*, vol. 39 (March 1929), pp. 41-57.

29. See Jane Mansbridge, *Beyond Adversary Democracy* (New York: Basic Books, 1980); and Amy Gutmann and Dennis Thompson, *Democracy and Disagreement* (Cambridge, Mass.: Harvard University Press, 1996).

30. For discussion of critics of, and alternatives to, Schumpeterian democracy see Ian Shapiro, "The state of democratic theory," in Ira Katznelson and Helen Milner, eds., *Political Science: The State of the Discipline*, third edition (Washington, D.C..: American Political Science Association and Norton, 2002).

31. See Samuel Huntington, *The Third Wave Democratization in the Late Twentieth Century* (Norman: University of Oklahoma Press, 1991), p. 267.

32. See James Buchanan and Gordon Tullock, *The Calculus of Consent: Logical Foundations of Constitutional Democracy* (Ann Arbor: University of Michigan Press, 1962), pp. 125-26, 132-42.

33. The "Death Tax Elimination Act of 2000" was passed by Congress in the summer of 2000 and vetoed by President Bill Clinton. President George W. Bush signed a similar provision into law as part of his Administration's $1.35 trillion dollar ten-year tax cut enacted in 2001, with the cost of the estate tax repeal projected to be $138 billion over that period. See the Joint Committee on Taxation's publication, "Estimated Effects of the Conference Agreement on HR 1836" (May 26, 2001) at *www.house.gov/jct/x-51-01.pdf*.

34. The most formidable obstacle in the United States is the Supreme Court's equation of money with speech that is protected by the First Amendment. In *Buckley v. Valeo* 424 US 1 (1976) the Court held, *inter alia*, that although Congress may regulate financial contributions to political parties or candidates, it cannot otherwise regulate private expenditures on political speech. The Court has since allowed some minor constraints on corporate expenditures in *Austin v. Michigan State Chamber of Commerce*, 494 US 652 (1990), but for all practical purposes the *Buckley* rule makes it impossible to limit privately funded political advertising. For examples of reform proposals that do not run afoul of the *Buckley* rule, see Bruce Ackerman, "Crediting the voters: A new beginning for campaign finance," *The American Prospect*, no. 13 (1993), pp. 71–80; and Ian Ayres, "Disclosure versus anonymity in campaign finance," *NOMOS XLII: Designing Democratic Institutions*, ed. Ian Shapiro and Stephen Macedo (New York: New York University Press, 2000), pp. 19–54 (2000).

35. The Progressives did advance a version of this critique. See Leon D. Epstein, *Political Parties in the American Mold* (Madison: University of Wisconsin Press, 1986), pp. 17–71. The lone voice in the contemporary literature seems to be Donald A. Wittman, "Parties as utility maximizers," *American Political Science Review*, vol. 67 (1973), pp. 490–98.

36. See Gutmann and Thompson, *Democracy and Disagreement; and Jürgen Habermas, The Theory of Communicative Action, vol. 1, Reason and Rationalization of Society* (Boston: Beacon Press, 1984); and "Three normative models of democracy," *Constellations*, vol. 1, no. 1, pp. 1–10.

37. The exception here is James Fishkin, *Democracy and Deliberation: New Directions for Democratic Reform* (New Haven, Conn.: Yale University Press), whose deliberative theory is intended only to promote enlightened preferences, not agreement.

38. See my "Enough of deliberation: Politics is about interests and power," in Stephen Macedo, ed., *Deliberative Politics: Essays on Democracy and Disagreement* (New York: Oxford University Press, 1999), pp. 28–38; and "Optimal deliberation?" *Journal of Political Philosophy*, vol. 10., no. 2 (June 2002), pp. 196–211.

39. John Dewey, The Ethics of Democracy in John Dewey, *The Early Works of John Dewey* (Carbondale: Southern Illinois University Press, 1969), vol. 1, p. 243.

40. *Ibid.*, p. 242.

41. Popper offers a powerful, if controversial, argument that, unlike Plato, Socrates was a democrat for just this reason, to wit, that he recognized how little we know, and thought everyone—including slaves—could be brought to understand this through education. *The Open Society and Its Enemies*, pp. 128–33.

42. Dewey, *Individuality in our Day*, reprinted in John Dewey, *The Political Writings*, ed. Debra Morris and Ian Shapiro (Indianapolis: Hackett, 1993), p. 83.

43. *Ibid.*

44. Dewey, *Freedom and Culture* (New York: G.P. Putnam's Sons, 1939), pp. 148–49.

45. Winston Churchill, Speech to the House of Commons, Nov. 1947. See adamsharp.com/RAVES/QUOTES/index.asp.

46. John Stuart Mill, *On Liberty* (Indianapolis: Hackett, 1978 [1859]), p. 4; Alexis de Tocqueville, *Democracy in America* (New York: Anchor Books, 1969 [1832]), pp. 246–61.

47. Jean-Jacques Rousseau, *The Social Contract* (Harmondsworth: Penguin 1968 [1762]), p. 73; James Madison, *Federalist* #10, James Madison, Alexander Hamilton, and John Jay, *The Federalist Papers* (Harmondsworth: Penguin, 1987 [1787–88]), pp. 122–28.

48. Marquis de Condorcet, *Essay on the Application of Analysis to the Probability of Majority Decisions* (1785). Kenneth Arrow, *Social Choice and Individual Values* (New York: Wiley, 1951).

49. Madison, *Federalist* #51, *Federalist Papers*, p. 318.

50. William Riker, *Liberalism Against Populism: A Confrontation Between the Theory of Democracy and the Theory of Social Choice* (New York: W. H. Freeman, 1982), pp. 101–16; William Riker and Barry Weingast, "Constitutional regulation of legislative choice: The political consequences of judicial deference to legislatures," *Virginia Law Review*, vol. 74 (1988), pp. 373–401. See also George Tsebelis, *Veto Players: How Political Institutions Work and Why* (Princeton, N.J.: Princeton University Press, 2001).

51. Rousseau, *The Social Contract*, p. 72.

52. Stephen Holmes and Cass Sunstein, *The Costs of Rights: Why Liberty Depends on Taxes* (New York: Norton, 1999).

53. See Frank Easterbrook, "Ways of criticizing the Court," *Harvard Law Review*, vol. 95 (1982), pp. 802–32; and Walter Murphy, *Elements of Judicial Strategy* (Chicago: University of Chicago Press, 1964), pp. 37–122. For a more general argument that if voting really is as meaningless as Riker claims, this undermines his "liberalism" just as much as the "populism" he attacks, see Jules Coleman and John Ferejohn, "Democracy and social choice," *Ethics*, vol. 97, no. 1 (1986), pp. 11–22.

54. For further discussion of fairness as a superior criterion to transitivity for collective decisions, see Mueller, *Public Choice II*, pp. 390–92.

55. Guiseppe Di Palma, *To Craft Democracy: An Essay on Democratic Transitions* (Berkeley: University of California Press, 1990), p. 55; and Adam Przeworski, *Democracy and the Market* (Cambridge: Cambridge University Press, 1991), pp. 10–12.

56. Nicholas Miller, "Pluralism and social choice," *American Political Science Review*, vol. 77, no. 3 (1983), pp. 735–40.

57. Arend Lijphart, *Democracy in Plural Societies* (New Haven: Yale University Press, 1977). I leave to one side the great empirical difficulties associated with determining whether preferences in a population are mutually reinforcing or cross-cutting, and how, if at all, they can be transformed from the former to the latter. See Shapiro, *Democracy's Place*, pp. 177–80, 216–18.

58. See Mueller, *Public Choice II*, pp. 63–6, 81–2.

59. See A.S. Tangian, "Unlikelihood of Condorcet's paradox in a large society," *Social Choice and Welfare*, vol. 17 (2000), pp. 337–65; and Gerry Mackie, *Is Democracy Impossible? A Preface to Deliberative Democracy* (Cambridge University Press, forthcoming). See also Green and Shapiro, *Pathologies of Rational Choice Theory*, ch. 7.

60. See Gordon Tullock, "Why so much stability?" *Public Choice*, vol. 37, no. 2 (1981), pp. 189–202. For the argument that institutions reduce the likelihood of cycles, see Kenneth Shepsle and Barry Weingast, "Structure induced equilibrium and legislative choice," *Public Choice*, vol. 37, no. 3 (1981), pp. 503–19.

61. John Witte, *The Politics and Development of the Federal Income Tax* (Madison: University of Wisconsin Press, 1985).

62. Tocqueville, *Democracy in America*, pp. 255, 260.

63. Buchanan and Tullock, *The Calculus of Consent*, pp. 78, 96, italics in original. One indicator of the work's influence is that when Buchanan was awarded the Nobel Prize for economics in 1986 almost a quarter century after its publication, the citation singled out "his development of the contractual and constitutional bases for the theory of economic and political decision-making." www.nobel.se/economics/laureates/1986/.

64. Buchanan and Tullock, *Calculus*, pp. 63–77.

65. *Ibid.*, pp. 77, 73, 73–74, 75, 75–76.

66. See Shapiro, *Democracy's Place*, pp. 19–29.

67. This is not strictly true if vote trading is allowed. Under that assumption, and assuming also no decision-making costs, there is no optimal decision rule for the same reason as Coase showed that, in the absence of information costs, wealth effects, external effects, and other blockages to exchange, such as free riding, no system of tort liability rules is more efficient than any other. Whatever the system, people will then make exchanges to produce Pareto-optimal results. R. H. Coase, "The problem of social cost," *The Journal of Law and Economics*, vol. 3 (1960), pp. 1–44. Assuming, however, that a pure market in votes does not exist, and Buchanan and Tullock acknowledge that some constraints on it are inevitable, they maintain that unanimity would uniquely be chosen in the absence of decision-making costs. Buchanan and Tullock, *Calculus*, pp. 270–74.

68. See Douglas W. Rae, "The limits of consensual decision," *American Political Science Review*, vol. 69, no. 4 (1975), pp. 1270–94. For Barry's earlier discussion, see his *Political Argument* (New York: Humanities Press, 1965), pp. 243–85.

69. When the number of voters is odd, the optimal decision rule is majority rule, n over two, plus one-half; when n is even, the optimal decision rule is either majority rule (n over two plus one), or majority rule minus one (simply n over two). Douglas W. Rae, "Decision-rules and individual values in constitutional choice," *American Political Science Review*, vol. 63, no. 1 (1969), pp. 40–56, 51.

70. R. B. Parker, "The jurisprudential uses of John Rawls," *NOMOS XX: Constitutionalism*, ed. J. Roland Pennock and John Chapman (New York: New York University Press, 1979).

71. Bruce Ackerman, *Social Justice in the Liberal State* (New Haven: Yale University Press, 1980); Ronald Dworkin, *Law's Empire* (Cambridge, Mass.: Harvard University Press, 1986); and G. A. Cohen, "On the currency of egalitarian justice," *Ethics*, vol. 99, no. 4 (July 1989), pp. 906–44.

72. Robert Dahl, *How Democratic Is the American Constitution?* (New Haven: Yale University Press, 2002), pp. 132–39.

73. Sociologist T. H. Marshall famously distinguished three types of increasingly comprehensive rights: *Civil* rights include "the rights necessary for individual freedom—liberty of the person, freedom of speech, thought and faith, the right to own property and conclude valid contracts, and the right to justice [the right to assert and defend one's rights]." *Political* rights include "the right to participate in the exercise of political power, as a member of a body invested with political authority or an elector of the members of such a body." And by *social* rights, Marshall meant "the whole range from the right to a modicum of economic welfare and security to the right to share in the full social heritage and to live the life of a civilized being according to the standards prevailing in the society." Terence H. Marshall, *Class, Citizenship, and Social Development* (New York: Doubleday, 1965), p. 78. Marshall was more optimistic than the historical record has turned out to warrant in that he conceived of societies as moving from civil to political to social citizenship rights as they modernized.

74. There are terminological issues at stake here on which substantive issues turn. For instance, in the *Lochner* era the Supreme Court struck down much legislation in the name of protecting individual freedoms, but the legislation in question was aimed at increasing social and economic guarantees— promoting civil rights at the expense of social rights in Marshall's terminology discussed in footnote 73 above. See *Lochner v. New York* 198 U.S. 45 (1905). For discussion of the *Lochner* era, see Lawrence Tribe, *American Constitutional Law* (New York: Foundation Press, 1978), pp. 567–86, for a general

discussion of evolution of American constitutional law through the years of the Warren Court (1953–69), pp. 558–1720.

75. See Rogers Smith, *Civic Ideals: Conflicting Visions of Citizenship in U.S. History* (New Haven: Yale University Press, 1997), pp. 165–409.

76. Robert Dahl, *A Preface to Democratic Theory* (Chicago: University of Chicago Press, 1956), pp. 105–12; and "Decision making in a democracy: The Supreme Court as national policymaker," *Journal of Public Law*, vol. 6, no. 2 (1958), pp. 279–95.

77. See Dahl, *Democracy and Its Critics* (New Haven: Yale University Press, 1989), pp. 188–92; and *How Democratic Is the American Constitution?* (New Haven: Yale University Press, 2002), ch. 3; Mark Tushnet, *Taking the Constitution Away From the Courts* (Princeton, N.J.: Princeton University Press 1999); and Ran Hirschl, *Towards Juristocracy: A Comparative Inquiry onto the Origins and Consequences of the New Constitutionalism* (Cambridge, Mass.: Harvard University Press, 2002).

78. See Ran Hirschl, "The political origins of judicial empowerment through constitutionalization: Lessons from four constitutional revolutions," *Law and Social Inquiry*, vol. 25, no. 1 (2000), pp. 91–147.

79. See Ian Shapiro and Casiano Hacker-Cordón, "Outer edges and inner edges," in Shapiro and Hacker-Cordón, *Democracy's Edges*, pp. 1–16.

80. Nelson Mandela, "Address to the court before sentencing," in J. Ayo Langley, ed., *Ideologies of Liberation in Black Africa, 1856–1970* (London: Rex Collins, 1979), p. 664.

81. See Shelly Kagan, *The Limits of Morality* (Cambridge: Oxford University Press, 1989) and, in a similar—though not explicitly utilitarian—spirit, James Fishkin, *The Limits of Obligation* (New Haven: Yale University Press, 1982). This is not to mention Peter Singer, who extends his utilitarian concerns to nonhuman forms of life as well. See *Practical Ethics*, second edition (New York: Cambridge University Press, 1993), pp. 63–68, 134.

82. See particularly Brian Barry, "Statism and nationalism: A cosmopolitan critique," in Ian Shapiro and Lea Brilmayer, eds., *NOMOS XLI: Global Justice* (New York: New York University Press, 1999), pp. 12–66; and Hillel Steiner, "Just taxation and international redistribution," in *ibid.*, pp. 171–91.

83. Nozick, *Anarchy, State and Utopia*, pp. 23–4, 108–18.

84. See David Held, *Democracy and the Global Order* (Stanford: Stanford University Press, 1995). For the criticism mentioned in the text, see Alexander Wendt, "A comment on Held's cosmopolitanism," in Shapiro and Hacker-Cordón, *Democracy's Edges*, pp. 127–33.

85. See Geoffrey Garrett, *Partisan Politics in the Global Economy* (Cambridge: Cambridge University Press, 1998).

86. See Wendt, "Comment on Held's cosmopolitanism," pp. 130–31, and Shapiro, *Democratic Justice*, pp. 234–37.

87. Barry, in "Statism and nationalism" is the exception here, since he holds out a cosmopolitan standard as the goal to be promoted within democratic systems.

88. See Thomas Pogge, "Cosmopolitanism and sovereignty," *Ethics*, vol. 103 (October 1992), pp. 48–75; Alexander Wendt, "Collective identity-formation and the international state," *American Political Science Review*, vol. 88, no. 2 (June 1994), pp. 384–96; William Antholis, "Liberal Democratic Theory and the Transformation of Sovereignty," unpublished Ph.D. dissertation, Yale University, 1993; and Seyla Benhabib, *Transformations of citizenship: Dilemmas of the nation state in the era of globalization* (Amsterdam: Koninklijke Van Gorcum, 2001).

89. See my *Democratic Justice*, particularly pp. 1–63, 143–95, 230–40.

Chapter 8: Democracy in the Mature Enlightenment

1. In this connection one interesting proposal is Ian Ayers's suggestion that campaign contributions should be thought of on the model of the secret ballot rather than the speech clause of the First Amendment, kept secret, that is, from everyone including their recipients. "Disclosure versus anonymity in campaign finance," in Ian Shapiro and Stephen Macedo, eds., *NOMOS XLII: Designing Democratic Institutions* (New York: New York University Press, 2000), pp. 19–54.